Quotes and Te:

Cloud Coffee House describes the kind of wc mind philosophical questions on how people in this future will mix their business and leisure lives. In the USA we're seeing a culture emerge where people are increasingly blending the two but maybe that will change too.

Alph Bingham Founder and Chairman, INNOCENTIVE INC.

Most organisations are rooted in the past and struggling day-to-day to keep pace with the rapid changes in the way our world works. Very few have the capacity or ability to do what Ian Tomlin has done with *Cloud Coffee House*, that is, to take a step back and view with clarity how we will do business in the future, and the exciting opportunities this presents. I would recommend that anyone influencing a company's strategy should take a moment, raise their heads from the day-to-day survival game and read this book..

Alanna Lawrie, Founder and CEO, textyouhome.com

If you could ever describe any business book as a page turner Cloud Coffee House would be it. Awesome!

Anthony Jamieson, CEO, Encanvas Co. Za

I was in two minds whether to pick up this book. From the first page I couldn't put it down! Astounding.

Nasser Elaheebocus, Hometrack Data Systems Ltd

A business book that articulates an idea that helps business people to explain what it is that they are trying to do.

Henry Dotterer, CEO, www.Proz.com

A book for anyone who's interested in the future of social networks.

Jamison Roof, technology lead, User Centric Design for a major consulting firm

Cloud Coffee House presents the future of cloud computing and the new workplace with such clarity that you can almost touch it.

Manoj Agarwal, CEO, US Tech Solutions Inc

A *bright idea* that sheds light on how technical innovation and culture change is re-modelling society and the business-world around the individual.

Anne Swift, President and Founder at Young Inventors International

Successful business books need a bright idea, and they, in the nature of business, come along infrequently.

John Collins, The Economist

Cloud Coffee House

The birth of cloud social networking and death of the old world corporation

Ian Tomlin

2000

First published in 2009 by Management Books 2000 Ltd
Forge House, Limes Road
Kemble, Cirencester
Gloucestershire, GL7 6AD, UK
Tel: 0044 (0) 1285 771441
Fax: 0044 (0) 1285 771055
Email: info@mb2000.com
Web: www.mb2000.com

British Library Cataloguing in Publication Data is available
ISBN 9781852525842

PROPOSITION

The Internet feels old yet it's only been with us for less than 15 years. The *next* 15 years will see the rapid growth of a new digital cloud that will surround our planet – the *cloudspace*.

It will be on a scale that no human could ever have imagined possible at the dawn of this century. Its digital sphere will hold data many times larger than the volume of the current World Wide Web. This amassed data cloud will expose where each one of us exists through our digital entrails of relationship ties. Our interests, friends, relationships, beliefs, behaviours, location, the people we've schooled with and worked for, the organizations and federations we share, our skills and capabilities, knowledge and wisdom will all be joined together in a single digital sphere that we will as individuals share a part of yet no government or organization could ever hope to own.

The cloudspace is the next stage in the human race's love-hate relationship with computers. It will replace *the office* as the place where most of us will work; the place where business is done. It will ultimately protect us from the corruption of power, give the web its heart, and it will offer every individual the choice to assert their personality.

In this new age, the Internet becomes the equivalent of a global switchboard that links one person to another. Exploiting this *switch* might soon enable every person to connect to any other person in the world in six connections. It promises unrivalled opportunity to build new relationships.

The cloudspace will change how organizations work and how they are designed. It will facilitate a new set of market dynamics, new resourcing structures and new challenges. How people will find their work, do their work, where they work; all these things are going to change.

This book describes this transformation in the world of business.

This book is about how the cloudspace will forever change the business world. But there is a social context too.

The cloudspace will form, not as the result of political decree or through the greed of corporations, but because of a native desire for people to want to socialize, share life experiences and assert their individuality; their emotional need to express to others 'I exist' and 'my opinion matters'.

It will cause every person to face two decisions that might ultimately determine the survival of our world.

The first decision is 'Do you want to be in the cloudspace or not?'

The second is more crucial, and brutal. It will be how those individuals who choose to join the cloudspace answer the human race's biggest challenge, namely, how to overcome the planet killing problem of over population.

But what is the cloudspace? Why does it challenge us to make life changing decisions? And where did it come from?

Message from the author

The surfer said, "It's about freedom, freedom to communicate with anyone you want to. And you don't need to pay. You can interact with others at any time of the day. It makes you feel grown up because you're *trusted*. You feel people listen to what you say. I couldn't *be* without it. I wouldn't be alive."

This is how dedicated *'surfers'* feel; the verve about being *on the grid*. Fill out a simple form and suddenly you're a *member,* connected and exposed to millions of others. They share your passions. What you say matters. When you're *on the grid* you *become* someone [Verb: To be. To exist in actuality; have life or reality: *I think, therefore I am.*].

The job of this book is to understand and innovate, to describe and imagine. It raises practical questions: Should you be investing more of your time *surfing, blogging, connecting* and *twittering*? Finding out about how *Facebook* and LinkedIn work? Are you unwittingly harming your career potential, your future prosperity, because you're not connecting to others across the Internet, people you barely know, trying to strike up a relationship? How many names are in *your Facebook*? How many people follow *your 'twittering'*?

I would encourage you to find out more about social networking. It's an opt-in that anyone who wants to get more from life should tick 'yes' to. Children of the 21st century consider it their birthright. Read this book and find out why it's a good idea to start learning about being *on the social net* now. If you find the idea of engaging with others across the web and exposing your personality abhorrent (and that's not an uncommon emotional reaction!) then I'd recommend you read this book anyway to learn what cloud social networking is about and how it's going to change the world you live in. You can decide if it's for you or whether you'd rather move to the Outer Hebrides and become a goat herder. Opting out through ignorance is not making a choice.

This book explores how social networking and cloud computing is changing the symbiotic relationship between society and business. It fascinates me how people jump from work to home life and back again. My first book, 'Agilization', is a kind of *management cookery book that* contains everything business leaders need to know about how to engineer organizations to always fit their most profitable markets. A topic I cover in *Agilization* is a change in social consciousness in younger generations; a desire to assert their personality on a society that doesn't seem to want to listen to them – what social scientists call 'Individualism' – how individuals choose to assert their personality on their life-course, life-style and buying decisions on others using the Internet as the main vehicle for communications. Social networks are a significant enabler to Individualism and they're causing the biggest change in business behaviours we've seen for generations. The more I explore the future path of people networks, the more positive and excited I get about our future.

Writing a book that will appeal to a broad age range has its challenges. Huge gulfs of understanding exist between the generations of how the digital age – the era of digital data communications ushered in by the World Wide Web – is changing lives. My mother and father, now in their later years, have barely noticed the changes brought about by the digital age of the World Wide Web, mobile communications and 24-hour online living. The telephone remains their preferred method of communication. They don't use a mobile and each time a bill turns up, my mother struggles to justify the expense of a PC and broadband to my father. The digital age hasn't changed their lives one jot.

In contrast, my children are always online with their friends – always *connected*. In the chronology of generations they're part of Generation Z ('Gen Z' for short – not sure what comes after that!). My kids grew up with computers and think nothing of chatting with friends, sharing pictures and buying products online. They're completely at home on the web and they're lost without it. They assume broadband is 'just there' like any other utility – gas, electricity, water. Time and again my kids lap up new innovations and think nothing of how clever they are. When Nintendo brought out the *Wii* games console, my kids weren't thinking about the innovations in motion sensing built into the wireless handheld controllers (kids in the know call them 'nunchuks'), all they knew is that they wanted one for Christmas.

I'm in the Generation X team; part of a population expansion trailing from the good times of the '60's and in my particular case because of the celebrations brought about by England winning the 1966 World Cup. I was born nine months later and my wife 6 months after that (it was a long party). We *Gen X's* were born into the heady days of pop culture and so we learnt about computers as we've gone along. It's probably because we had to learn the hard way and saw too many early stage failures that we over analyze innovations in computing and telecommunications rather than naively assuming technology works.

How business works has always fascinated me, probably because I grew up in a family run business. In my career I've experienced different types and sizes of business. As a child I was a reluctant helper in my fathers' small engineering company. In fear of having failed my A levels, I felt the need to quickly find a job and found a management trainee placement with an American Corporation. Six years later, after a brief encounter with the public sector, I found myself managing the marketing of a mid-sized computer technology company. I rejoined the corporate world again briefly in the form of an international software company before finally plucking up the courage to establish NDMC Ltd ('NDMC') with Nick Lawrie.

I started my career thinking the bigger the company was the more sophisticated its management processes would be. Coming from a family business *run without people with degrees* I assumed the gods of the boardroom were super humans. My experiences have taught me that business is different to home life but it's a practice, not an art or science.

The more I study social networking, I realize how fundamental it has always been to the way business works. As relationship ties become more visible, social networks re-draw our values and the map of commerce. Such a fundamental change creates opportunities for some, threats for others. Reading this book I expect you will see how YOUR world is likely to change too and the likely impact it could have on your lifestyle, who you work for and where you work. In the final section I explain how social networks will be the change agent that solves the biggest business challenge facing 21st century management practitioners since it was set out by Peter Drucker, the father of the modern day management consulting industry, who wrote:

"The most important, and indeed the truly unique, contribution of management in the 20th century was the fifty-fold increase in the productivity of the MANUAL WORKER in manufacturing. The most important contribution management needs to make in the 21st century is similarly to increase the productivity of KNOWLEDGE WORK and the KNOWLEDGE WORKER." [45]

I sincerely hope you enjoy reading my book.

Contents

OUR DIGITAL SOCIAL NETWORKING JOURNEY SO FAR

There have always been social networks. The human race has successfully employed social networks to survive and enjoy deep emotional support.

Social media technologies enabled by the World Wide Web started as a bit of fun on a University campus when a graduate decided it would be a good idea to build a website that made it easy to share information with friends. What made this website special is in the way it presented each member with a wall across which they could pin up everything they wanted to say about their individuality (and their friends too!). These ego-walls gave individuals the ability to connect with friends with whom they possessed strong relationship ties and similar interests.

1

Small world

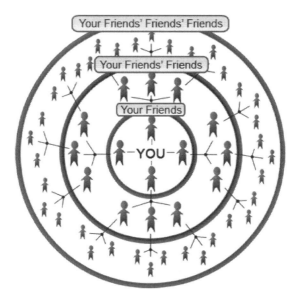

In 1929, a Hungarian author with the memorable name of Frigyes Karinthy published a book of short stories titled 'Everything is Different'.[1] One of them, 'Chain-Links', suggested that, with a population explosion and better communications, the world would become a smaller place. It highlighted the challenges that scientists in future would have to grapple with in the field of network theory (must have been a real page turner) and his work kicked off a debate in social science leading to a popular theory – now called *six degrees of separation* – that states:

> **'If a person is one step away from each person they know and two steps away from each person who is known by one of the people they know, then everyone is on average six "steps" away from each person on Earth.'**

Back in 1929 the world had a population approaching 2 billion. Today it has a population of 6.7 billion – and it's still growing.

Of course, today we also have the benefit of the Internet, mobile phones and the ability to call people in Australia over the internet for free using services like *Skype*. In 1929 you couldn't write a blog, connect to everyone you know with *Facebook*, or publish a video on *YouTube* for the entire world to see. Will it be possible to one day reach out to ANYONE else in the world in six connections?

Makes you think doesn't it.

> A psychologist called Stanley Milgram attempted to prove the influence of social networks in the 1960s by giving letters to a random bunch of people with instructions to get the envelope to its final destination by mailing it to people they know. He later reported that the letters arrived at their final destinations in an average of six hops. Even though Milgram's results were later discredited (*Psychology Today* reported that only 30% of Milgram's letters made it to their final destination), another study by Columbia University in 2003 published results of an e-mail study involving 60,000 people from 166 countries. It took an average of six hops to get a message from one stranger's inbox to another.[2]

Social networks. Two words that are on the lips of many technologists and social scientists today. They are descriptions of social structures that map out relationships between individuals. While we form a tiny part of a 6.7 billion strong global network, most of us relate more to the smaller, tighter, *sub networks* that also exist with our friends, families, where we live and work, school, interests, hobbies, pressure group or political party.

For entrepreneurs social networking describes an IT phenomenon that guarantees untold riches to those clever young software entrepreneurs who are able to magically harness the enthusiasm of their youth to build websites that have huge click appeal. For social scientists the very same term conjures up a vision of a new age in human-kind – the *participative age*. The participative age describes how a new generation of technology familiar boys and girls are re-writing how society works. They feel disengaged by politicians and poorly served by society's traditional emotional support mechanisms like family and community. So they participate in social networks in search of online emotional support causing the identity of the *users* and the *creators* of knowledge on the Internet to become blurred.

They get involved online because *they can*. This is how their world works. 'Hasn't there always been an internet?' they ask. The Internet is the innovation that has promoted the idea of connecting with people around the world from the comfort of your home. Even though social networks have always existed, today they're so much more visible.

But it's hard today to look at *Facebook* – the best known of the social networking websites – and see a tool for business. As society changes to embrace the digital age, consumer markets have become tribal and social media sites like *Facebook* become the glue that binds people together. We now see companies selling their products on *YouTube* and praying for consumer advocates to buy into their ideas and communicate their messages. Individuals are expressing their individuality in video, chat, reviews and blogs and can influence thousands of others through expanding networks in the 'CLOUD'.

From his Harvard dorm, Mark Zuckerberg conceived *Facebook* and he unknowingly started a revolution; a small idea that would ultimately be as far reaching as the invention of the wheel, printing press, steam engine and cotton spinning machine.[3] His idea to enable individuals to connect with each other sounded peculiar to business people at the time but not now. His thinking mirrors that of thousands of young people who *want to network* and who share a native affinity with technology to do it.

> **Adult interaction in social media is significantly on the rise. According to a 2007 comScore study[4], visitors to social media sites jumped a staggering 774 percent between 2006 and 2007; and the Pew Internet Study[5] reports that some 50 million Americans now read and create blogs.**

The cultural shift to social networking has not been lost on politicians. Barack Obama's campaign to be president of the United States employed a uniquely 21st century mix of digital communications mediums to reach out to the youth of America. He engaged the youth of America in a political debate using *their tools* on *their terms* and asked them to join with him in an effort to change the landscape of American politics. He knew he was using a medium that they could relate to; a digital channel they would be listening in on. During the 2008 Presidential campaign, Barack Obama's *YouTube* site received over 84 million hits while his

Facebook site had more than 2 million supporters.[6] The euphoria of the Obama campaign might still have been orchestrated by clever PR firms and funded by corporate money but it was driven by a surge of energy from a reinvigorated youth who re-discovered a passion for politics.

Not every communication in the Obama campaign was *orchestrated* by his clever campaign team. The domino effect that happens when individuals start to communicate through their social networks allowed the quiet voice of Obama to touch millions of young and disenfranchised voters within just a few weeks. How is it that these messages were able to cascade so readily through to millions of people? Sure, the Internet and mobile texting has a lot to do with it but it's mainly because the invisible social networks that bind people together are largely in place – in the same way that the whisper of a teacher being pregnant at the school gates can mean every child is armed with the news by the time the teacher gets to her desk for registration. It's all thanks to the grapevine.

What *is* a Social Network?

The term "social network" has its origins in social sciences. It's been around since the 1950s, but the meteoric rise of social-networking has been driven by the celebrity of social media sites like *Facebook* and *MySpace*. Increasingly it has been adopted by technology companies, another fad term. The computer industry is arguably the worst in the world for creating new acronyms that lead to new fads egged on by technology analysts who profit from conjuring up new markets.

I don't see social networks as a technology phenomenon as some technology commentators and academics do. I see it is a description of associations between individuals that come together for *social reasons* such as family ties, hobbies, shared interests and so they can share ideas and debate topics. Neither is it a new subject. I've described below three examples of notable academic works:

> **Professor J. A. Barnes of the London School of Economics[7] used the term 'social networks' systematically as far back as 1954 in a research paper that reported on his community study of a Norwegian Island Parish in Bremnes, Norway. He used the term to denote patterns of ties that cut across the concepts that had traditionally been used by social scientists. In his study he discovered an abundance of formal organizations existed, but that most individuals appeared to**

make decisions with reference to personal contacts that often cut across these organizational boundaries. Barnes categorized the social relations he'd seen into three categories: relatively *stable formal organizations* serving many different purposes, *unstable associations* engaged in fishing and *interpersonal links* that combine to form a social network and on which perceptions of class are based (Sounds like the typical office found in business doesn't it?).

In 1973, the American sociologist Mark Granovetter wrote a paper published in the American Journal for Sociology titled 'The Strength of Weak Ties'. He suggested that in marketing or politics, the weak ties enable people and organizations to reach out to populations and audiences that aren't accessible via strong ties.[8]

Another notable writer on the subject was Anatol Rapoport who identified that large networks could be measured by profiling traces of flows through them. Rapoport wrote a paper on how information flowed within a school showing its rapid progress through a population to almost all—but not all—school members. (Rapoport is on my list of 'interesting people I'd like to connect to when *Facebook* lets you go back in history'). His work contributed to discussions around the *six degrees of separation theory* – where this chapter began.[9]

How they begin

There have always been social networks.

Through history you would have encountered them around camp fires, in candle lit rooms, over the garden fence, in public houses and cafes. A network though can be a pretty intangible, invisible thing. It's much easier to spot when the participants are connected by cables but most social networks aren't like that. The participants and the connections between them aren't finite or easy to spot. But we know social networks exist when we are part of them. The 'spark' that forms social networks starts when one person says hello to another and in the back of their minds they try to work them out. Whenever we meet someone new I think most people have subliminal thoughts like – 'Do I *like* you? Can I *trust* you?' and... 'Do other people think you *popular*?' and even thoughts like 'How might you help me in future to get me what I want?' I don't think it's me being shallow; I think it's something everyone does and no doubt comes as the result of our social need to quickly develop survival skills in the playground. We need to know who is going to smile at us and who is likely to throw a punch or pass messages behind our backs in the next maths lesson.

From these thoughts we start to form ideas of the types of people we're dealing with and how they can be a *useful* person to know; useful in terms of being able to influence the bullies, become friends with or get invites to parties. From these humble beginnings we learn who to trust and who not to trust. We develop our lists of people who will help us and those who won't; people who we're prepared to help and those that we won't. Before you know it, you have a network.

And there are always the 'go to' guys that you need to get to know and befriend because for one reason or another life has given them a gift. Perhaps their parents are rich and they have the only house with a pool in the district, perhaps their mom doesn't mind if you pole up in the afternoon with a bunch of other kids, maybe their dad runs the local ice cream van and will give you the occasional free ice cream, or better still, they were born in a rough neighbourhood and grew up with the tough boys that will punch you as quickly as look at you unless your new best friend says 'this guy's okay, leave him alone'. What precise characteristics make a good *go to guy* is difficult to say but perhaps the biggest issue is the social network they already have – their friends, their family links, the tough boys they already know because of where they grew up or the kindergarten they went to. The ability to network does vary from one person to another. Some people appear to be naturally better at networking than others and are prepared to spend more time doing it. Why do they invest the time? Is it because they're less secure in their own company and therefore seek the company of others? Is it because they come from a family background that lacked deep emotional support and so they seek it elsewhere? Alternatively, is it because their culture – for example, English are naturally restrained when it comes to talking to people they don't know while Italians are much happier to greet people. Even when it comes to sitting on a bus, English people will generally work hard to find the seat furthest apart from the other people seated on the bus, whilst in Italy it's more common for people to find the first available seat and sit next to you.

Do you have a social GOLD CARD?

We don't all have the same standing in the social networking game.

The currency of social networks is your social capital and some people clearly have more social capital than others.

Social capital is not defined by its *ingredients* – i.e. the things that make up your social capital armoury, but in terms of *outcomes* – what those ingredients can do for you or the community you are associated with. The fact that people don't exist in a vacuum but exist within a plurality of formal and informal networks is central to the concept of social capital.

> **Some people have tried to make sense of social capital. One of the most notable of these was a man called Robert Putman who became interested in the breakdown of trust between people and their civil authorities that resulted in his writing many articles on the subject. His work concluded that social capital exposes itself through social networks in different ways (Putnam, 2000). Putnam recognized that the impact of social capital depends on the form it takes in different circumstances.[10]**

I describe these attributes as:

- 'Bond strength' – the influence of social capital on the strength of relationships

- 'Bridgeability' – the extent to which social capital can engender connections through weaker ties

- 'Uplinkability' – how social capital enables individuals, or groups, to engage with others in positions of power (i.e. those who for whatever reason are on a higher plane).

Measuring social capital is not so easy (a crude numeric assessment is to count how many *Facebook* contacts you have). Social capital will become something we all think more about in the future as social networking grows in importance. Finding a new project or job might depend on your bond strength, bridgeability and uplinkability.

Building relationships, one person at a time

Personal relationships naturally accumulate as people go through life and mix with one another. Each individual progressively builds relationship ties with family and friends, work colleagues, the people in their neighbourhood. We each make choices to hang on to the relationship ties we value or we release them. To sustain, social networks demand an investment of time. People have to make the effort to interact.

This effort might be encouraged if someone wanting to keep in touch for social reasons such as staying in contact with school friends, family or work alumni, or because they recognize an advantage through the relationship. For example, individuals may want to expand their gaming network by leveraging relationships with some of the people they go to college with. Other social structures have a location context such as the places where they live, work or keep fit.

Most of these networks result from a *commonly shared interest*. They don't necessarily result in an outcome or people having to 'do' anything. The network exists – and continues to exist – because people want to communicate to keep their shared interest alive. The rewards for the individual vary. It might be a tacit form of emotional support, to belong to a community, or it might be more implicit such as a learning experience.

Other times people will come together through a *shared outcome* that they want to achieve; people who had no previous relationship or reason to know one another. For example, a group of neighbours who find themselves in the path of a planned new runway development might decide to create a protest group to raise objections. The existence of the network is inextricably tied to the achievement of the outcomes of the project; i.e. to prevent the runway from being built.

What happens when the decision to proceed or cancel this runway project has been made? Does the network just disappear? Are all of the fragments of relationships forged for this common purpose instantly forgotten? The answer invariably is no. Once relationships are forged, many of the connections will remain in place.

Not all relationships have the same 'strength'. Examine your own address book. How many of these people wouldn't object to you calling them out of the blue? How many of them would do a favour for you? This is what is meant by the strength of a relationship – it is the level of effort someone is prepared to make to help you and invest time in keeping in contact with you. We all of us have school friends that we could have kept in contact with but chose not to do so because we weren't prepared to invest this time (perhaps because there wasn't enough in common, or the person did not appear to be very friendly last time a conversation took place).

Strong ties are harder to maintain than weak ties because they demand more frequent contact and attention. There's a limit to the number of strong ties an individual can maintain. Weak ties, on the other hand, are practically limitless, given they include people you may have met only once or know in a specific social context (like your boss's wife). But with both strong and weak ties, new relationship opportunities can present themselves. Weaker ties can provide stepping stones to new relationships. For example, you might be at a party and find someone you once knew as the geeky spotty kid who kept distracting you at college happens now to be the successful best friend of the host. Simply saying that you know each other from college may turn out to be the best thing that guy ever did for you.

We each of us have a 'live' set of relationships (i.e. the people in your address book who wouldn't be surprised if they were to hear from you) that sustain because there is an active reason to engage with them. We also each have a longer list of 'dormant' contacts that are known to us but would not expect to be approached unless there was a suitable context and the request for contact, the required time investment on responding to the communication, was judged to be *reasonable*. Just imagine how you would feel if someone you fleetingly met at a pub phoned you up at home and asked for an introduction to your boss! How would you feel? Put upon?

In the Georgian era, etiquette prevented someone from saying hello to someone else unless they had been introduced. Today we can pretty much talk to anyone we want to without a formal introduction – but whether they'll talk back is another thing!

Attitudes towards 'what is reasonable' when it comes to people communicating are forever changing and they differ between generations. Most of the people I know in my Generation X are reluctant to share their personal contact information on the web. They wouldn't dream of sharing their personal family photographs online where others can see them. But the friends I have in Generation Y (children of the baby boomers born from 1978 to 1995) and my children of Generation Z think nothing of it. It's wrong for us to base how people will interact with one another in future ('what is reasonable' in terms of how networks are formed, and what level of contact is appropriate) based on our own perspectives of what is socially acceptable today within our own fields of experience. Future generations might find it totally 'cool' to pass on their contacts to others without requiring too much justification.

The debate on social capital, the value individuals and groups lever within social networks, has moved up a gear in the 21st century as government recognize the future potential influence of these formal and informal networks on economies and society.

More liberal attitudes towards sharing and exploiting social contacts are emerging. Today, more than ever, it's okay to ask someone you know for an introduction to someone else. Why? Because you can bet they'll be asking you to do the same at some point later down the road. The heightened awareness of social networks exposed by consumer-led social media tools like Facebook and MySpace is relaxing standards of propriety.

Birds of a feather flock together

This well known English proverb suggests that those people of similar taste congregate in groups. Social networking proves it to be true.

The almost organic formation of social networks brings together like-minded individuals who share the same interests, adopt similar behaviours etc. For decades, big corporations have treated consumers as face-less transactions. This impersonal engagement approach with consumers is no longer working. Marketing communications that take no interest in the type, personality or cultural background of an individual are falling on deaf ears. For commerce, social networks are interesting because the individuals within them often exhibit shared norms and values. What commerce sees in these new micro-cultures are micro-markets for products and services. Vendors have the opportunity to infiltrate the trust bond between members of a group to lever personal endorsements for their offerings that dramatically increase the probability of sales. Understanding how to access these micro-markets and communicate in ways that develop trust and don't challenge the norms of behaviour that exist within them has become a business critical issue.

Deep 'emotional' support

Social networks are important to us as individuals because they provide *emotional support*.

In the Victorian era it was normal for people to have large families. No doubt this was partly cultural and also because of the horrendous life *expectancy of child due to disease. It was also for economic reasons.* Children represented *more hands* to work to support the family and put food on the table. Large families also offered a more substantial emotional support network where every member of the family group had people – other family members – that could be relied upon when times were hard.

Children growing up rely on the emotional support of families and friends. But we all know that not every child has the same level of opportunity. Consider the advantages enjoyed by a child from a wealthy background who attends public school and an Oxbridge education compared to a child from a 1950's housing project who goes to a comprehensive school, and only because his mum says he has to. The public school boy can look forward not only to a good education but the opportunity to develop a social network with peers that come from a similarly advantaged background. These relationships (and those of his parents) with will foster social advantage in later life.

The emotional support available to individuals can be shallow (close family and friends) or it can be deep, far reaching and highly influential.

This support network is for me the biggest advantage and reason why children of a public school education profit in later life; suggesting that the biggest difference between the 'haves' and 'have nots' in a classless society is more about the size and credentials of an individuals' deep support network, not the affluence of their family.

Social networking has always existed, manifest in a deep support network that helps advantaged children find the better jobs and opportunities while children whose parents have weaker connections and little social influence struggle to find a way in life. The advent of social media sites means that individuals are better able to harness contacts in their deep emotional support networks. Moreover, individuals with limited access to a support network can seek to develop a larger network by harnessing contacts they meet in day-to-day life, and leverage relationships to people that *these contacts* know.

Most people know that the best way to *find* a job is through *networking*. The economic slowdown in early 2009 led to a dramatic increase in the use of business social networking sites like *'Plaxo'*, 'Xing' and *'LinkedIn'* as a means to generate job opportunities. Individuals who used to treat business social networking as a happy pastime – something to do during the lunch break – are now adding more information to their profiles and spending more time promoting links to others in their network with the ambition of finding new work opportunities.

Online social network media sites have become both a social and economic enabler. They form a social support mechanism for young people to be heard when other mechanisms appear not to be listening. In her remarkable book 'The Support Economy' author Shoshana Zuboff describes how society has changed faster than institutions of capitalism stating, "People have changed more than the business organizations upon which they depend. The chasm that now separates individuals and organizations is marked by frustration, mistrust, disappointment, and even rage."

Social networks are a place where individuals find emotional support; feeling connected, having a voice, encouraged by the success of others. Few corporations have any visibility or understanding of this new support fabric of society.

Modern attitudes of individualism are exposed through the type of relationships consumers seek through their buying behaviours. No longer are consumers volunteering to be treated like pawns in a corporate game; a faceless transaction on a balance sheet. Instead they look for relationships with suppliers that support their values and emulate their attitudes. Digital social networks become the start-point; the place where consumers look for guidance on new products and services.

Tribal brands

For business the cost of finding new customers is increasing as traditional vehicles of promotion such as onscreen TV advertising, newspaper and magazine advertising are losing ground against new social media sites. Companies are investing more heavily in new ways to influence social networks. Unlike the old rule book of marketing that said corporations could *tell* people what they could buy and for how much, the society of the 21st century dictates that suppliers must adopt an inclusive engagement approach. Social networks *amplify* the power of the individual. People, particularly young people, won't buy from sharp suited faceless corporations when they have a choice.

Comparison sites like *gocompare.com*, *comparethemarket.com* and *uSwitch.com* and *confused.com* demonstrate how the World Wide Web provides greater depth of choice in a single place, and how *that* can rapidly change the dynamics of markets. They did not exist a decade ago, but now the price comparison website industry is worth over a billion pounds a year in the UK alone. For many firms, price comparison sites now provide the majority of their business – so getting onto the first results page on web search results is vital. In the case of comparison sites, all consumers see happening is one sharp suited corporation being replaced by another. On TV adverts for these websites, we do at least see caricatured 'normal people' promoting services to us, wearing jeans and jumpers and portraying themselves as the sort of people you'd expect as neighbours if you lived in a middle-class area somewhere in Surrey.

The next change in buying behaviour I expect will be even more dramatic. As individuals adopt social networking environments as a day-to-day place to communicate and 'live' we can expect the focus of advertisers to move there. It won't be on their own terms because like any relationship on a social network, only people who are invited can play. This makes it likely that social networks will evolve 'advocates'; people who source products and services to serve the needs of the buying communities they represent.

In my book *Agilization*, I describe this new kind of *tribal* market. The term 'tribal' when used today seems to hark back to some primitive era but I don't mean the term to be in any way derogatory. We all belong to one tribe or another and to me, social networks are part of that native instinct; an important part of human behaviour that through the centuries has helped us to survive. A tribal market is one that embraces small communities of people who come together through a common interest or set of values and then apply their buying power to assert their personality on the marketplace. This assertion of values and expectations of products and services today has the potential to influence supplier behaviours such as how mobile phone companies design their phones to have replaceable covers so people can enjoy 'images' that suit them.

Consumer markets will get ever more tribal in the participative age due to the assertion of the power of social networking communities. Just imagine how easy it will be in future for a community of workers or friends to establish a buying group; to procure holiday rentals overseas or electronics products (like cameras) that support a hobby (say, photography). Where today every individual would search for the best deal online, we can imagine that creating a buying community could soon be a mouse-click on the social network portal. Instead of offering products online via their own website or a price comparison site, suppliers might soon be serving the needs of 50, 100 or 1000 consumers through social networks. And what would happen if communities increase their buying advantage by offering their endorsement with *other* individuals in their network? If social networks harness their buying power, they will need to recruit advocates that work on their behalf (not on behalf of the suppliers) to facilitate deals and manage relationships.

This scenario paints a picture of a new *tribal* consumer market. Consumer product and service suppliers will serve new market needs by working more intimately with communities found in social networks. It won't be possible for suppliers to dictate how to package or sell their wares. They are to become the servants of capitalism, not dictators.

As yet the social structures forged by digital social networking haven't translated into *buying communities* able to leverage their influence on product and service quality or selection – but that will come. I suggest in Agilization that ultimately some of these social networks will 'brand' themselves to organize and harness their buying power.

> A 'tribal brand' describes an emerging consumer-driven market organism born of a common expression of values held by loosely-coupled communities of individuals and manifested in 'sticky values'. Tribal brands leverage buying influence of consumers to engineer deals with suppliers prepared to meet the specific needs of their communities. Through tribal brands, individuals can collectively assert their buying power. Corporations will invest in the development of tribal brands because they provide a cost-effective means of reaching buyers who adopt common values and interests.

Relationships with market intermediaries such as these will be life threateningly important for suppliers. We're ahead of this curve and only just beginning to see the evolution of social networking into a daily habit but there are already examples of consumer-facing organizations that project similar behaviours to those tribal brands will emulate.

One of these examples is the FAIRTRADE movement that encourages consumers to buy produce like coffee on terms that ensure money gets back to the disadvantaged farming communities that source the goods rather than retailers and merchants retaining the lions share. Consumers who buy FAIRTRADE produce force suppliers to adopt behaviours through organized buying power. Another example of this is (PRODUCT) RED.

> (PRODUCT) RED is a not-for-profit organization that supports the global fund to fight against aids by encouraging companies that sell consumer products and services to design (RED) branded products. When products are sold a portion of the profits is paid to the global fund. Companies that support (RED) today include American Express, Apple, Converse, Dell, Emporio Armani, Gap, Hallmark, Starbucks Coffee and Microsoft. The amount of funds generated by (RED) to date is the equivalent of providing more than 660,000 people with HIV lifesaving antiretroviral therapy for a year. Consumers who want to assert their values through (RED) can purchase anything from gadgets and designer clothes to credit cards.

Upside down markets

As social networks sites become mainstream and a daily activity for the majority of Western World people, more organized consumer groups will inevitably evolve. This transformation will lead to niche interest groups and then clusters of niche interest groups until the online digital market place won't be about corporate websites that consumers 'go to' but aggregations of advocacy-led social networking clusters that will no doubt work through new types of brokers and agents to offer buying solutions to their communities. Consumer brands will want to rush in and get closer to these new consumer clusters. The old rule book of marketing and of corporate brand policy that keeps customers at arm's reach will leave many brands out in the cold.

> The brand expert, Alan Mitchell in his book 'Right Side Up' paints the picture of an age where the focus of competition migrates to whether you are 'on my side' or not, and if so, how efficient, effective and enthusiastic organizations are at acting on behalf of their customers.

What happens next is that a traditional manufacturer's value-chain design-build-warehouse-ship-market-sell is replaced with a new model where advocates of tribal brands first describe their needs, to brokers who find the best fit solutions from suppliers. This reversal of the value chain puts consumers who are able to leverage their social networks into organized buying power at the head of the food chain of capitalism.

A key difference in this upside down model is the *ownership* of the customer relationship. Where today companies spend millions of dollars on their direct marketing and customer relationship management systems, this final step in the marketing chain is more likely to be dominated in future by brokers and tribal brands. It is they who will manage the relationship with consumers, it is they who will own the databases of customers and manage the final act of provisioning. In future, unless suppliers have 'permission' to approach consumers, the likelihood of them being able to execute successful marketing campaigns will be extremely small; so small I expect that it will probably not be an option. If suppliers aren't 'on the inside' working in consort with tribal brands, then I expect they will experience their own ice age.

This race for affiliation has already started, hence the amount of money being invested by large consumer brands to try out new ways of reaching out to online communities.

Brands are an extremely valuable business asset. They serve to build an emotional picture to consumers of the *values* of an organization that are intended to foster an emotional affiliation with consumers – almost as if to say 'We *get* you; we know how *you* feel'. Already brands like Shell (now the *Energy* not *Oil* company) and the Cooperative Bank are promoting ethical and environmental values to influence buying decisions. But consumer-facing organizations are going to need to do more than make brand promises if they are to succeed in tribal markets. Consumers are quick to see through corporations who attempt to create a false façade of 'sticky values' (emotional values that organizations seek to associate with their brand like 'youthful', 'socially conscious' or 'hip') that might have appealed once to consumers in the 1990's.

In the participative age, the only way brands can influence behaviours is to become *a part* of the social landscape. Companies like Apple® do this very well. Today, if you were to look online for information on Apple® products, you are more likely to see a video created by a customer in their bedroom than an 'official' corporate release. As happened with the *iPhone,* Apple® will encourage consumer endorsements by taking the videos cut by consumers and editing them rather than make their own.

In this way, social networking, an interesting study of social behaviours in the 20th century, promises to be the *primary platform* of consumer markets in the 21st century.

2

A place to network

When I grew up, people said it was in the clubhouse at the local golf course, in the Wine bars of London Walk or smoke filled Men's Clubs where the real networking took place. Now the places where people network are more plentiful, more varied.

Networking is harder to spot.

Stand in a tube train or a hotel lobby on a Monday morning and they will be overflowing with people on their *iPhones* and *Blackberrys*, probably networking with others over the digital web. Social networking has moved from discrete exclusive locations that few could access to an activity that happens everywhere. Any time of the day you will find people growing their social capital. The digital age of the Internet and mobile phone is uniquely creating and enabling social networks by providing access to 'a place' where people can find like-minded individuals who share their values, interests and shared outcomes. The Internet is a place where markets form; markets for products and markets for knowledge.

The term 'social media' refers to the user generated content that is created when people share their knowledge and experiences with others, although digital publishing applications like *MSN*, *MySpace*, *Twitter*, *YouTube* and *Facebook* – i.e. the technology platforms that support these aggregations – are seen as such integral components to the medium that they generally fall within the same description. Social media websites create ways of finding people you have a relationship with, offer mechanisms to engage with them, exchange information and then manage the content relating to those relationships. They enable individuals to strengthen their existing relationships, harness 'weak' ties that would probably have otherwise fallen dormant and to also find new relationships by using as stepping stones the relationships individuals already have. Digital social media websites powered by the Internet, create a market for relationships – 'who knows who' – on a global scale.

MSN, MySpace and *Facebook* are some of the most widely known social media sites. They achieved their success through teenagers and college graduates recognising that they could present their personality online and expose it to others. Through these vehicles they could find like-minded people with similar interests and communicate with them. Social media sites display the social consciousness of people who use them to register their right to exist, be different, and to live and express their individualism as they want to. But *Facebook* isn't just a hangout for young people. More and more adults use it too.

21st century social networking behaviours

Social networks today use the World Wide Web and social media tools as a place to meet and keep in touch. Unlike a letter or telephone, people who use social media sites are always online and connected.

For many individuals, like my daughter and her friends, the Internet and mobile phone becomes a life essential. The social networks they facilitate are an essential social fabric to this youthful generation; part of what they understand society to mean in the 21st century. The values and experiences found in *MSN* and *Facebook* have more relevance to young people than political parties, trades unions, local community structures and religion. The ideals of 'everyone is equal on the web' and it is the right of every individual to assert their personality online and express their opinions is a reflection of our 21st century society. The Internet is not seen to *cost the planet* anything. It is a treasure that everyone can use without feeling guilty. The advent of social media and always online access to the Internet via browser or mobile phone has led to the emergence of new pastimes:

Wikis

A 'wiki' is a collaborative web-page that enables anyone with a rudimentary knowledge of plain text scripting (which isn't so difficult to learn) to contribute or modify content. It's like sitting around a table with a note-pad and giving everyone a pen to contribute their thoughts and opinions. Before you know it, you have a very full pad! Wikis are a way of gathering knowledge collaboratively and putting it in one place used to create and to power community websites (visit www.Wikipedia.org for the best example). Computer scientist Howard G. 'Ward' Cunningham came up with the wiki idea in 1994. His 'WikiWikiWeb' site went live in 1995[11] and formed a model for all of the wikis sites that followed. Later he said he'd thought about patenting the idea. I bet he wished he had.

Blogging

'Blogging' is about having a web-site you can write on so that others can read what you're thinking and comment on it. The connected nature of the web gives bloggers the ability to enter links to other blogs to assimilate stories on the topics authors are interested in. They act as *collections of insight* for others to read. Therefore, the bloggers become thoughtful 'informediaries'. Blogs started out like online diaries that used simple design wizards and authoring tools to empower individuals with only limited IT skills to publish their thoughts and make them available for others to read. Once a document has been authored, bloggers can use free online services like *Pingoat, Pingomatic, kping* and *pingyourblog* to inform search engines that it's there to be read. Really Simple Syndication (RSS) is the underpinning web feed communication format that is most commonly employed to feed blogs to search engines. It is a common standard that can be read by many different programs. Where users want to monitor a specific blog they can use an RSS reader like *Google Reader* or *RssReader* to check subscribed feeds regularly for new work and download any updates they find. RSS feeders provide a user interface to monitor and read the feeds. In order to attract the attention of search engines, blogs must be updated frequently to develop content and substance (for the top blogs that means on a daily basis) – because search engines like fresh content. For this reason many blogs have moved from becoming personal diaries to team sports. More successful blogs adopt industrial media techniques such as having a single story focus or picking off topical subjects in the news.

I Can Has Cheezburger? is an example of a blog that works. Launched in January 2007, the site focuses on light humour and has estimated revenues of $5,600 a month[12] through its monthly 15 million page views. The site has everything you would expect in a blog – lots of instantly rewarding clips and articles, a fistful of online advertisers and a grungy, inoffensive design style. Other examples of blogs that work include *Boing Boing* that key-lines into cyber-culture with revenues exceeding $1 million a year from its 22 million page views every month and *Mashable* with 4 million page views per month and a somewhat remarkable estimated revenue of over $166,000 per month!

'BoingBoing'. Blogs like this are serious business making $millions each year

Podcasting

Podcasts picked up their name from the Apple iPOD. They're a means of disseminating previously recorded sound files that people can download to their portable media player so they can listen to them later. Anyone with a computer, internet connection, and an audio recorder can record an MP3 format file and then upload it to a server on the internet where they can be found and downloaded by 'podcatchers' (the programs that identify podcasts.) The podcatcher reads a feed to identify the podcast and download it to a computer. It's possible to do a similar thing using video formats but then they're called a vidcast.

Twittering

Twitter was launched in 2006 and describes itself as 'a free social messaging utility for staying connected in real-time'. *Twitter* gives people the choice to be voluntarily stalked by millions of others. It makes it possible for people to communicate using simple text-based messaging.

The technology that makes this possible is a digital messaging website that communicates your messages to other members who have asked to follow the entrails of your daily ramblings. Like an 'always-on blog' you can send little 'tweets' to the site to explain what you're doing at any point in the day and the content immediately gets distributed to anyone who chooses to 'follow you'. Celebrities like Britney Spears and Al Gore, even institutions like the BBC and No.10 Downing Street have their own *Twitter* accounts. *Twitter* offers capabilities on its website to connect people to others; what is now being described as micro-blogging. When you create your membership on the *Twitter* site, it invites you to interrogate your email services like Yahoo and Gmail to find accounts of people that might want to follow you. It was recently reported that actor Stephen Fry has over 50,000 people following his twitters![13]

Twitter works on mobile networks in some countries which means people can *twitter* whilst on the move; sending new messages and being updated on the people they follow. The whole experience is extremely interactive and, according to some of the users that I know, becomes quite obsessive. The real-time aspect of *twitter*ing 'anytime, anyplace, anywhere' makes it unique. *Twitter* fully leverages the always on possibilities of the digital era to connect people around the world and enable freedom of thought. It offers Generation Y unprecedented freedom of expression, the ability to live in other people's pockets 24 hours a day if they really want to.

Like other social media, *Twitter* becomes yet another form of communication that third parties can leverage for their own purposes. One highly visual example of this is '*Twitter*vision' that was created by the entrepreneur Dave Troy. It's an independent website that presents *Twitter*s on a world map as they're happening. Viewers see the thoughts of millions of people from different nationalities communicating.

What's driving demand for social media?

Digital social networking made possible through mobile and web-based social media tools such as those listed above is a 21st century social phenomenon. Young people are prepared to invest hours of their time to publishing their inner most thoughts and experiences on social media sites because they feel a need to be online and engaged. Of course when dad starts joining in, suddenly these sites can become *un-cool*, so there's lots of space for new ideas.

At different life stages, young people find good reasons to become part of the social networking phenomenon.

Children are growing up spending less time outside, on parks and interacting with the kids in their town. This is partly because of parental concern for their safety. It's also because they choose to plug themselves into gaming consoles and TV screens. Children as young as five are turning their bedrooms into multi-media hubs with computers, TVs, games consoles, mobile phones and home entertainments systems. According to one survey of 1,800 children aged five to 16 conducted by *ChildWise*[14], children can spend an average of 2.7 hours a day watching TV, 1.5 on the internet and 1.3 playing games. In February 2008, HM Government's schools minister emphasised the risks of parents creating a generation of 'battery farmed children' by encouraging children to pursue these 21st century behaviours indoors. But it's easy to see why connecting to social media sites becomes liberating for these children and, with an absence of 'street scene' social interaction, that little Jane and little Jonny relish the thrills of communicating with other children around the world in real-time.

Teenagers and college students who have grown up with computers and the Internet have similarly been ignited by social media tools.

The internet has become the binding communications fabric of a generation. My first book (*'Agilization'*) introduces the term *Individualism* to describe how young people today want to assert their personality through the digital web that spans the world. Many young people feel unsupported by the traditional emotional support vehicles such as community, family, religion, political parties and trades unions. They feel disenfranchised; that this world is *not theirs*, and they choose instead to login to the digital world of the Internet to connect to old friends and to also find new friends who share their interests and values. More children are growing up in single parent families with no male role models around, some (not all) see religion to be irrelevant to their world – similarly politics and politicians – and as they look to the future they don't see how they will make a difference. It's as if everything that could be done *has* been done. One of my younger friends said hers was the *hope-less* generation, a generation without hope. They feel isolated and alone. They crave freedom of self-expression.

The whole idea of exposing your soul on the Internet to thousands of other people you don't know is alien to older generations. Many of my baby-boomer friends are quick to identify the risks attached to sharing information like who we are and where we live. The young people of Gen X and Y don't think that way. For them logging into the Internet and connecting to others through social media sites is natural and well worth the risk of sharing a little personal information. NOT being online is like cutting yourself off from the rest of the world. You're not SOMEONE if you're not on *Facebook*.

The adoption of new collaborative web technologies is progressing at two speeds; almost instantly for Gen X and Y and, for the rest of us, as long as it takes for a sibling or young work colleague to mention it!

It's a value based market. No level of marketing spend can convince millions of other people to adopt these technologies. The user communities decide for themselves and users are getting accustomed to seeking opinions of like-minded users over corporate ads that are losing their impact on buyer behaviours. New innovations are broadcast by web communities that find them and start to use them. The same sites – *Facebook, YouTube, Twitter* etc. – become the vehicles to share great ideas. Sites like *YouTube* prove themselves to be valuable evidenced by the level of user adoption (*YouTube* could boast many thousands of subscribers by the time they found their way onto the radar of news writers and technology journals).

Genres of current 'social media sites'

There are two main categories of social networking websites:

Social media sites provide emotional support for individuals through contact with their peer groups on social matters such as party planning, sharing opinions. Family matters etc. To example this category of social network, my daughter used to belong to a sleep-over club when she was younger (what Americans call a slumber party). She and her friends would take turns to keep consecutive parents awake all night in a ritual that demanded lots of chocolate, make-up and pillow fights. To keep in-touch with one another they would regularly communicate on *MSN*. When they hit their teens, the sleep-over clubs migrate to *MySpace* and *Facebook* but whatever the conduit, the network will continue to exist until it loses its relevance to the participants.

The other major category is **business social networking sites** that are designed to harness social capital and through it create wealth by enabling individuals to harvest their relationships and exploit the influence of relationship ties. It's not unheard of for a salesperson to leave one company for a competitor and promise to bring a contact book along full of new prospects. Tangible value comes from relationships acquired through business but there are even more possibilities if commercial organizations can tap into the deep support networks of individuals. These categories are more theoretic than real. I use them to describe the original *reason for being* of different *genres* of technical platform. In the real world, sites like *Facebook* have since become an essential part of business life for many people and sites like *Ning* enable people to create their own social network <u>for any reason</u>. Sites like *Facebook* and *Ning* show that, as happens in the real-world, people *work where they live* and they *live where they work*.

Social Media Sites

Language changes. In addition to great terms like *va-va-voom* and *wiggle room* that have recently made it into the Concise Oxford English Dictionary, we also have words like *spyware* and *blogosphere* entering vocabulary. New words that fall into such common use that dictionaries record them evidence societal change. The digital age introduces new verbs like *Googling* and (to) *Twitter*, *YouTube*, *Flickr*, *Skype, MSN, MySpace* and *Facebook*. They reveal the impact of computing behaviours on society. These verbs are associated with social media sites that enable people to share information in different formats; text, video, images, or personalised collections of everything.

If you're sub-20 years of age I expect you already know about them, probably use them. Even if you've passed the 20's I expect at some point you've heard someone talk about these websites. You might have even *Googled* them. Having done so, you would no doubt draw the conclusion that the average age of user communities is, well, young. What these consumer-focused social media tools have in common is they're all relatively inexpensive and they enable almost anyone to publish or access information. They differ therefore from 'industrial media' like a printing press that generally requires significant financial capital before you can publish anything to the masses. Here's a roundup of the most influencing social media sites just in case you've not encountered them before.

Facebook.com

From its origins in the dorms of Harvard, *Facebook* has become the best known social networking site. Individuals use it to share their public face. *Facebook* is what most people see as the invention that really started digital social networking. While there were websites out there doing similar things, *Facebook* managed to capture the imagination of a large enough group of Harvard campus students and media publicists to bring the possibilities of digital social media to the attention of the world.

Facebook allows people to gather together all of their social media content in a single place on the Web so that others can find them and learn more about their personality. It's like an ego-wall where you can, as an individual, express your personality through your images and digital content, relationships, likes, dislikes and associations.

Valuations of *Facebook* range for £3 billion to $15 billion; clearly evidencing the leadership position that *Facebook* holds in the consumer social media market. The facts about *Facebook* are astounding. According to *Facebook*'s own statistics, the average user has 120 friends on the site, collectively users spend more than 3 billion minutes on *Facebook* each day (worldwide) while more than 18 million users – 70% of them outside the United States - update their statuses at least once each day. So if you think about it, at anytime of the day, there will be someone somewhere updating their profile on *Facebook*.[15]

Flickr.com

Flickr is a website for sharing photos. Given the mass of digital cameras (and mobile phones with embedded digital cameras) millions of people walk the surface of the planet today with a camera. *Flickr* provides a common place on the web for people to publish their collections and view others.

YouTube.com

YouTube lets you broadcast yourself. It provides a home to the video clips you might produce and a place for you a place to share them with others. It also means you can view their videos too. Corporations publish videos on *YouTube* to promote their products through informal videos and encourage individuals to produce their own videos about their products.

'Somegreybloke' created by Mike Booth[16] is an animated character that regularly features on *YouTube*. It examples the tongue-in-cheek satirical humour that youth culture brings to cyberspace older folk aren't meant to understand. It's visual humour that has a slightly despairing tone to it that appeals to today's young people and inevitably draws large numbers of website hits. One example of Mike's work is a video titled 'What is *Facebook* For' where our self deprecating guide *Somegreybloke* sits as he always does before his PC in a dressing gown and goes on to describe *Facebook* as, '..a massively multiplayer role-playing game where the objective is to collect as many friends as possible.'

YouTube has created a market-place for individual creative talent that has fundamentally changed the creative industry by alerting corporations to the skills of young people who are using the medium of video to project their ideas.

MySpace.com

MySpace was one of the first places on the Internet that people would go to create a community with their friends to share thoughts and pictures. It soon became the place people visited when they wanted to connect with friends in cyberspace. Interestingly, the launch of *Facebook* created in some communities like the US army a two tier social networking stratosphere where officers would use *Facebook* (probably because of their campus education) and rank and file soldiers would use *MySpace*!

MSN and Windows Live

For my kids, MSN is the place they go to meet their friends in the digital sphere. According to Microsoft's statistics[17], more than 120 million people connect to what they now brand as *MSN Windows Live Spaces* on a monthly basis. The site provides individuals with their space on the Internet where they publish their thoughts, communicate with friends, share music and photos. Microsoft's social networking platform was one of the first to emerge and continues to be one of the most popular sites for individuals to communicate with one another.

This is a small list of the many collaborative tools and communications vehicles that innovative companies are coming up with to serve the consumer social networking market. There are many hundreds more. Others you might want to *google* include *Ning, BeBo, Friendster, Hi5, TagWorld, PerfSpot, Zorpia, Netlog* and *Yahoo 360*.

3

People vectors

Metaconcepts of social networks

Against a backdrop of morning after news stories about people getting unstuck by putting things on *YouTube* or *Facebook* (they later wished they hadn't) there are things going on with social networking that have important implications for the world of business. Scientists, academics and entrepreneurs are looking at the bubble of hype and trying to strain out factors that will have a sustainable impact on the way people will live and work in future. It isn't terribly charming but in the science of social computing every person is a 'node' on a series of networks created by 'ties' (the relationship links that form associations between nodes). In computing, the *data that describes data* used to catalogue and make sense of *classes of information* is called 'metainformation' or 'metadata'. When people network, they're creating more information about themselves and their ties:

Who they know
Their likes and dislikes
What groups and communities they frequent
Where they live
What they think about
Who they meet and connect to
Their relationship ties

Gathering this new metainformation and exploiting it is interesting to social scientists who are trying to work out what makes people 'tick' and how society works. Its use has the potential to revolutionize the way we live and work. The *participative age* as it is becoming known is the first era of human history where identities, relationships, preferences and behaviours are being voluntarily entered by individuals into computers to build a social map of the world; a map of unimaginable proportions. Here I briefly describe the metaconcepts that hide beneath the social networking habits of people that are creating a different kind of society.

Metaconcept 1. Ego-lens and ego-walls

EGO-LENS

Two basic factors drive how, as individuals, we relate to the world:

1. Our perspective of the outside world as we look upon it (what I call the 'ego lens').
2. ..and our understanding of how we want the world to view us as individuals (what I call the 'ego-wall').

We all have our own uniquely weird perspectives of the world of information. We stand on top of our very own mountain surrounded by a panorama of insights that we view through a lens shaped by our personal learning experiences and perspectives of 'how the world works according to me'. The *ego-lens* is a view cast by our individual personas. It is the reason why the inventiveness of the human race can never be replicated by computers. It's impossible to separate the human aspects of personality, our value traits, passions, beliefs and phobias, and how we apply them to distort how we each see the world from a unique perspective. Not only do we each rationalize insight in different ways based on our personal life experiences, but when working in teams or communities, very often the interplay of individuals will further change how we collectively make sense of information. The human race has the power to think irrationally; to make mistakes in the way information is consumed and interpreted. This can lead to completely new perspectives that no computer would have come up with through logic alone.

> **When Sir Isaac Newton famously observed an apple falling from a tree to the ground, he didn't think "that's handy, I**

> fancy some fruit" like others might. The event happened at the time he was making sense of a particular subject (that turned out to be 'gravity'). His world of insight at that moment was being viewed through an acutely distorted lens.

The 'from where I'm standing' *ego-lens* takes many factors into account when exploring information including the basis of knowledge the individual already has, their interests, the time criticality of information or the location of the individual. And we sometimes opt to proactively distort our view of the world.

> **At NDMC we believe our economic success comes from harnessing the talents of our people in a way that makes their lives fulfilling and bring a positive contribution to society. We wouldn't entertain projects for customers that force our people to do work they're not suited to or don't enjoy, or that knowingly results in an outcome that negatively impacts on society. As a business we have purposefully imposed a *filter* on how we see the world.**

Whether we choose to slap it on *Facebook* or not, we each of us have in our minds an ego-wall that presents us. It is our emotional picture of who we are and our lives. The ego-wall is a collection of values, styles, caricatures and preferences that we use to describe ourselves to others. Social networks map across these individual spaces but they never subsume them. Generation Y leaving the University campus today isn't anything like as worried about sharing personal information that previous generations have.

A characteristic of the *participative age* is that a person's individual space is exposed on the web like a calling card so others can lever this information to create new ties. Individuals who want to communicate with others first present their own *ego-wall* as credentials to join the network. In some ways this is what 'the ego-wall' of the social media site *Facebook* does that I profile in the next chapter. Platforms like *Facebook* expose everyone's individual space to make judging a person and their potential social capital easier. It's an open club that you can join. The importance of this ego-centricity has been lost on many providers in the computer industry and it took the success of *Facebook* to wake the business world up to its relevance. It's been a major reason why so many attempts to harness knowledge management have failed. Industry has focused too much on gathering and husbanding content without giving sufficient consideration to the ego-centricity of users. Not *Google*.

> *Google*, **the well known web search engine, catalogues the metainformation of how websites interact. By harvesting this information it let's users search and find the insight they're looking for and it does this by analyzing the frequency of ties between websites, between websites and people, people and content.** *Google* **exposes this hidden matrix of meta-information and all users see is a weighted list of the insight that is most likely useful to them.**

The role of ego-centricity on learning and knowledge sharing is important to register because, as I explain later, there are two schools of thought on how the future direction of social networks, computing and the workplace will go. Ego-centricity is at the very heart of this debate.

Metaconcept 2. Mapping ties (Joining the dots)

Social networks are made up of the ties between the nodes. Relationships form these ties between us. Social network maps and models reveal these ties. Presented as an illustration, like the six degrees of separation diagram in the first chapter, these ties appear like a spider's web with the ego-centric 'me' at the centre. What illustrations like this hide are the vast differences between the characteristics and strengths of ties.

STRENGTH

This is the degree of emotional bond we feel for another 'node'.

The relationship with your mother is stronger than the tie you share with a distant cousin. Even *first degree* ties are of different strengths. The *strength of tie* is the degree of intimacy measured by how much someone will do for someone else (in most cases not much!). Individuals are more likely to ask people with whom they share a deep bond for advice or guidance. These are more *elastic* relationships. Having not spoken to a person for a long time, people are more likely to reconnect with them if they share a deep bond. But Gen Y is happier to share ties with others *even if* the strength of that tie is weak. There is a social acceptability within Gen Y to share ties on the web, in a virtual world, recognizing it to be somehow different to the social standards of the real world.

TRUST LINES

Whilst the bond we have with another person is a factor in how we inter-relate, so too is the confidence we have in a relationship. Trust is generally earned but it might also be inherited. For example, it might be that we trust nurses, religious leaders or police to be *good people*. They inherit an assumed good character because of their role in society. If we trust people we are more likely to ask their advice or go with their recommendations and endorsements. I imagine there to be *trust lines* that lay across social networks. They point to relationship ties where trust exists. It is these ties that commercial organizations seek to tap into because they know the power of an endorsement when it comes from someone whose opinion is valued.

> **"The Strength of Weak Ties", was a famous article written by American socialogist Mark Granovetter and published in the American Journal of Sociology in 1973. In it Granovetter set out his observations on how people leverage their weak ties to bridge into new relationships and forge new connections. His study reviewed published research articles of the day and led him to conclude that "the strength of a tie is a (probably linear) combination of the amount of time, the emotional intensity, the intimacy (mutual confiding) and the reciprocal services which characterize the tie." In Granovetter's view, a similar combination of strong and weak bonds holds the members of society together.**

ASSOCIATION, IDENTITY AND ROOTS

It's a commonly held belief that people are more attracted to similar than dissimilar others. A study of the social networks of Finnish immigrants in Estonia by Heli Hyvönen of the University of Helsinki in 2008[18] found that most people tend to socialize with others from a similar background and/or in a similar situation. These bonds of culture, faith, beliefs etc. increase the likelihood that bonds will form.

SHARED LIFE EXPERIENCES

This principle states that if you went to the same school I went to then it's more likely we will form a tie. In a similar way, the Alumni of a University or company are more likely to build relationships with others who share an association of an institution or life circumstance even if two individuals have ever met before. Shared life experiences

FREQUENCY

The more time we spend with people, the more likely we are to form a relationship. The more time we spend with people we know, the more intimate a relationship is likely to become.

Metaconcept 3. Entrails of activities and habits

Social networks carry within them a record of the activities and habits of individuals. Social media technology platforms like *Facebook* and *Twitter* encourage people to input their thoughts, activities, preferences, likes and dislikes etc. For the first time in our history, gigabytes of data on the activities and habits of millions of people are being captured by vast computers. Can you imagine how interesting it would be to view maps of these behaviours and see what sort of people do what sort of things with their time and with whom?

This *activity and habit* data holds enormous wealth to commercial organizations able to leverage it to target products and services to individuals who share common interests, habits and behaviours (and who might be more influenced by recommendations from their friends).

Metaconcept 4. The thoughtful web

You might have noticed when browsing the Web that somehow an advert pops up that seems to know your tastes and preferences; the book you like, a favourite holiday destination. Sites like *Amazon, eBay, Facebook* and *Google* are spending millions of dollars to perfect the technology that makes this happen.

Computing is less about silicon chips these days and more about tracking patterns of user behaviour. Having captured your click-trails, product wish-list choices, the sites you visit and the people you talk to on social media sites, those clever computer folk can start to build a picture of 'you' on the web. Once they've done this and worked out what you like they can start to pluck out the information that you want.

The technology exists today to enable people to receive the sort of information they want as they want it, when they want it. The more click trails web users expose, the more able Internet sites are to exploit this data to profile users and start being *thoughtful* and proactive.

The *thoughtful web* is what's waiting for us just around the corner. Not the sort of Internet we live with today that makes us have to do all the running and steals the last few hours of leisure time away from us when we arrive home late from work and just want to 'veg out'.

There's a feeling deep down that the data we give up will be used to manipulate us, throw irritating adverts and promotions in our face. Technologies like 'cookies' placed on our Personal Computers track our personal activities and behaviours can sometimes feel a lot like bugs.

I might be describing your worst nightmare; a [19]George Orwell 1984 story of computers taking over and giving Governments the ability to control us like puppets. But I never read 1984, partly because it sounded too heavy and painted an all too depressing future. Perhaps that's why I have a more encouraging outlook.

The web today has a TRUST problem and many people of my generation don't like the idea that we're being watched by the web (perhaps too many people read 1984?).

Let's take a more positive perspective. Cookies that have the potential to steal our confidential information and plant nasty things on hard drives can also be used to simplify login processes by remembering details like your name and address that you don't want to repeatedly enter every time you need to complete a form. In future, the *thoughtful web* will provide the information you want when you want it. Perhaps in future we will even *choose* to volunteer data and the *thoughtful web* will act on your behalf to find the information, products and services important to you.

Google Latitude is a service offered by Google that provides you with an ability to find your friends and show other people precisely where you are on the planet by tracking the location of your mobile phone (might also turn out to be useful if you lose it!). You're probably wondering how Google Latitude manages to work out where your mobile is with an accuracy of 20 meters! Well the answer is triangulation. Just like the early sailors it takes readings from the positions of satellites, mobile phone masts and Wi-Fi access points and works out through some Sherlock Holmes deduction where you're standing. Typically, mobile phones don't have the brainpower to work all that out so Google Latitude's onboard software gets your phone to send through a few pertinent details about its location and then relies on Google's hugely powerful data crunching servers to spill the answer. Not everyone's happy with Google Lattitude. Privacy International was scathing

about the risks that *Google Latitude* introduces to personal safety, recognising that whilst *Google* insists that you agree to sharing information with their servers it's not impossible for piggy-back applications to hook into the *Google Lattitude* service and commandeer it for more illicit means.

Location-awareness is cool stuff. It brings information to the place in the world where you are sitting right now (you are sitting aren't you?).

Have you ever been out and about and wondered when the next bus might turn up? With location-awareness you can type in the fact you want a bus into a phone from wherever you may be and the mobile phone won't only show you which bus route you're closest to but it will also give you your nearest stop and show you on a map where the next bus currently is on its route at that moment. Imagine that you're in your car with your young and hungry family and you want to know what eateries are between you and your home that can offer you a sit-down meal for two adults and two children for the amount of cash you have in your wallet. Give vendors knowledge of where you are at any particular time and product and service suppliers can help you to find places to buy that are close to you as you drive through town or finish your country walk. The technology exists to do all this today.

Google Latitude shows your location on Googlemaps

There are a lot of new technologies making the thoughtful web happen and location-awareness is just one. Sensor networking technology is another. Millions of little computer micro-chips that use tiny sensors to capture movement, clicks, payments etc. are now concealed all over our world – in meters, on adverts, in our computer devices, watches, pet collars, event tickets and motor cars feed back their data to hosts miles away so that information (that in the 20th century never existed) can serve us to make our lives easier. These tiny sensors will in future let you know precisely where buses are because you'll be able to see them moving around streets on your mobile phone.

Let's not also forget the tremendous impact the humble camera is making to our digital society. We are seeing the digitization of our world. It's thought by 2020, every part of our world will have been photographed. Just visit www.flickr.com and type in the name of any town or village you can think of and it becomes easy to believe. Microsoft now offers tools that automatically apply the address of the location where a photo was taken based on GPS coordinates. Instead of numbers, users get the "real" names of the sights they photograph together with location data that is saved as metadata along with your photos.

Other software products can stitch landscape photos together to create 360 degree views, gather up your photographs and turn them into three dimensional structures (see an example at http://photosynth.net/default.aspx). You can imagine with so many people using so many cameras that the world is a much smaller place.

The *thoughtful web* means that our children won't need to travel too far to find the information they want. Trips down to the local library in the rain on a bitter Saturday morning will soon be a distant memory for most in the Western World.

Advances in telecommunications have so far been the greatest contributor to the *thoughtful web*. This has been helped by Asia, USA and Europe competing for the fastest broadband and mobile networks.

In case you were wondering, and according to the Information Technology & Innovation Foundation's 2008 ranking of the world's broadband internet connections, South Korea and Japan have the fastest broadband internet while Finland is the fastest in Europe with a median download speed of 21,7 Mbps according to the study.[20]

Mobile phones have also had a huge impact. According to market analysts[21] something like 3 billion people use them and in 2009 the mobile phone industry is expecting to sell over 1 billion handsets.

Most people in the Western World (and beyond) are online for large chunks of the day. With *iPhones* brimming with applications and most of the population seemingly connected online, we're all getting used to the idea of being *information consumers*, generally without having to pay anything for the privilege.

We inherit these attitudes and behaviours from our experiences as consumers and transfer them to the workplace, and it's in the business world where information consumerism is set to make its biggest impact.

Here's why.

For years, corporations have happily managed their own stock-piles of corporate information assets. But now there are more information assets outside their corporate firewalls than there are within. Workers growing up with the Internet and free-to-use tools like *Google*, *Facebook* and *Skype* suddenly find themselves trapped within an environment where their access to information is privileged. Even *iPODs* might be seen as a security threat. This doesn't go down well with post graduates!

The way corporations think about information systems is out of sync with the new generation of office workers. IT people think in terms of *platforms* and *applications* when users only think in terms of useful information. It's surprisingly difficult even today to get useful data out of business information systems.

The 21st century is the era of the *information consumer*.

The information services they consume, in the home and at work, are delivered *where* they want them, *when* they want them, *as* they want them. There is no room for compromise. An alternative service is just one click away. In this uncompromising supply and demand world, the winners are *information consumers* who are turning the high handed computer industry into the submissive plaything of children.

The *thoughtful web* is arriving to a browser near you soon.

Metaconcept 5. Information consumerism

In the 1980's when Personal Computers arrived, many of us believed that this innovation would lead to computing for the common man.

But the common man had no grasp of what personal computers were really for. I remember my father asking my mother why she spent over £1200 on an Amstrad PC. What did it do that a typewriter couldn't? Sure, my brother and I had fun filling up its 8 Megabytes of hard disk with silly programs that didn't do very much, and we were able to exploit the spreadsheet application for our homework, but essentially this early PC didn't change the world very much. We still walked down the road to pick up our groceries and went into town to buy our records.

Thirty years on and we're as a society more accustomed to buying products and services online via the PC that takes pride of place in the corner of the dining room or centre stage in our home offices. We know window shopping is easier online while ordering online is normally cheaper. It has been technologies like the Internet, search engines (like *Google*) and Internet browsers like *Microsoft Internet Explorer* that have really started to make the PC worthwhile. In its new role, the PC isn't really doing much more than providing a window to another world. The processing of data and the organization of websites and data is occurring somewhere else. The democratization of computing did not happen with the PC like we thought it would. For the common man, the Personal Computer isn't *personally* computing very much at all. It has become another appliance in our home; like a television or telephone that provides access to a world beyond the comfort of our homes that provides information. The gradual growth of information services delivered to our door via the Internet is the source of a silent revolution. It's not the big bang that some might have expected but it is changing the way the world works.

Most normal people today still don't understand how to programme. For decades, the expertise to apply computing technologies has been held within a small community of experts. The idea of democratized computing will never happen and the notion that we will all need to code or script in order to be a part of the future human race can thankfully be forgotten. Instead, computer science has delivered an environment for producing information services that can easily be consumed with simple tools to create new ways of serving up information.

My kids *consume information services* like *iTunes* and *Googlemaps* and think nothing of it. They use *MSN* and *Skype* without an instruction manual. The clever computer technicians that work for these companies serve up computing in a way that we humble people can just USE it. The 'bricks and mortar' of computing platforms is a background issue that a proportionately small community of IT professionals still have to worry about but for most of us, we no longer need to think too much about HOW information services are delivered – they just are.

> **Information consumerism describes a cultural change in the expectations of information users that it is *information services* and not web-sites, software applications or**

> computing platforms that the consumers of information should expect to pay for.

It leads to a computing behaviour where individuals and organizational entities make available an *information service* that may be consumed on a utility basis.

> Today I can download my applications as a service from *Google*. They supply me with Internet search as a service, my email as a service, my maps as a service and my news as a service. I no longer need to worry about the computer systems or software required to deliver the information services I want to consume. *Google* takes care of that. All I need to think about is what information I'm looking for and what do I want to DO with it.

Information consumerism *democratizes* IT.

The focus of the software publishing industry is rapidly transitioned from the supply of 'applications' (i.e. tools) to information services. As a consumer, for practically any shrink-wrapped software application that I would have previously purchased from a retailer to install on my home PC I can now access a copy-cat application as-a-service. I can even replace my land-line phone with a *Voice over Internet Protocol* phone service like *Skype*. Organizations like *www.OpenOffice.org* and *www.zoho.com* provide credible alternatives to the sorts of packages I would have expected previously to buy and install.

The world of corporate computing is a little slower to change but it too is slowly adopting *information consumerism* in its own way.

Since the start of the century, software companies serving the enterprise computing market-place have started to offer their products on a pay-as-you-use basis; what they called 'Software-as-a-Service' (SaaS). *Salesforce.com* was one of the first software companies to popularise this new commercial model, providing their Customer Relationship Management software to business customer on a per user per month basis.

Success stories like Salesforce.com have encouraged other companies to adopt this commercial model to offer their software. For suppliers it means that they must provide instantly useful software that appeals to a target group and works right-first-time. If software does not deliver on its promises, users can choose to stop using it (normally without any tedious contract clauses) meaning vendors don't get paid. This has driven up standards of usability exponentially across the software industry over the past few years.

In adopting the SaaS commercial model smaller companies have more of an opportunity to enter markets that want to use the information services their software enables. They only need to deliver *something useful* that consumers or businesses are prepared to pay a small amount for every month. But it's not so simple. Customers are naturally demanding and there's a lot of software out there. To shine, vendors must provide a service that is important to the information consumer.

Within an industry accustomed to receiving reasonably hefty license revenues as soon as they sell their applications, Software as a Service's revenue model is painful for vendors to swallow. It drives down the cost of software, by giving purchasers more choice and freedom to move between vendors, and also means that vendors must wait longer to recover their research and development costs as revenues trickle in over a period of months (potentially years).

It's not just software publishers who can jump on the bandwagon to service the needs of information consumers. News and media companies, governmental departments who use and manage information, research companies, federations and professional organizations – all of the organizations who own content are finding new ways of using it to deliver value to information consumers.

The ultimate manifestation of this new information services world is the idea of a virtual cloud that surrounds our world that we can't touch or see. A cloud that has the potential to provide tailored information services to every human-being and organization in the world.

The cloudspace.

Metaconcept 6. Informediaries

Informediaries are people (or web-served information services) that find, source and aggregate insight around a subject. They add some level of perspective of what they've seen (like a research consultant) and progressively they might develop wisdom and deeper, more valued, perspectives because they're learning from what they're sourcing.

New businesses are springing up as entrepreneurs recognize that, with new light-weight software tools and access to sources of useful information, they can create 'information intermediary businesses'.

Software applications like *JackBe*, *Coghead*, *Microsoft Popfly* and *Encanvas* enable people to harvest data sources and *mashup* new information services in quick time.

Innovations in operating systems and integration tools encourage the growth of *information consumerism*. In recent years the Internet browser (that used to possess very limited scope for presenting information because of its reliance on HTML) has received a massive overhaul. Today, new technology innovations are arming software publishers with the necessary tools to deliver highly sophisticated user interfacing through the web browser now seen as the user interface platform of choice.

Metaconcept 7. Trust lines

I introduce trust lines as a characteristic of metaconcept 2 (mapping ties) but it's so important it's justified in being highlighted in its own right. Trust is an important credential in the valuation of relationships. It is a bi-lateral relationship; one person trusts, the other is the trusted.

Trust can be subject-specific.

For example, you might trust a friend to choose the Pizza topping you like because you know they appreciate your tastes, but you might not trust them to book a holiday for you or represent you in court. So the whole concept of trust is tied to the peer-to-peer relationship between two people and is based on what one knows of the others knowledge, behaviours, credentials, values etc.

The existence of trust between individuals removes the necessity for protocols and a great deal of red tape. Consider for example the workings of a jazz band compared to an orchestra. In an orchestra, everything has to be written down. In a jazz band the roles of the different musicians are clear but there is a much higher level of trust that each person knows instinctively what they are to do and how they should inter-play their contributions towards those of others in the band. Of course there are some unwritten protocols, but essentially very little is documented.

In business, when trust breaks down companies rely on contracts and procedures to take over. The less trust there is between parties, the more contracts are necessary. If there were total trust between two individuals then there wouldn't be a need for contracts at all! But greed underpins business and so contracts and lawyers always have a role.

Trust plays a major role in how buying decisions are made. People tend not to trust institutions but other people. Therefore social networks play a major role in leveraging trust. Organizations that wish to sell products and services must encourage individuals to trust their customer value promises. This is what 'brands' are about.

Trust lines are relationship characteristics that overlay social relationships. Where they can be identified they're very powerful enablers of relationship building and commerce. To be trusted by many people represents significant economic value if it can be harnessed by individuals and corporations.

An important contributor to the level of trustworthiness attached to an individual on any given subject is the level of *wisdom* an individual is believed to possess. There are many definitions of wisdom but I see it as an ability of individuals to make the best use of available knowledge to judge a situation and determine the most appropriate course of action.

I don't think wisdom is a particularly cool topic either in the world of consumerism or business. I suspect it's because we associate wisdom with grey hair and wrinkles. In the 21st century where it's cool to be young, wisdom is not something we talk much about. Capturing knowledge about wisdom is actually a vital ingredient of social networking. Why? Because we are more likely to trust people with wisdom. If you agree with this statement then it stands to reason that the fastest way to create trust is to expose wisdom. Follow this line of thinking and you reach the conclusion that if social networks expose wisdom, then more trust lines emerge and the more trust lines that emerge promise better decisions to be made faster because individuals can cut through the red tape that forms when trust does not exist.

Trust lines aren't well understood today but someday soon they might be. For individuals seeking to tap into talent pools, the ability to expose trust lines and wisdom could transform how project teams are selected. Just think how powerful this knowledge might be to commercial organizations that rely on personal endorsements to sell their products and services. If commercial organizations can access this meta information it could lead to a seed-change in the way organizations promote their products and services.

And what about politics? Do you trust your political representatives? Will an increased appreciation of trust lines result in new structures of political representation to emerge?

Metaconcept 8. Infinite federations

Social networks aren't finite or mutually exclusive. Being part of one network does not prohibit an individual from being a part of another. Social networks provide the opportunity for infinite forms of federations between people, between people and institutions, between commercial organizations and institutions and people.

This makes the whole concept of social networking hard to grasp. These intricate webs of relationships that are constantly joining, breaking apart and reforming. It creates a conundrum with very little measurable logic to it.

It's like the schoolyard. Imagine befriending a child who invites you to join in a game of football, but then you fall out and find another friend who invites you to build a den in the corner of the play area where you meet up with other children who like to play rugby. As an individual you are building ties, creating trust lines, forming social structures and influencing these groups as these federations form and break apart.

The federations that form aren't disciplined and pre-planned. They seemingly fall together and break apart one event at a time. These concepts are difficult for business people to grasp because we've gone through a century of management concepts based on mechanization, of rigid procedures, of organized markets and disciplined protocols, contracts and rules. The contracts, processes and rules that have become the norms of business behaviour weren't there from the dawn of time. Commerce made these attitudes and behaviours to protect shareholders.

The real world is much more like the schoolyard.

BIG BUSINESS AND GOVERNMENT

Social networking has become a more serious pastime in recent years. Social media tools are exposing strong and weak relationships ties between individuals, giving them a digital context.

In the world of business, social media tools are emerging intended to serve the very different needs and expectations of individuals in their work-life roles. Individuals (particularly those in Generation Y) are transferring their experiences of the social web into their business lives. They have, as individuals, come to recognize they can employ similar tools to tap into their business (social) relationships to exploit weak ties to bring about new business opportunities.

Employers are experimenting with these new tools to afford their workforces better means to share ideas and knowledge.

The horse play of individuals on consumer social networking sites is slowly awakened the sleeping giant of big business to the realization that relationships can be harnessed when 'digitized' and – were organizations able to tap into this web of social connections, to leverage the goodwill and trust lines that exists within it – then new business-to-consumer and business-to-business relationships await them.

Governments identify the potential for wealth by being the ideal hosts for knowledge work and knowledge workers. Around the globe governments are implementing strategies to be *knowledge superpowers*.

4

Clouds with silver linings

BUSINESS

Social networking sites that mean business

If you're a few years over puberty then what goes on in *Facebook*, *Youtube* and *MySpace* might appear pretty juvenile. Suggestions that social networking is going to change the planet comes across as media hype. If you're a *non-believer* that's okay because it probably means you haven't seen any practical reasons for networking yourself yet. But there are tools that are geared more towards the networking objectives of business people.

In the absence of a title I call these 'business networking platforms'.

They share many of the technologies adopted by social media sites (like *Facebook*) but their focus is towards meeting the networking needs of business people who want to explore how their address book maps into six degrees of separation. Many sites began as an online card index that could provide an always accessible store to house contact data but now the technology has morphed into something different.

The ethos behind this technology is that everyone knows someone who might be useful for you to know. The difficulty is how to expose the names of people that reside in the personal address book and card index that every business person has. Business social networking platforms publish contact data to a website and then compare address books to alert members about people they know or might know. The result is a list of online connections between people within various categories of separation. When signing up to a site for the first time, personal contact information is captured through a profile screen that users voluntarily complete in as little or as much accuracy as they wish. To protect users from spam and unwanted approaches, these platforms won't normally release personal details or support direct communications between members –the assumption is that you already have the email address of the person you want to connect with. They use your own email server to communicate messages.

Leaders in this category are *LinkedIn, Xing* and *Plaxo*. Last time I looked, *LinkedIn* had over 35 million contacts registered on its system and the number is still growing. *Plaxo*'s 15 million users have given it a $200 million valuation. All of these platforms are similar in the way they work and make you feel like part of a not-so exclusive club. For millions of people, managing connections has become another task to perform as part of the daily grind.

Xing

Xing only entered the market in 2006 but in its first nine months generated revenues of €25.09 million[22]. Like *LinkedIn*, *Xing* concentrates on bringing value to business people by helping them to manage contacts and forge connections through a 'who knows who' model adopting a similar model to *LinkedIn*. As a late entrant, *Xing* has been able to consider what works and what doesn't work in this market and then apply a very European multi-cultural feel to its website by supporting 16 different languages and, through the use of its modern web-based platform, offers attractive user interfaces and purpose built tools that make the administration of relationships easier

LinkedIn

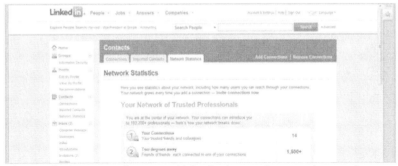

The marketing strap line says *LinkedIn* 'strengthens and extends your existing network of trusted contacts'. The word *trusted* is pivotal here because it emphasises the role of *LinkedIn* is not to find people you don't know but to sustain links to people that you've met before. It's easy to use and automatically trawls through your outlook contact address book and emails to find names of people that might be on its network. Once connected, *LinkedIn* gives you details of people you know – so if I'm linked to John, John is able to view the basic contact details of all my contacts on the *LinkedIn* system. If John wants to contact my marketing manager who is also on *LinkedIn*, John can ask me nicely to forward his message. This ability to expose and connect with the contacts of people you already know is perhaps *LinkedIn*'s most differentiating feature. LinkedIn is very proactive and regularly sends emails to inform you of new people who have joined the network that you might know and can connect to. It also updates you on what other people are doing.

Plaxo

Plaxo's focus is to manage contact information; a step-up from a card index but the net result is an online repository of people you know. Like *LinkedIn*, *Plaxo* offers an email dredging utility. It allows you to update your own details and share them with others – a change in your own "business card" will be replicated across the address books of online users who know you. You can also email your address book requesting that people update their own details.

Where to network

Every social media and business social networking site will have its own following. *MSN* appears more popular with kids in Europe while *MySpace* is the place to be for kids in the USA who want to chat, follow celebrities and arrange parties. *Facebook* started on the college campus and has always maintained its core following from these early roots with more educated folk. There are apparently many more married men and women on *Facebook* who aren't looking to find young free and singles but want to keep in touch with their friends and social contacts. The result of this multi-layered web of possibilities is that digital networkers juggle between *Facebook*, *MySpace*, *Twitter* etc. and personal blog sites.

With so many places to network online, the challenge for users is deciding where to place their social map of friends to encourage collaboration and stay in touch. This is causing a degree of fatigue for networkers who want to keep engaged with their different communities.

One of the sites that attempts to provide a 'single place' for your social map of friends and relations to hook into is the website *FriendFeed* which automatically picks up the stuff you share on over 40 websites, like *YouTube* and *Flickr*. I doubt any provider is going to manage to effectively harness all of the tools and capabilities that social media offers to provide 'one space'.

There are other ways of solving this problem.

Some communities are going offline to bring the party out of the clouds and back on to solid ground. Located in Santa Monica in the heart of Silicon Valley, '*Twiistup*' is a business that connects people from technology, media and entertainment by hosting events that feature start-ups who are chosen to show off their products and services to the media, investors, influential bloggers, fellow technologists and anyone else whose interested in learning about what's new. They provide an alternative to traditional – more formal – networking events. Apart from being a good excuse for the social elite of Silicon Valley to get from behind their laptops and let their hair down, *Twiistup* events provide an opportunity for this community of networkers to meet face to face on the ground to cement their relationships, many of which started online.

I can only imagine that this morphing of social networking from 'cloud to ground' is likely to increase and we can expect to see more business like *Twiistup* emerge promising new rewards for those who invest time in maintaining their profile on the digital map.

Why it's good to network

No effort, no gain. Building social capital demands an investment of time. An increasing proportion of the world's population spend a small part of their day blogging, updating *Facebook* and *Twittering*, accepting or requesting *LinkedIn* associations and making sure they're up-to-date on email via their Blackberry. If there isn't a financial reward for performing these activities, you'd have to question why they bother.

I know why I explore all of these different sites; it's because I'm naturally inquisitive and forever wondering if I'm missing anything. How many of the 200+ million members of *Facebook* and other similar websites registered like I have and only ever visited once or twice because they were inquisitive? I wonder.

There are some obvious reasons why people do invest in social networking through digital social media sites. I cover them here.

Emotional support

Social networks provide a level of emotional support. It comes from the *need to feel connected* – the emotional support thing I covered in the previous chapter. Older generations used to keep the radio on low as a background noise so they didn't feel they were the only person on the planet. Younger generations feel they must network or feel at risk of being overlooked. So they make the effort to get online and connect with their friends.

Some of these tasks: checking email, *Twitter*ing, *Facebook*ing etc. are quite addictive. There's the anticipation of it all; thinking 'Who's online?' or 'has anyone been in touch with me since the last time I was connected?' The exercise of connecting becomes a ritual. Of course, as individuals, we don't HAVE to do it. We have a choice. We could always SWITCH OFF if we wanted to. There can be no doubt that some people are more engaged in social networking than others. Still, I don't know anyone who has their social networking performance associated with their pay grade or job description. Perhaps one day this will change but for now, the advantages of social networking are less finite.

Social capital addicts

For some people the addiction is not performing the networking tasks themselves, it lies in a constant need to build social capital (other egomaniacs write books!). We all knew someone at school that was always organizing the house parties and trips into town. These socialites appear to be born with the belief that networking generates social capital and this forms part of their make-up. Similarly, I know business people who are aggressive communicators and work hard on their networks. They harbour a belief that these relationships offer them 'currency' in the new age of 'who knows who'. It's more difficult today to access people who don't want to be accessed; so much easier to turn the answer-phone on, switch on the email spam filter and direct unwanted mail into the trash. For people who want to find other people, leveraging social networks has become as important as returning phone calls. As the stock of these relationships grows, individuals who operate a large network become more valued. I expect for sales and marketing people in the future, a study of an individual's social networks will form part of their credentials.

There are more 'power networkers' than there used to before applications like *MySpace*, *LinkedIn* and *Facebook* emerged. Some still use a card index and a phone, but even these traditionalists are succumbing to the potential of social networking sites to add another dimension to their networking activities. Digital social networking makes it possible to lever opportunities from weaker ties – people who would not be pleased to receive a phone call but would be happy enough to accept a *Facebook* invitation, the barriers to networking have come down a little.

Mastering 'Egonomics'

Social networking has moved from 'sharing pictures with Grandma' to a business activity.

Few people have turned their ego-centric social networking habits (or social capital) into sustainable economic engines that offer full-time employment. In researching this book, I've encountered business power networkers whose nature of employment (sales people, business consultants, the self employed) means they depend on their networks for future prosperity.

Most sales people I know tell me how difficult it is these days to obtain appointments with prospective customers in business-to-business markets without the intervention of a third party to introduce them. Whilst it would be hard to evidence how this increased networking delivers tangible revenues, it is inevitable that some people have found just rewards by investing time in the use of social media sites to extend the tentacles of their relationships to new areas of opportunity. Whether the outlook is to find employment or a new client, business social network sites have become a useful new vehicle to tap into new business opportunities and cement relationships with other business people. Sites like 'LinkedIn' provide the opportunity for individuals to join special interest groups and these forums provide additional mechanisms to gain introductions that can lead to business opportunities. The bigger the network, the more potential there is for commercial opportunity. Whether for business or pleasure, the rewards from social networking are long term. It takes time to develop trust. Rushing into forming tenuous network relationships can send the wrong messages and probably evolve the wrong sort of relationships (needy people are rarely seen to be the best people to hang with!).

An article titled 'The new Valley Girls' in FORTUNE Magazine published in January 2009[23] profiled a social network of powerful business women predominantly from the Silicon Valley area who gained attention for their social media habits. The network, that partly came about from social media networking on the Internet, now includes such women as former CEOs Carly Fiorina of Hewlett-Packard and Meg Whitman of eBay, Caterina Fake, who co-founded *Flickr* and sold it to Yahoo!, author Sharon Meers, a former managing director at Goldman Sachs – a veritable who's who of the Silicon Valley A-list. These women use *Facebook*, *LinkedIn* and *Twitter* to stay connected, trade tips and sustain a self-reinforcing community of individuals with common shared interests. They identify that by socializing with one another they put themselves in the pathway of opportunities that otherwise would not exist. The women, with very hectic lives are able, through social media sites to maintain a level of

> society as they negotiate travel from school gate to office desk. The social network represents a marriage of social camaraderie, deep emotional support with the always present promise of professional advantage by leveraging the influence of contacts. This is not a hidden 'boys' club that seeks to help its members to prosper by cutting deals behind closed doors synonymous with smoke filled rooms and funny handshakes, this is up-front, brash positive endorsement of digital social networking that aspires to bring deep emotional support within a social and professional context.

Is it likely that individuals will one day find sufficient economic mechanisms to live from their social networks?

Will the traffic that these sites draw provide advertising income that covers the cost of running and growing networks?

Can users contribute to a sufficient number of paid online surveys and reviews to make a living? Unfortunately, the industry is so new it's difficult to answer any of these questions but no doubt there are opportunities here for entrepreneurs with creative minds!

How business people are already benefitting from social networking and the social media

The social media sites

The most obvious business beneficiaries of the rise and rise in social media have been the site providers like *Facebook*, *Flickr*, *Twitter*, *YouTube*, *MySpace* etc. who have grown their ventures into multi-million – sometimes billion dollar businesses. To give some idea of the scale, the owners of *Facebook* sold just 1.6% of their business to *Microsoft* in October 2007 and made $240 Million, *YouTube* sold for $1.65 billion in October 2006. At the last valuation *MySpace* was worth $580 million while *Twitter* (that only launched in 2006) was valued at $250 million. If you were in any doubt, social networking is big business.

The blog kings and queens

As I covered earlier, there are some pretty wealthy bloggers out there. Some are members of the business elite – celebrities that *happen* to blog – like Pierre Omidyar who founded *eBay* with his wife. Others made their money from blogging like the blogs I profile in Chapter 2 (*I Can Has Cheezburger? Boing Boing* and *Mashable*) who make many thousands of dollars a month from advertising revenues. These 'mega-blogger' businesses take on the form of more traditional industrial media companies than the 'man-in-a-home-office' hobbyist. Supporting such vast community of surfers demands a mix of business, technical and literary skills that make it a team, not solo, sport (they've come a long way from being one persons' online diary).

The undercover marketers and paying advertisers

Those businesses that find a way to reach new customers through social networking grapevines can make a real impact on their revenues.

When social networks bring people together to form web communities, they create ripe targets for marketers and advertisers. Engaging with social networks requires more guile and thoughtfulness on the part of the supplier. Successful suppliers expose their offering to a online communities in subtle ways; perhaps by publishing social media content that is humorous and engaging that users feel happy to endorse and hopefully will send to others in their community.

When suppliers use crude or provocative media content to encourage endorsements this is called 'viral marketing'. Few brands are happy to be associated with content of this nature to a more common form of recommendation marketing is sometimes called 'stealth', 'buzz' or even 'undercover' marketing. The ethos behind this genre of marketing is to post digital media that targets individuals who don't realize they're being marketed to. The intended response of the recipient is that the communication is spontaneous and unsolicited leaving the recipient feeling that 'one good turn deserves another' and this encourages them to pass on the marketing message.

Some viral and undercover campaigns are fantastically funny, while others are morose and tasteless. True, everyone likes a laugh and sex sells but the intimacy of a personal email inbox or social network site aren't places where people expect to be invaded by porn and crude humour. Getting the balance right is important for brands who don't wish their brands to be tarnished by 'tat' adverts but do want to connect with new audiences for their offerings – in more intimate ways.

There's a big risk of a backlash when marketers engage in these methods. Individuals can feel duped by clever marketers into doing something they wouldn't have done had they realized it was a *campaign* rather than a spontaneous communication. People are already tired of unsolicited mail and content. The risk of computer viruses makes opening any flash file, attachment or executable undesirable. The life of endorsement marketing might not last for long but the desire of businesses to engage with consumers in different ways is so great that no doubt marketers will find new creative ways to gain our attention through the social net. Advertising through social media sites is already big business – and it's growing fast.

> **According to the research company eMarketer, global advertising spend on social media sites shot up 155% in 2007 to $1.2 billion, and is expected to push beyond $4 billion by 2011. Most of the volume of online advertising is placed by agencies just the same way as they do in printed media.[24]**

Google is eyeing social media sites as a target for placement digital advertising. In August 2008 they were assigned a patent for their methods used to 'display advertisements to members of a network of one or more communities of members, identifying one or more influencers in one or more communities and placing one or more advertisements at the profiles of one or more members in the identified one or more communities.' (You couldn't make it up).

Free advertising

Advertising your business using a *Facebook* account is free unless you want to pay for 'paid ads'. Platforms like *Facebook* provide a free-to-air promotional space that's much easier to create and manage than a website you have to design and pay techies to support. With more than 200 million active users, not only are your friends probably on *Facebook*, but so too are your prospects, customers and competitors. The informal style of social media sites provide an instant door opener to develop your brand and all the time raise your placement on *Google* – because it prioritizes results according to the frequency of connections.

Sourcing ideas

Social networks provide great opportunities – if they can be harvested – to find new ideas. At one time Intranets were seen to be the way to harvest ideas from employees. By the early 1990's many of these complex IT platforms were relegated to informing staff about company raffles and enabling employees to sell cars and unwanted furniture to one another. Businesses are now adopting social networking technologies in their droves – embracing technologies like instant messaging, wiki's, blogs, PODcasts and *Facebook* style user interfaces to encourage people to share knowledge, ideas and find solutions by thinking outside of the box. Forward thinking companies are searching even further, beyond their businesses, to harness a community of people to source great ideas.

Powering information worker productivity

The consulting business I started with Nick Lawrie, NDMC, conducted research in Europe during the early 2000's to explore inhibitors to information worker productivity in offices. Any organization, from the smallest team to the largest enterprise, contains within it a web of practically invisible social networks. People use these networks to share and solve problems, test theories and learn from the know-how of others.

Like the social scientist Rapoport, we identified that there are many information flows that cascade across these informal networks of people. These were not articulated as formal business processes. Most managers could not describe them or register their existence. But the people we spoke to – marketers, sales people, technical experts, project managers – knew of their existence and depended on them to get work done. For practically every subject area there were *seekers* who needed help and *solvers* (the 'go to' guys) that either had knowledge of the solution or who knew who to speak to in order to find answers.

Many of the people in these networks who were answering requests were in effect performing tasks not seen by their employer to be part of their job remit. These contributions to the success of the enterprise went unnoticed.

But what would happen if these individuals left the business? What would be the consequence on operational effectiveness? The organization would lose knowledge and contributions to operational effectiveness that it had no knowledge of. It would feel the consequences. Suddenly tasks that 'just happened' would suddenly not happen anymore and colleagues would feel the strain of attempting to fill the void. Speak to most office workers of their experiences and these issues will emerge.

It's no secret that people rely on colleagues to direct them to answers and overcome day-to-day problems but these invisible networks are important to understand. Why? Because genuinely useful and valuable people, doing the right thing in the best interests of the organization they serve will feel undervalued. The organization might elect to make decisions on employing staff or shedding staff that can have an immense consequence to their operational effectiveness and yet they probably wouldn't know at the time. Managers might not register the true value of individuals who are filling the voids of knowledge and procedure that exist within the enterprise. Then, reward schemes might ignore the contributions of valuable employees who then feel poorly treated and elect to leave, resulting in valuable knowledge bleeding out of the enterprise.

> **In 1949, Eric Trist of the Tavistock Institute for Social Research[25] (the Tavvy) spent his time at the Haighmoor seam in Durham analyzing the team working behaviours of coal miners. Trisk identified that when imposed team structures were adopted (the conventional model), miners that were organized by managers would commit only to their allocated task and would consequently only enter into a few very limited social relationships sharply divided between those within his task group and those outside. With 'outsiders' these task- constrained miners shared no sense of belongingness and neither would they feel any responsibility to them for the consequences of their actions. In contrast, work teams that organized themselves would take ownership of the shared outcomes of the team, they would have more relationships, deeper emotional ties and they would discharge more tasks. Of most interest, workers operating within these informal work-team structures were more productive than those who discharged specific tasks as part of the conventional model.**

Analysis into team behaviours, like the one above, proves that workers are more productive when they utilize their informal social networks. People resent being told how to work, who to work with, where to go for work. They hate being told that they have to share information! When imposed organizational structures of work-teams are adopted people depend less on their social network for emotional support. The reality for most organizations is that social networking underpins their commercial success and operational excellence. In their ability to fill cracks in processes organizations profit from the existence of social networks every day but business leaders don't see them, so they can't harness their potential.

Making money from *the 'promise'* of social networks

The fastest growing community of business people profiting from the social networking growth curve are found in companies who 'path find' and provide expertise to consumer-focused brands. I'm referring to those market research, advertising and marketing communications agencies that have been quick to identify demand from consumer brands who seek to understand and harness new social media.

Consumer brands are investing $millions into online social media centric research, marketing, advertising and communications.

Small wonder. A survey on consumer buying channel preferences carried out by the digital response media agency Equi-Media in 2006 found that more than 50% of consumers in the UK now prefer using the internet compared to other media when researching consumer service products like car insurance, loans and travel products.[26] The popularity of online purchasing has brought the social networking of the young into focus because of its influence on millions of online shoppers.

Corporations can ill afford to ignore social networks and their influence on buying behaviours for online retail. It's worth investing a few million dollars just in case they really do make a big difference.

> **A 2008 survey of 17,000 people in 29 countries by the media communications agency Universal McCann titled "When did we start trusting strangers" concluded that social media is directly impacting the way consumers buy their products and services, finding that consumers are sharing opinions in unprecedented numbers.[27] Instant Messenger and email are still top online channels for informing people about products and services – but more importantly, social channels have become hugely significant, with over 29% of respondents to the survey commenting on a product or brand on a blog and 27% having posted an opinion on a social networking profile.**

GOVERNMENTS

Winston Churchill said, "The empires of the future will be the empires of the mind." It turned out to be a prophetic statement. Much of our service-based economy requires people to serve it; people who use their brains and not brawn to earn their living – *Knowledge workers*.

The term knowledge economy is all we have to describe an emerging economic era that represents a marked departure from the twentieth century industrial age. In Europe, almost every other person is employed performing information-centric roles. Little wonder that states want to be knowledge economies. It's foremost in the minds of politicians and when European leaders met at the March 2000 Lisbon summit, they set a goal of becoming 'the most dynamic and competitive knowledge-based economy in the world' by 2010'.

Like most industries, the knowledge economy needs infrastructure and resources to thrive. In the UK we once had a strong manufacturing industry. Britain has a lot of mineral deposits that can be mined, and a willing work-force. Our infrastructure of canals, railways, local cafes and tool manufacturers all grew around this compelling opportunity to cut raw materials out of the ground and make things.

The raw material of the knowledge economy is information. The 21st century sees the need for broadband and fast Internet access, for mobile phone masts and easily accessible and affordable office space. These things are no less important as the canals were to the support the logistics of the manufacturing era. But unlike industries that depend on natural resources being pulled out of the ground, the knowledge economy has very little physical imprint. Any government who is willing to invest in education, a little telecommunications infrastructure and advertises itself as being friendly for the knowledge economy has the opportunity to be a leading international location for knowledge work by 2015. Any banana republic or world power can get into this industry and the bar is very low.

Portugal for me is one of the best examples of a Government that has opened its doors to the knowledge economy. It boasts one of the finest telecommunications infrastructures in Europe, it has made sure that all government services have to be accessible online, and it works extremely hard to attract business. Dubai would also have to come into this list. The country that has realized its natural oil resources will eventually run dry has made itself the number one venue for business in the world by creating the right conditions to make it easy for businesses to move there. Both Dubai and Portugal do possess some natural resources in common that appeal to knowledge workers and we lack in the UK – namely an excellent climate and good beaches. All other things being equal, perhaps these factors will ultimately determine the knowledge economy super powers.

Any changes to the way a knowledge economy works will have a dramatic affect on society. Even those people not directly engaged in the knowledge economy will profit or suffer from the successes of a state in its ability to harness the rewards of working with knowledge. Sometimes a knowledge economy is defined in terms of knowledge-based industries with high ICT usage that employ large numbers of graduates and professional workers – 'knowledge workers'. Knowledge working is a broad church. Think of all of the people engaged in education and academia, scientific, public sector administration, politics, bio-medical and engineering research, customer services, information technology, teaching, business process outsourcing and back office administration, accounting, public relations, media and communications, finance and banking, business consulting, authors and publishers. Get started and you realize how many of us rely on our know-how to make a living.

Knowledge working is not peculiar to any specific vertical market or industry. All industries employ some knowledge workers. But neither is it something that *everyone* does, or *will do*. Today, businesses work in much the same way as they always have. Supervisory and management layers, professionals, creatives – people who use IT more as part of their roles – are more likely than not to be knowledge workers.

> **The fourth European Working Conditions Survey (EWCS) conducted in 2005 provided data for the first ever report on Europe's 'knowledge workers'. The report 'Exploiting Europe's knowledge Potential' by the Work Foundation found most knowledge workers are full time employees with permanent contracts who change their employment infrequently, on average remaining with the same employer for 12 years. Most work is in the "Social Service" sectors (health, social work, education, etc.) and are primarily office based with only around 35% having the flexibility to work from home.**

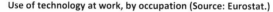

Use of technology at work, by occupation (Source: Eurostat.)

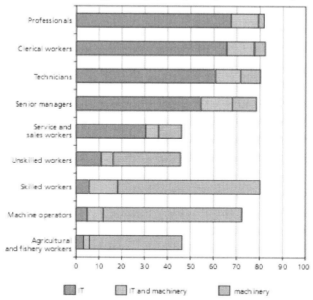

Today markets for knowledge are generally seen by business as an 'interesting project' if you're looking for a relatively cheap side-order of creativity. If governments were to take pro-active action and offer social welfare to life-workers through programmes that encourage people towards self-employment around this model, then the number of people who jump ship from full-time employment will create small tsunami of knowledge market activity – remembering that, when asked, around half of full-time people claim to be unhappy with their work-life balance.

I think at some point a government, somewhere, will start to become proactive and others will follow because of the economic need to be a leading *empire of the mind*. It will happen – the question is when.

BIRTH OF THE CLOUDSPACE

In the period between 2010 and 2015 a cloudspace of metainformation will grow and become the common fabric between domestic and business life.

The cloudspace will describe the relationships between individuals, their associations; and expose their 'digital self'.

The Internet will become the global communication switchboard of a 21st century world where any individual will be able to connect to any other in six steps.

NEW BUSINESS IMPERATIVES

The dynamics of business in the early 21st century will make adoption of work behaviours that exploit the use of the cloudspace a business imperative. Without it, old world corporations will be unable to compete.

Competitive advantage of business organizations will depend much more on the ability of organizations to always fit their most profitable markets. Organizations will demand a level of agility only made possible by harnessing the creativity and knowledge of individuals in new ways.

Demand for 'human resource innovation' and a step change in information worker productivity will lead to more investment and risk taking in mechanisms to harness talent in business.

At the same time, new forms of knowledge worker, technology innovation and self-organizing markets will emerge to make this happen.

5

A global war for talent

If social networks are ever to become a mainstream function of business operation there must be a **stimulus**. This is it.

There is a global war for talent.

We live in a knowledge economy, or at least around half of us do. Employment in knowledge-intensive services in the UK increased from 37 to 43 per cent of all jobs between 1996 and 2006.[28]

A shortage of 'knowledge worker' talent

Both nation states and businesses have a selfish interest to make sure they can acquire the best talent to thrive in an economy driven by brain-power. The problem for industry and governments is the pool of talent to serve this brain-centred economy is too small.

Employers need lots of talent.

In most organizations, people are still the most important asset. These intelligent, enterprising, creative 'doers' are needed to make success happen.

Departmental leaders (The 'corporals')

It's essential to have leadership in an organization, but that leadership must extend to every level of an enterprise for an organization to sustain its agility and deliver differentiating standards of customer service. Good organizations and great leaders know this.

As far back as 1988, the management consulting firm McKinsey conducted research across 77 large US companies in a variety of industries to understand talent-building philosophies and additionally surveyed nearly 400 corporate officers and 6,000 executives from the "top 200" ranks in these companies. Their research pointed to a severe and worsening shortage of the people needed to manage critical functions, let alone lead companies. Since this report, the shortage has worsened.[29]

Historians believe that the success of the German Blitzkrieg, the sweeping advance of German troops across Western Europe to the English Channel in 1940, was largely due to the ability and encouragement of *lower-ranking officers* to take the initiative and lead small teams of soldiers to overcome the challenges they faced in the field as new situations emerge; events where devolved leadership and ingenuity needs to happen unfettered by prescriptive process.

In 'Agilization' I explain how poorly devolved decision making leads to organizational inflexibility; the visible consequences of which can be experienced by customers in the form of poor customer services.

In December 2008 NDMC had its mobile phone contract coming up for renewal. We weren't convinced we were getting the best value from our supplier and so we decided to hunt around the market to 'see what was out there'. From our investigations we hit on a mobile phone provider that appeared to be more business focussed and even had a business sales representative who came to see us. We took out a contract with them but within 7 days we found the network coverage so poor that it made the phones unusable. We wrote to the sales person advising that we wanted to

> cancel the contract. Her reply said how sorry she was the contract had not worked out. A few days later (after no action had happened) we called the customer service desk to find out what was being done to arrange collection of the mobiles and arrange for the *PAK numbers* of the phones to be released. Their customer service desk knew nothing of our cancellation. After a few phone calls they accepted that we had cancelled. We had several mobile phones to return. A few days later they sent us one returns bag. We called them and asked for enough to send back all of the phones. Next day another bag arrived. Then another. It took 4 weeks of phone calls to get a sufficient number of bags. We returned the mobiles. Three weeks later we received a call from their credit control department insisting that we pay for our first quarter of usage. Apparently, because they had 'created' PAK codes (we don't know why) the account had been left open and there were, as the result, charges to pay.
>
> Constantly through this story we hit *processes* of one sort or another; 'I can only send you one bag' or 'I'm not allowed to transfer you to the team that organizes returns', or 'we can't give you your PAK codes without raising an invoice'.

Like this example no doubt you have encountered contemptuous customer service from a supplier; organizations that don't appear to have any form of devolved leadership. They operate on scripts that carry operators through pre-scribed processes.

Robotic customer service agents are unable to react to any diversion from the instructions on their computer screen. With no corporals in the field, the only way these organizations can hope to discharge even a reasonable level of customer service is to write down how they want customer service agents to act in the event of any conceivable situation arising.

But customers aren't robots. Neither do they want to be treated like robots.

Organizations lacking devolved leadership overcompensate with rigid, formalized procedures prevent good corporals from delivering the service standards they know customers want.

In 2001 I opened an account with one of the world's largest banks. I insisted to the bank manager that I would only open an account if I was assured a personal relationship – someone I could talk to – if ever I needed any assistance. But the bank had policies which meant they didn't offer a personal account manager unless you achieved a certain band of revenue. My enterprising bank manager offered her direct dial number and said, 'If you need anything just call – but don't tell anyone because I'm not allowed to do this really!' We've had the account open for 8 years and sure enough, whenever we need anything we speak to our manager and she fixes it. The bank is profiting from our business because its 'corporal' is breaking the rules to do what's best for the customer.

Management thinking today says that corporals are less necessary than they once were. Current management philosophy says they've been replaced by processes and scripts – but they haven't. The consequences are found in dreadful customer experiences and stories like mine on the opposing page. The lack of recognition of 'corporals' means the business world isn't generating demand for the talent that makes organizations work better. Without demand, education systems around the world concentrate their efforts in more rewarding pursuits like the development of individuals with *knowledge* rather than *know-how*. This cycle is heightening demand for those people with both.

A shortage of skilled workers

Some industries depend on a steady stream of people who have been educated to a high standard or have a thorough appreciation of the craft, science or discipline at the core of how organizations produce their customer value. Many industrial sectors are experiencing an acute shortage of knowledge workers, and projections suggest a worsening situation. A global market for talent with increasingly open economic borders means that skilled workers have more opportunity and can drift around the world to find the best opportunities for themselves and their families. The more scarce skilled workers become the more corporations battle for the best people. Indian companies surveyed by *The Economist* reported that over 50 percent of their employees had been contacted by another organization, resulting in a 40 percent turnover rate.

Creative thinkers

Even if there wasn't a global war for talent, there would be a similarly aggressive war for ideas and innovation. Corporations need to source those next big ideas that assure their future growth and success – the next cure for Cancer, iPOD or *Google*. Today's global economy has an unquenchable thirst for ideas and knowledge. Intangible assets such as knowledge, skills and ideas have become competitiveness differentiators.

Aging population is widening the talent gap

Companies aren't short of raw numbers of people, they're short of skilled talent and innovation. Businesses today already work hard to cut frictional costs in their processes through computer automation. An information worker that keys data into a computer is a cost. A knowledge worker that finds a new way to satisfy customer demand is an asset. If you were a business leader, which one would you employ?

Employers want more thinkers and less doers, but this shift in demand has outpaced the labour market. Organizations are left considering their answers to two important questions: How do we cultivate a workforce of a capacity to accommodate future growth, and what's the best way of harvesting the greatest value from their contributions?

An aging population means the number of skilled workers available for work is dwindling. In 2006, [21]40 percent of companies around the world reported difficulty filling jobs. Just maintaining current levels of skill and experience has become difficult for employers because now there is a global market for talent and skilled people have many more choices.

Trends and projections for the population of working age in Europe from 1950 to 2050
(Source: The Economist survey 2006)

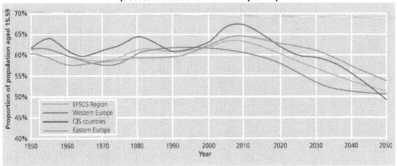

THE DEATH OF OLD WORLD CORPORATIONS

The cloudspace will redefine business value, attitudes and behaviours

Consumers will have more choice and more power. Markets will become even more collaborative in order to serve customer value and business agilization will offer the greatest competitive advantage.

The value of personal and organizational relationships (brands and wisdom) will increase in currency whilst the perceived value of information and computing technology will be dramatically reduced. Know-how will become more important than raw knowledge. The role of informediaries will increase and then decline.

The market for recruitment will flatten as employers are more easily able to connect to the wisdom and skilled workforce they need, as they need them.

Globalized large corporate brands will continue to increase their domination.

Business organizations will through economic necessity develop a social conscience.

6

New business behaviours

Like a hoard of drunken joggers, global corporations have stampeded across the planet in search of the next super growth consumer market or economic back-water offering lower labour costs not thinking about where they tread or who they tread on.

The fact that consumers feel increasingly betrayed by the big brands that ignore them hasn't given board directors too many sleepless nights. They've felt bullet-proof. Nothing a consumer did could really hurt them (could it?). CEO's have been more worried about the risk to their pension of skittish investors and accounting blunders.

But that was then.

The days of running with the same business plan forever without having to consider what customers think are fast coming to an end.

What do corporations have to be scared about in the 21st century?

The first big change is *globalization*.

It's still going on and big business is getting bigger. Unfortunately for big business being too big isn't always good news because governments don't like it. They have a habit of strapping trading sanctions and lots of red tape around corporate elephants that trample through their countries. And globalization cuts both ways: consumers can buy products from anywhere around the world 24 hours a day.

Another big change is the *participative age*.

When consumers get stamped on by fat corporate mammoths today they can tell thousands of people about it (that's enough to keep any mammoth tiptoeing on their pinkies!). Whether they work for them or buy from them, generations Y and Z expect corporate brands to show a working *moral compass* towards social responsibility and ecology.

But the biggest step-change on the life expectancy of corporations is the subject of this book – *cloudspace social networks*.

Cloud social networking brings the conscience of the world together. Corporations that carry on trampling over people will find their brand reputation disappear faster than an autographed poster of Zac Efron in a teen girl slumber party.

The jungle drums of social networks can also play a positive role for business. Organizations that learn how to harness the potential of social networks to connect to groups of consumers will leave their competitors behind in the dust.

Social networks will act like a huge amplifier: Success will echo more success, while organizations that offer poor quality products and services, or have no moral compass, will be mercilessly put to the sword.

If the last year of financial institutions running on the rocks and big corporate names getting their accounting shoe-laces crossed and falling on their noses has taught us anything it's that no enterprise is a rock. All organizations flirt with the possibility of death unless they change to meet new market conditions.

On the whole they're changing.

Organizations are a fabric of policy, procedure and instutionalization that binds together a bunch of people. And over time the people change. New generations enter the workforce with a different mind-set and shared norms of behaviour inherited from the social side of their lives. It's not instant but this burst of 'new' changes the beliefs and values of the organization.

When I scribbled in the title 'the death of old world corporations' to the head of this section, I wasn't thinking that corporations would end their lives, rather that the forms and structures they take today will die.

The cloudspace will cause corporations to resource differently and adopt new organization designs. Social networks will blur the perimeter, the *rubicon* of corporations. They will use so many contracted workers that it won't be obvious who the corporation employs. Expect also to see a blurring of markets with many more intermediaries in the supply chain, including tribal brands, adding to and enriching customer value.

This *enterprise make-over* will see fat and rude 20th century corporations disappear and in their place will appear slim and socially schooled 21st century global organizations.

Welcome to the AGILIZED world

If he were around in the 21st century Charles Darwin could have been a great organizational engineer. When, in his book *'The Origin of Species'* Darwin described the process of natural selection – i.e. the process by which favourable traits that are heritable become more common in successive generations of a population of reproducing organisms, and unfavourable traits that are heritable become less common, Darwin provided the 21st century business world with its greatest metaphor.

In today's rapidly changing market, it is those organizations more able to adapt to new market conditions – to FIT their most profitable markets – faster and more effectively, inheriting traits favoured by customers, that will survive. This is the subject of my first book 'Agilization'.

This capability demands new technologies and innovations. It also needs business leaders to re-think their management principles that they've trusted for over a century. It's a lot to expect of big corporations that feel bullet-proof and continue to make money adopting their current behaviours. In 'Agilization' I describe the 10 key subject areas that influence the ability of an enterprise to agilize itself and advise readers on how they affect a change from the organization structures and behaviours they adopt today to a new 21st century design.

I won't attempt to cover the content again but the 10 subjects are:

1. Vision and essence – Understanding what the enterprise lives for
2. Leadership – Identifying skills and behaviours that leaders must instil
3. Alignment – Turning what the enterprise does into more value
4. Operating approach – Re-wiring the enterprise to act smarter
5. Process performance – Optimizing work behaviours
6. Behaviour – Changing minds

7. Insight – Learning how to learn
8. Curiosity – Re-focusing on the importance of thinking
9. People – Adopting new ways to exploit human potential
10. Technology – Applying new technologies to new situations

Agilized markets introduce a new employment climate

Fine-tuning a workforce to meet business needs has been made more difficult by the propensity of markets to change their structures and redefine what an organization 'must do well'.

The *ability to fit best* is the key competitive differentiator in a business world where market structures are transforming faster than ever. Almost any industry you can think of – retail, advertising, publishing and media, utilities, finance – is today undergoing dramatic market restructuring. These changes make it next to impossible for organizations to get the right balance of talent to projects.

The dynamics of human resourcing are changing as the result of markets working differently. Market factors influencing the dynamics of human resourcing include:

New ways of working are enabled by technology

There has been a huge demand over the past 50 years for software coders and people with deep technical computing expertise.

Companies would employ many different types of operating systems and lots of specialist software tools that developers would use to create business applications. But that is changing. Today, organizations like *Google* and *Microsoft* provide business professionals, who have limited computing expertise, with simple *point-and-click* software tools that enable them to serve themselves with the applications they need for business. Now companies are on the look-out for people who understand business and can *apply* technology – to interface between business units and exploit these new easy to use IT tools. Programmers suddenly find themselves with the wrong skills for the market. Organizations carrying fat IT teams full of developers suddenly find they've got the wrong talent.

Industries are being re-defined

In advertising and communications, the Internet has contributed to the destruction of traditional industrial media and television broadcasting channels which are being displaced by a more substantial number of virtual social media sites and digital channels. The skills needed to advise clients on modern digital media marketing are a blend of quasi-technical skills mashed-up with traditional marketing skills and a deep understanding of how to work with mediums like *Adobe Flash, Facebook, Twitter,* push-email, online video streaming HTML websites, viral and endorsement marketing. The type of resources demanded by commercial organizations becomes so diverse that it's not possible to recruit individuals equipped with all of this know-how and talent for the relatively small amount of time it's needed.

Online retailing is reshaping buyer behaviours

In business-to-consumer and business-to-business markets, more people are buying more often online. Some high-street retailers, operating in areas like music retailing, have been crippled by the influence of online players like *Amazon.* Other organizations that operate cascading sales channel structures (i.e. with local reseller or partner channels) can find themselves suddenly uncompetitive because of the costs associated with financing their channel compared to online vendors selling direct.

This was the experience of *Hewlett Packard*'s PC hardware business in the early 2000's when they found themselves head to head with *Dell* the online PC manufacturer. *Hewlett Packard* operates a sales channel through reseller partners and distributors. All these people need paying and expect sales commissions for their efforts. *Dell*, on the other hand, with its online retail model sells products direct to end users and businesses via the Internet and benefits from significantly lower costs of sale. When this type of shift in business model occurs, competitors have to adapt to similar or an alternatively disruptive business model.

The emergence of 'cross-industry' economic pathways

In some industries and disciplines, public and private sector organizations share common outcomes and must work collectively to achieve them.

For example, since 2005, Social Services organizations across the UK have be working together to make sure 'every child matters'. This UK-wide initiative has been driven by Central Government and came out of the failings identified through the Victoria Climbié enquiry.[31] Victoria Climbié was an eight-year old child who was abused and murdered by her guardians in London, England, in 2000. In 2003, the UK Government published a green paper called Every Child Matters alongside the formal response to the report into the death of Victoria Climbié that identified significant failings in the information sharing and cooperation systems between different support agencies involved in child welfare and protection. The task of newly appointed directors of children's services is to ensure that information used by each of the agencies involved in child welfare and protection across a region is joined up and focused towards putting 'the child' at the centre of 'the system'. This cross-industry cooperative approach means that no single organization can hope to be successful without contributions from others. It doesn't matter if one organization hits its operating targets if the collective outcome of the industry isn't achieved (i.e. to make sure children are safe and can prosper). What emerges is an *economic pathway*; a value chain that spans an industry. Several organizations are likely to contribute to any process. The 'subject' of the *economic pathway* – How it produces its 'value' (in this case *a child*) becomes the common focus and value outcome of all activities. This single perspective ensures that 'value' is delivered. Other examples of cross-industry economic pathways include roads networks management in highways management sector, care pathways in healthcare, underground asset management in the utilities sector and offender management in the prisons and offender management sector.

Example of an economic pathway

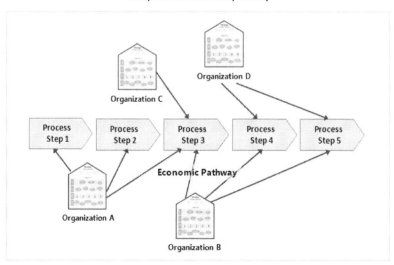

As cross-industry economic pathways mature, it becomes difficult – almost impossible – to notice where one organization ends and another begins. Each contributing organization will share its information with the next, employees work together on shared projects with common outcomes, working practices become *normalised* as do computer platforms and employment terms.

Cross industry partnerships present new possibilities for employers to rationalize and harmonize resourcing strategies.

> **Collaborations leading to outsourcing and shared services.**
>
> **In 2006, I was working on a business transformation project for a local authority in the UK. Half way through the project, it was announced that the customer facing operations of the organization were to merge with two other authorities to provide a single point of contact for people who lived in the region. This announcement made a lot of sense. Each of the authorities was operating their own customer service desk and a disparate portfolio of IT systems. Each organization had strengths and weaknesses in their processes, knowledge assets and staff skills. Creating a single point of contact for local people and harnessing the collective talents of the organizations, meant that a single, better customer service experience for local people could be provided. What this transformation also meant was that non-core activities that had limited influence on the quality of front-line services but were critical to business continuity (like finance and HR) were MUCH BIGGER operations and this provided the opportunity for managers to consider outsourcing these back-office services to suppliers whose core competency and investment in innovation was such that the 'new organization' could achieve additional benefits. Prior to this change, the effort and potential value of outsourcing to a third party would have been marginal.**

A number of industries are now working together to pool demand for talent so they can balance demands for labour and skills with supply. This can take the form of a collaborative procurement portal, a knowledge market or a framework agreement with a select number of supplier organizations. Economic pathways make this more achievable.

Outsourcing to lower priced labour markets

Organizations that operate on a global scale seek to achieve operating economies by exploiting lower labour rates in different regions. At the same time, they seek to harvest the skills that exist within their business across the different locations they operate internationally. Organizations that can exploit these global resource pools and lever advantage from the lower operating costs of regions can disrupt the status quo of markets.

This is exampled by the rapid growth in outsourcing to Asian markets where highly skilled workers are available at lower costs.

> **The information and outsourcing market in India is expected to be worth $60 billion by 2010 according to research conducted by *Nasscom* for *McKinsey & Co.*[30]**

Resourcing projects exclusively from labour sourced within the enterprise makes organizations uncompetitive when competitors are harvesting lower cost talent from across the globe.

Big consumer brands are gate-crashing markets

Over the last decade it's become more common for well known brands to lever their strengths into new industries.

Think of how *Sainsbury*'s and *Tesco*'s in the UK have moved into finance and pharmacy services and in the case of *Tesco*'s how they also now sell mobile phones, car insurance and offer catalogue shopping (competing directly with companies like *Argos*). In a similar way, *Dell* now sells computer printers, *Amazon* has moved into computer services and *Apple* now manufactures mobile phones (*iPhone*). Major brands have the opportunity to do this because they already are trusted by consumers and often can exploit assets and skills they already have. The consequence on markets is that incumbent players that might have enjoyed leadership in their market can suddenly find their business under threat by a huge aggressor.

This ability for a large brand to gate-crash a completely different market for products and services means that the dynamics of human resourcing change. Tomorrow, should *Tesco* start selling IT equipment (they already sell software) they will suddenly need IT expertise and domain expertise for the markets they will sell into. The scale of 'shift' in human resourcing patterns can be instant and dramatic.

The world gets smaller while corporations get bigger

We are seeing consolidation in most industry sectors.

Banks are swallowing up smaller banks because liquidity is king in financial markets these days, utilities are merging or acquiring other utilities because they need so much money to manage such vast asset portfolios and fund the investments needed to balance risk when discovering new sources of fuel. Larger retailers have all but killed local village shops and high streets because of their colossal buying power and ultra-efficient logistics operations.

In business-to-consumer markets, individuals are more likely than ever to select a brand they know over one they don't. They feel a deeper emotional bond with a known brand. Brands have an ability to connect to people on different levels by leveraging their quality of being a familiar friend. This means that big brands are getting ever bigger.

Big corporations impose their *norms of behaviour* on society from behind their firewalls. This trend towards bigger corporations, bigger brands, means that the cultures and attitudes of corporations – protecting intellectual property, compliance, risk adversity, IT sustainability regimes etc. – are imposed on the working patterns of knowledge workers if they want to be considered for work.

These disruptors to market structures mean that organizations can ill afford to be constrained by large immovable numbers of full-time employment contracts. They need as much flexibility in their labour resources as they can muster. Yet, at the same time, they need to secure the best people with the best knowledge.

Agilized enterprises are thinking differently

INNOCENTIVE Inc. (who I describe later) showed that, by combining demand from an industry and sourcing a supply of appropriate knowledge skills, knowledge markets can thrive. By accessing knowledge markets – that tap into talent beyond the organizational firewall – *knowledge seekers* can harvest the ideas and creativity of thousands (perhaps one day millions) of experts. No single organization could ever hope to employ such a vast resource pool for innovation. In light of early successes, employers are now more prepared than ever to consider new resourcing models to satisfy their talent requirements. But while some corporations are beginning to think differently, not all are. Only a small number – perhaps 1 in 10,000 – are even considering new ways of working; attempting to understand how changes in the social landscape, brought about by social networking technologies and behaviours, are re-drawing the ring-fenced talent landscape they understand today.

Factors such as cross-industry collaboration (required to satisfy industry *economic pathways*), the changing workforce, the desire of workers to roam free of the office and benefit from flexi-time, the needs of organizations to tap into talent from outside the enterprise means that organizations are quickly becoming *enterprises without walls.* As Art Coviello, Executive Vice President, EMC Corporation states, "Businesses are becoming 'hyper-extended enterprises,' exchanging information with more constituencies in more ways and in more places than ever before."

Organizations learn to listen and adapt – or die

Commerce has been slow to register the new economic drivers of competitiveness in the agile economy I describe in Agilization: the ability to listen to, and engage with customers in new ways; the ability to adapt to new market situations; to know how to plan; resource on demand in response to changes to business models; to employ adaptive computer platforms; to know how to modify enterprise logic (ways of doing things, norms of behaviour) – and more than anything else, to appreciate that the quality of talent at its disposal (driving innovation) is the primary determinant of an organization's ability to move up the value chain and stay competitive in global markets.

Seeing employees as consumers and customer advocates

Commerce has also been slow to register the value of social networks. Until the advent of social media sites, the idea that employees had relationships inside and outside of work that could be useful to an organization (if understood) was not on the corporate radar. Now it is, but most business people still don't have a good idea of what social networking can do for their organization; how it can influence business processes and produce demonstrable value.

What growth in popularity of social media has done is to draw attention to the existence of social networks in business. The penny has dropped in many a boardroom that the organization chart by no means reflects the reality of how their organization works, who it is that makes things happen, who the 'go to' people are that are vital to retain – and how these relationships can potentially introduce an organization to new business opportunities. The traditional 'us and them' relationship of management and workforce is blurring; so too is the line between employee and consumer.

Learning how to harness the talent within reach

Employers see a miss-match between their requirement for skills and the talent available. This is evidenced by slow career advancement as well as financial reward for knowledge work. Employees rarely get paid for ideas. It is a legal right of employers to own any ideas their staff come up with but if they're not rewarded, why should staff come up with ideas for the organization they work for; particularly if they're able to profit from their ideas by selling them via online knowledge markets outside of work? Unless there are specific clauses in their employment contract there's no reason why staff shouldn't do this. To source innovation, organizations have to reconsider their reward models for employees and how employees are measured in terms of contributions to business outcomes. Employers need to think more about 'what productivity looks like' and how staff are rewarded for positive performance behaviours. Without this new thinking (to get their house in order), employers won't be able to harness talent and skills beyond their corporate firewall.

Employers must balance quantity demands with quality of life for employees

Overall, although most knowledge workers in Europe enjoy a relatively high level of autonomy in their jobs, they have yet to achieve the economic freedom to exploit their knowledge independent of full-time employment. This is reflected in the numbers of knowledge workers who continue to be employed full-time (I would estimate something like 90% of workers) even though, when asked, fewer than half of these people will say they have a good work-life balance.

The purpose of the European *Lisbon Strategy* is to make Europe the 'most dynamic and competitive knowledge economy in the world'. It is also to create 'more and better jobs'. However, this raises the question of what a 'better job' looks like – better paid, better work-life balance?

Balancing efficiency and social justice

There is an assumption that employers seek to milk the lifeblood from their workers to achieve the maximum amount of work time (and therefore 'productivity') and that there is an inevitable trade-off between productivity and social justice. But this attitude doesn't exist in many knowledge-based businesses because managers know people are made less productive when they work too many hours and don't look after themselves. A knowledge economy operates fundamentally different productivity dynamics to manufacturing based economies. Employees aren't prepared to see their quality of life or sense of social justice compromised by the conduct of employers. Employers know that, to attract the best talent, they need to be socially conscious employers and support the social needs of their workforce as well as their career progression and salary expectations.

> **A survey conducted by UK communications group BT of 120 young professionals found that more than one-third thought working for a caring and responsible employer was more important than the salary they earned.**[32]

To be competitive, organizations know that they must achieve greater *agility* in their labour resourcing matched with access to the best people with the best ideas. Commerce has enjoyed a level of relative stability in markets for half a century and with it a plentiful supply of human resources. Business managers could afford to think about their business models once every decade. The rules of business were handed down to managers by their peers.

Now commerce finds itself facing skittish markets with more discerning customers and a global shortage of talent.

Something's got to give.

The axle of the knowledge economy is reaching stress levels pushing it to breaking point. An agile business world demands an agile workforce. The simple truth is that it no longer makes sense, either *economically* for employers or *emotionally* for employees, to maintain a relationship based on full-time employment contracts.

NEW FORMS OF KNOWLEDGE WORK AND KNOWLEDGE WORKER

The growth of the cloudspace encourages individuals to make their way in the world by harvesting their relationship ties, associations, knowledge, skills and wisdom.

Changes are already happening in labour markets. More and more people seek a different blend of work-life and the opportunity to dedicate more time to their family, domestic pursuits and work activities more closely aligned to their skills, passions and interests.

The cloudspace introduces a new market dynamic in labour markets. It puts people in contact with even more opportunity to find economic freedom. It grows the number of groups and associations that people can join in order to make money from their skills.

It exposes a rich new layer of metainformation on people that creates a more sophisticated job market where employers can find people with the right experience, knowledge and know-how to serve a more graduated series of job roles. Through it, employers can cherry pick specialists for the roles that emerge through new business situations.

LIFE WORKERS

'LIFE WORKERS' are born when individuals find the demands of employment move beyond its rewards and start to conflict with personal life-style ambitions. They choose quality of life and *lifestyle* over full-time employment.

Not everyone CAN be a life worker. These individuals have gathered relationship ties, credentials and experience by working *on the inside* of the business world and have developed valued skills and wisdom.

Through an increasing demand for highly skilled workers available 'on-demand' to resource new business situations, life workers have found their economic freedom and are taking the opportunity to find better ways of re-balancing work and life, better places to live.

LIFE WORKERS choose to be self-employed contractors, with one foot inside the corporate world, who are able to exist with economic security on the outside of full-time employment to dedicate themselves to their specializations and harness their potential to bring value to the businesses they serve.

7

Escaping the organization

The majority of people today are employed on full time contracts. It's important not to forget that. In this chapter I profile people who walked away from the world of salary cheques and long hours in search of something else – but I don't want to leave you thinking that within a couple of years we will all be self-employed workers. We won't be.

Big corporations are getting progressively bigger. It's the gravitational force these huge organizations generate that sets in place how other smaller commercial operations revolve about them. Workers have always had their life choices to make. In the solar system of business they can find themselves a place on one of the bigger planets that rotates at a slightly slower pace where they can enjoy the richer resources available to them. Alternatively they can choose to plant their flag on one of the smaller moons that whirls around the big planets at a faster pace.

For all their plentiful resources, it's not always greener on the bigger planets. Big corporations have much to give but they expect a hefty pound of flesh in return. And to some extent when you take their pay cheque they own a part of your life. It's not quite the same as in Victorian days of course, when employers would pay for your house and if you didn't perform you lost your job *and* your home in one go. But still, if you come up with a great idea, remember it's theirs. And maybe going home at 5.30pm is what you've contracted to do but it's rarely enough. Anyone who has worked in an office knows that if you want to progress in your career, you need to put the hours in. But nobody puts a gun to your head and forces you to work on a full-time contract do they?

Lets' be honest there are lots of reasons why working for someone else is good news. For one, you get perks like a pension, health insurance (if you're lucky) and maybe even a company car. During the hours of work there's a warm office or workplace that's heated without you paying the bill; perhaps even a canteen.

Still, it's not for everyone. Sometimes it's not even an option.

In the late 1990's and early 2000's a considerable number of companies in IT and telecommunications sectors cut back on the number of people they employed. Corporations whose core business was not IT or running call centres were also pruning these non-core business areas by outsourcing them to third parties. Transformations in organizational structures that led to jobs being axed were performed under the new terms of 'downsizing' and 'rightsizing' giving managers new ways to convey bad news to unlucky employees. Many of these people who took early redundancy packages weren't ready to retire. This trend resulted in a large number of highly skilled people re-entering the job market and looking for new things to do.

These individuals also had new lifestyle expectations. It so happened that this activity coincided with a rise in the level of dissatisfaction felt by many people on the one-sided relationship of working for employers who were happy to nurture an office culture where it was considered seriously un-cool to leave your desk before 6.30pm, even if your salary cheque did only pay you up to 5.30pm. When the European Union Working Time Directive came into force in 2001 – that made it illegal in Europe for employers to insist their staff work beyond 48 hours a week – it was common practice amongst employers to 'invite' employees to sign a waiver.

The business world's open disregard for work-life balance has taken its toll on how people view their lifestyle.

People appraising the amount of time they spend as corporate drones and the amount of time they have left for family and personal time, are coming to realize that the figures don't add up.

In their ones, twos, tens and hundreds, skilled middle-aged people with many years of work potential ahead of them are electing to work for themselves as consultants and independent knowledge professionals; possibly even performing the same role and leveraging the same skills, but on *their* terms.

The era of the '*Life-Worker*' is upon us.

The emergence of Life-Workers

Life-workers are people who turn their back on full-time employment in pursuit of a better mix between lifestyle and work. For many, work and play activities are significantly merged and somehow morphed together into a new *lifestyle of work* culture. These knowledge workers have learnt they can balance their work and home life better by becoming self-employed or working for smaller niche businesses. Some become contractors, others entrepreneurs who setup their own business simply to be able to balance work and home life. They can operate in a market where know-how is scarce and can enjoy a good existence. Work feels like another *project* or *pursuit* rather than a period of the week when you sell your soul for a salary. Life-workers identify that they can achieve long term financial security for their families working on *their* terms.

> **A survey conducted by *Critical 2 Limited* for *MORE TH>N Business*, a UK-based business insurance firm, found that 70 per cent of new business owners were not financially or career-motivated. Fifty nine percent of those surveyed said they started a business to 'gain more control over their lives' and 54 percent said they did it in order to 'be happier'. There are more than three million micro businesses in the UK which account for around 90% of all firms, generating over £3 billion in revenues and employing more than five million people (That's around 10% of the population). According to this research, life-workers represent something like 70% of Britain's micro businesses.[33]**

Many styles of life-worker exist, from people who start a small manufacturing or merchandising business from their garage (like 'Mulberry' who started as a mother and son team in 1971 and has grown its business to become a British Lifestyle brand), to marketers, designers, consultants and other professionals who elect to mix work and home life in their own way.

Having the opportunity to benefit from a more balanced work-life does not prevent life-workers from being comfortable with the idea of making money and becoming famous while they're doing it. Even the great Richard Branson confesses that he doesn't work all of the time and profoundly states it's not a recipe for success to do so.

> Life-working does not necessarily mean a compromise to career opportunities. A study by Yellow Pages reported that mums who've set up home based businesses now have a combined turnover of £4.4 billion in the UK. Many of these mums started a home career in order to balance their home life.[34]

Life-workers represent a sizeable economic group that is already successfully profiting from its knowledge. Walk into any hotel lounge located on a motorway interchange and you will find yourself in the company of life-workers conducting their business; probably meeting with clients or other life-workers.

For employers they are a resource that can be turned on and off like a tap to serve specific needs for knowledge and skills as they're required.

> I joined the swelling ranks of life-workers in 2001. Today, when I'm not writing, I spend much of my time working for clients from home or meeting other knowledge workers in hotel lobbies and home offices either creating or sharing knowledge. Whilst I'm a director of a software company and a management consulting business, I'm also very much a life-worker, paid for my know-how on-demand by different people. As my wife confirms on any occasion she's asked what I do for a living, I don't perform any specific role or work for a single company. I'm an IT market specialist and I enjoy the economic freedom made possible through the knowledge I've gathered through my career in sales, marketing and management working for large organizations either directly or as a contractor. Advising companies allows me to step between projects and generate sufficient income for my wants. Like many other people I'm sure, I didn't realize that I could make a living doing a mixture of things instead of taking the salary of a single employer. And today, it's still not an easy decision. Whatever the bureaucrats of Brussels may talk about there is no social welfare safety net for knowledge workers who choose to go out on their own.

Today, it takes courage and a blend of skills to become a life-worker. Being able to deliver knowledge that others are prepared to pay money for is only the beginning. Life workers must be their own sales person, receptionist, project manager, accountant and administrator.

While researching this book I interviewed Henry Dotterer, founder of the world's largest online translation business network (ProZ.com), to ask him about his community. As it happened, Henry's early career offered up a good example of a different attitude people who go into lifeworking now have. Henry said, "The idea for ProZ.com hit me in 1997. Having come from a computing background, I was finding work in Japan as a translator, copywriter, technical salesperson and more. I enjoyed the freelance lifestyle very much."

This multi-tasking, free-wheeling lifestyle is common to an increasing number of income earners who create their wealth by working on a range of different projects for different companies at the same time.

Living on the OUTSIDE of the INSIDE

What most life-workers have in common is that they learnt their craft working 'on the inside' for large employers. This real world apprenticeship affords life-workers much more than the ability to gain know-how and develop job skills, it also educates them on how businesses work, introduces them to important professional bodies and provides valuable personal relationships and emotional support networks that they wouldn't have had the opportunity to develop 'on the outside'.

The growth in size of big corporations makes the world even smaller and it shapes markets for knowledge. These businesses know that they need innovation and ideas but within the fabric of a far more regimented world of compliance, risk management and IT control. It's no good just offering an idea. Every 'new thing' needs to fit somewhere in the corporate machine. *The machine* needs to be listening in order for new ideas or innovation to take hold.

> **Steve Wozniak – a.k.a. the guy that came up with the *Apple* personal computer – worked for a time at *Hewlett Packard* designing handheld calculators. He shared his idea for a personal computer with them before eventually leaving to set up *Apple* with Steve Jobs. HP said 'thanks but no thanks'.**

Unlike the man in the street, before business can share knowledge it needs to know who owns it. Intellectual property ownership can make or break a company.

> People still can't agree who invented the telephone. When I was a child, everyone said it was Alexander Graham Bell. More recently it has been recognized that Bell's design looked VERY SIMILAR to the patent drawings submitted *on the same day* 12th September 1878 by Elisha Gray, a Quaker from Ohio.

If consumers offer an idea to your business, then who owns it? What if a member of your workforce comes up with the same idea a week later? Do you own the idea then? Wouldn't it be better *not* to invite customers to send you their ideas just in case they unwittingly compromise your intellectual property?

Over time, organizations adopt operating norms of behaviour and procedures (what I describe as 'enterprise logic') that shapes how they think and act. Larger organizations embrace more complex enterprise logic structures but none of this is visible to the naked eye.

Without the understanding of *how enterprises think,* life-workers are unable to engage their talents into the gear wheels that drive internal processes that ultimately grind out customer value. Their only opportunity then is to harvest knowledge rather than create it. Their potential value to prospective buyers is significantly diminished.

Few people who become knowledge based life-workers survive for long without having been on the inside first for sufficient time to earn a few grey hairs and develop some wisdom. Exceptions to this rule do exist. They include people who have learnt so much about new technologies, new online markets and other current fashions and behaviours that they can become knowledge intermediaries – people who perform the role of guides for bigger organizations.

Many people in business find mentors during their work career, people who can guide them, or provide them with a sounding board. These contacts become critical lynch-pins for life-workers who function largely independently of the corporate machine and who need to maintain a perspective of the corporate business reality.

Employers increasingly rely on life-workers

Life-workers play a positive role in the effectiveness of businesses for a number of reasons:

The 'always right-sized' organization

As I covered in the previous chapter, businesses face a faster pace of change than ever before. They never quite know what knowledge skills they're going to need.

Because life-workers are contracted for specific projects, employers can turn them on or off like a tap. Employers pay only for the time life-workers are working on projects. Any preparatory work or 'project overhead' is borne by the life-worker. In most cases the overhead costs of equipping life-workers with ICT and telecoms equipment and finding office space are passed on to the life-worker. And whilst employers will no doubt be charged a higher hourly or daily rate, they have no employee tax or benefits issues to consider.

Another big attraction for employers is the preparedness of life-workers to make themselves available at the drop of a hat. Their lifestyle means they can normally balance a number of projects at the same time. In previous years, it was common for IT and professional services companies to 'bench' people (i.e. pay them a peppercorn income) while they were not working on projects. Increasingly, the growth in the available life-worker community means now they don't have to.

Everyone's an expert these days

One of the primary advantages of life-workers to businesses is that they are 'to-order' experts on specialist subjects that can suddenly become important. This knowledge and know-how is probably needed by organizations some of the time but not all of the time which is when life-workers become a 'must-have' resource. Without them, employers either have to contract a 'supplier organization' – probably a more complicated procurement exercise – or they allocate one of their internal people with probably less domain experience and who still has to work on other projects while they battle to acquire the know-how they need to discharge the task. Learning on the job is of course something that everyone has to do sometime but without the proper guidance it can lead to costly errors occurring and things being missed. Life-workers are available to order.

Sub-process and new process expertise

As it becomes easier for specialist knowledge workers to find employment through online communities and knowledge markets, so it becomes possible to encourage richer specialization. Instead of marketing consultants there are 'product launch experts', rather than general designers employers can recruit specialist *Adobe* flash designers, web designers, brochure designers; people that are very good at a very specific tasks, or have specialist knowledge of a particular tool, technology or process.

Workers with wisdom

Life-workers jump from one project to the next, often across industries. They're exposed to many more experiences and perspectives of their chosen discipline because it's all they do every day and they're paid to do it well. Employers benefit from this world aware knowledge and richer interpersonal maturity without paying a premium for it. Many life-workers gather insight and project experiences month after month, year after year. They develop their own network of contacts and associations with professional organizations related to the subject they're passionate about. Employers are able to access this rich wisdom and specialist knowledge, relationships, know-how, experience, industry ties, insight, technical certifications etc. without having to pay someone to develop these riches.

An unfettered external perspective

It's difficult sometimes for employees to deliver an honest appraisal of situations to their managers or peers when it might be seen as critique, of their supervisor and there is the possibility that the individual giving the criticism may be affected (either positively or adversely) by the commentary. My experience is that employers normally value another independent viewpoint on the outside of their business.

In 'Agilization' I introduce the concept of a 'cocooned organization' that only seeks advice from within its four walls and bases its appreciation of what matters most to its customers on that single perspective. This isn't uncommon in larger organizations for management teams who make strategic decisions to be separated from customers by 3 or 4 layers of organization structure.

Every industry and organization has its own lexicon of language that influences how it interprets what it hears. In *Agilization*, I also introduce a phenomenon called 'talk-back' which occurs when internal staff who listen 'according to their internalized understanding of how the world works' and interpret what they're listening to on that basis. For example, if you were working in the financial services sector and overheard someone saying there was a problem with the bank collapsing you would instantly be thinking 'Which Bank? (i.e. financial lending organization) rather than appreciating that your colleague was talking about the river bank behind the building that was flooding because of the high level of rainfall for this time of year.

Having time to think

As the pressures on internal staff become ever more focused on 'coordination' of resources and project delivery, corporate workers find they have less and less time to *think*.

It's become quite a topic in business of late. People are spending so much time booking meetings, drafting documents, answering emails, writing budgets and attending project planning meetings. Precious time is lost for *thinking*.

> During his meeting with the Conservative Party leader, David Cameron, whilst on his presidential campaign visit to the UK, Barack Obama mused, "The most important thing you need to do is to have big chunks of time during the day when all you're doing is thinking." [35]

It's part of the culture of life-workers to have *and make* time to think. This is partly because they disassociate effort from reward. They frequently invest time to study and research their chosen topic unrelated to any given project or client (like painters that paint *because they are painters* or mountaineers that climb Everest *because it's there*). I know designers constantly on the lookout for new website designs or interior designers who will happily invest time in a haberdashery to see what's there that they might use for later. This is unpaid research work.

> Tony Buzan, inventor of the graphical thinking tool *MindMap* asked people where they are physically when they have great ideas, paradigm-shifting epiphanies, or a flood of memories they've been trying to remember. He says, "Regardless of continent, age, gender, education and race, the answers are the same: in the shower; the bath; the loo; shaving; walking in nature; in bed; looking at water; listening to classical music and long-distance travel such as running or driving."

In so many organizations a culture of rewarding constant activity pervades instead of encouraging workers to release thinking time to identify break-through insights. So someone else needs to do the thinking. This division of labour welcomes life-workers with open arms. They're becoming the *contracted thinkers* of the enterprise.

Why aren't there more life-workers?

Balancing the *war for talent* and a bourgeoning demand for innovation from commerce with the growth in numbers of people with grievances against full-time employment (and who possess the right skills to adopt a more individualistic work-life balance), you'd have to ask why there aren't *even more* life-workers than there are today. These are some of the reasons:

Access to markets

Even life-workers struggle to know what's *out there* sometimes. Until business networking tools like *Xing* and *LinkedIn* came on the scene there wasn't the opportunity for life-workers to connect to groups and markets. With business social networking this is changing as the illustration shows on the right of LinkedIn's 'Related Groups' area.

LinkedIn cleverly exposes member groups around a theme. Click on one group and LinkedIn exposes other related groups on the same theme (like 'change management', 'HR' or 'language translation'). In this case it reveals a number of independent and professional organizations who are creating networks for change management consultants. Networks can be totally open to everyone or closed, requiring membership. LinkedIn's 'Official Groups' go through a review process that evaluates whether the group is an established membership organization. If it is then the site verifies the owner's affiliation with the organization when they apply.

LinkedIn's 'Related Groups' feature

These 'open to anyone who's qualified' networks grow quickly by leveraging social networking facilities on sites like LinkedIn that update their members on what peers are doing. When peers join a new professional network, suddenly anyone else in their social network is informed. If the individual who joins a group is highly regarded, their colleagues become interested to find out why they joined and what makes the group so interesting. These 'alerts' bring disconnected people together in common interest groups.

Business social networking platforms create a storm of endorsement based marketing that directly targets people who are most likely to be interested in a discipline area. Sites like LinkedIn provide an essential enabler for life-workers to build their market reach, giving them the opportunity to leverage strong and weak relationship ties.

Most employers today continue to adopt full-time employment models and aren't contemplating alternatives

To create a market for anything there has to be supply and demand – and all parties have to visit a market. Many organizations haven't actively sought alternatives to full-time employment model; most because they haven't explored the possibility that other resourcing models exist. In truth, there aren't many places where organizations can discover successful examples of working knowledge markets.

Discriminative tax systems live on

Tax systems don't take life-workers into account perhaps because the existence of life-workers is relatively new and not well understood. Corporation Tax in the UK is meant to be a tax on profits. But most life-workers don't greet the end of year balance sheet with champagne and a big party; they are more likely to squirrel the money away to extend the time window before their bank account runs dry. As the result, for life-workers, in the UK at least, Corporation Tax (charged at 21 per cent of profits up to £300,000) acts like a punishment for success and cruelly reduces the 'survival' time window. For many individuals, this *cap on success* is a good reason to stay employed on a full-time contract.

Sometimes it's cool to be employed

I know I've mentioned it before but there are advantages to being employed. In the US for example, everyone needs healthcare insurance and normally it's paid for by employers. There's also the camaraderie with work colleagues – people buzzing round that people feel they would miss if it weren't there. Being a life-worker isn't for everyone.

Employers today aren't honouring their implicit duty of care to life-workers

It's not all great being a life-worker. Full-time employment has some distinct benefits such as (very often) a pension plan, health scheme, mobile phone, maternity and paternity needs – perhaps even a company car. Life-workers in contrast are left out in the cold. Employers have yet to honour their implicit duty of care to ensure the life-workers who contribute to their organizational success are supported.

Welfare markets today don't promote 'flexicurity'

In the meeting rooms of the EU in Brussels politicians and bureaucrats are discussing the subject of 'flexicurity'. A portmanteau of *flexibility* and *security*, it is a term used to summarize 'how to guarantee new forms of welfare security to workers through supporting employ-ability in return for more flexibility in the labour market allowing companies to adapt their workforce to suit a changing economy'.

> The European Commission in its *Employment in Europe 2006* report describes flexicurity as an optimal balance between labour market flexibility and security for employees against labour market risks).[36]

Governments and employers care about flexicurity because they know that knowledge markets won't become mainstream unless there are welfare mechanisms to give individuals economic security. This is a key question for governments today when it comes to economic competitiveness and social cohesion because human capital is the bedrock of any knowledge economy. Those regions that get better at tapping into the talent pools of knowledge workers are most likely to be the power houses of the world's knowledge economy in the future.

But, so far flexicurity does not support the needs of a knowledge economy. Employers are happy to profit from the ideas and innovation provided by life-workers but they're not prepared to honour their duty of care. No doubt it will take government intervention to ensure that markets supporting life-workers will one day soon provision for market standards of worker healthcare and pension planning that full-time employment provides. The EU Lisbon strategy for growth and jobs underlines the need to improve the adaptability of workers and enterprises and whilst it sounds a very bureaucratic problem and debate, it's important if knowledge markets are to become mainstream.

The technology needed to bring those who have knowledge to those who need it, is in its infancy

For there to be knowledge workers (i.e. people who make their money by delivering and applying knowledge) there must be knowledge markets where buyers can meet sellers. There are some early examples of knowledge market technologies around today (these I describe later in chapter 14 but these aren't mainstream yet or able to support full-time employment).

Larger organizations must do something different

The pressure on employers to win the best talent means that many large organizations are thinking more about how they retain the best people. One good way of doing this is to be sympathetic to requests of workers to gain more flexible work-time arrangements and find a better work life balance. When seeking employment young workers today look at an organization's track record on corporate social responsibility and aren't afraid to negotiate flexible working terms. There is a business case for work-life balance. For example, the UK telecoms company British Telecom, claims that it saved £52m in overheads in the year to March 2003 by increasing home working (it calculated an annual saving of £10m in fuel costs alone).[37]

More flexible employment contracts would encourage more people to keep taking the corporate pay cheque but there are a number of issue areas that I've covered in this chapter that would still be on the 'unhappy list' of many workers.

Mixing projects

Achieving more time with the family and time at home isn't the only life-mix that life-workers are looking for. They also want to devote their work time to a subject or key interest area without the distractions of other stuff employers ask them to do because they're on a salary. Life-workers I speak to often explain to me one of the big reasons they decided to change their lifestyle was because they felt their employer was only expending 30% of their talent. They don't feel they are giving 110% yet they want to.

> **According to Henry Dotterer, CEO of www.Proz.com, corporations aren't necessarily making full use of the talents of their internal and external workforces. "In the traditional model, a company defines a box in an org chart, writes a job description, and then attempts to fill the box with exactly one person. In other words, one person, one job. In some cases, a better approach is to form teams dynamically, based on the intersection between project-based need and individual capabilities. Many people have several marketable skills, and these often go untapped."**

Corporate workers have limited time to think

This issue of time to think is an important one. Many corporate workers are today overwhelmed by email traffic and back to back meetings. They are coordinators, not thinkers – through circumstance, not by choice. Their productivity is measured by the tasks they complete, the spreadsheets and PowerPoint they produce, rather than their positive contributions to business outcomes.

Being paid for innovation

It grates on people when they come up with a great idea and their organization does not reward them for it – particularly as nowadays there are other agencies on the web who will pay hard cash for knowledge skills, creativity and innovation.

Competing for business against smaller companies with more agility

Big corporations sometimes feel bullet-proof but we know from recent events that it doesn't matter how big you are in today's market, you still need to keep one step ahead of the pack (and not drop the ball) or you will get trampled underfoot. Smaller companies enjoy more adaptive organizational structures, fewer silos and are normally more in tune with their customers and markets.

Corporations today are failing to provide the social environment that young people want

Young people today particularly are accustomed to having always online access to information, technology and social media tools. When they go to work for an employer they expect to be able to walk in the door with their iPOD, plug into *Facebook* and use Skype. It can come as a surprise when they experience locked down corporate networks and IT teams that don't allow mobile phones or USB sticks because of fears of data security breaches.

The drivers behind life-working

The appeal of *life-working* is driven by a mix of push and pull-factors: On the push side, some became surplus to corporate requirements or reached 35 and suddenly became too old. Maybe late nights in the office, the absence of a mentoring network or their employers' inflexibility towards home working and lack of appreciation for great ideas finally got to them. Alternatively, it might have been the draw of pull-factors such as working from home and committing 110% to a subject they were interested in that made the difference. Or maybe working on the balcony of a villa somewhere in Tuscany with sea views was too much of a draw after all.

A micro-slice of the future

Life-workers offer a glimpse of a future style of knowledge-based economy.

With no welfare state model for life-workers, early stage markets, immature support technologies and most enterprises adopting norms of behaviour that only think of full-time employment, there remain significant and complex barriers that prevent the rapid proliferation of knowledge markets fuelled by life-workers. Let's not forget that life-workers are still pragmatic people who still have to think about mortgages and their standards of living. They are only prepared to 'risk it' so far. They value a standard of living they've probably become accustomed to over a number of years through full-time employment.

They grew up *learning* technology, not *living* with it. Sharing their personal contact details with others still feels a little alien to them. They might still read the terms and conditions that fly up on web-sites to understand what they're committing to. Life-workers are migrating from what was to what might be. They are still very brave people because they're crossing the tight-rope of a self-employed existence without a safety net. But to all intents and purposes, like me, they are cloth cut of a world before the Internet and they inherit the cultural attachments of the last century.

But there is another community of knowledge workers arriving on the scene that has a totally different perspective to knowledge working.

And they live on the edge.

.

KNOWLEDGE BOHEMIANS

They come from the highly educated class of Generation-Y now entering the workforce on their own terms.

A new generation of highly skilled post-graduates are leaving their early years of education recognizing that their perspective on work life, and their emotional obligation to potential employers, is hugely different to that of their parents.

Their employment horizon is not measured in a job for life. Their aspiration is not to dedicate their lives to an employer or a career.

An emerging new form of organically formed social support network gives them a level of confidence in personal economic security and the encouragement to *do their own thing*; to live life on their own terms; achieving economic security and freedom by working on many different projects for many different employers.

8

A bohemian life-style

In my father's day, a job for life was ALWAYS seen to be a good thing.

A good employer could guarantee a lifetime of income security. Working for a single employer all of your life has a definite upside to it. The British United Shoe Machinery Company ('The BU') was the company I joined after leaving school. It was the place my father worked as an apprentice and his father worked in the purchasing department years before. Small world. As life would have it my grandfather managed to last a lifetime at 'The BU', my dad made it to 15 years and I exited in 5.

I took a trainee management job at *The BU* because I was desperate. I was 18 and waiting for my A-level grades to arrive in the post. Then a close friend who I thought to be much brainier than me flunked his grades. So I added 1+1 to get 3 and thought I'd better get a job quick. I didn't wait for my grades. I applied for as many jobs as I could. That was how things worked in my day. If you didn't have the *nous* upstairs you got a job so your parents didn't have to worry about your future anymore

Attitudes are different for people leaving higher education today. These are the individuals that governments and industry hope will replace the dwindling ranks of baby boomer knowledge workers who are thinking more these days about their retirement. Many of the class of 2009 and 2010 hope to fall into the security of full-time employment as people have for centuries. Others won't make the grade and find employment opportunities outside of the knowledge economy.

But a growing number will find a third way to make ends meet.

Meet the knowledge bohemians

Knowledge bohemians are part of Generation Y ('Gen Y'). They are well educated and they've grown up with computers so the web's their playground, their community, their oracle, their mouthpiece and home from home. Information services like *Googlemaps*, *Twitter*, *Wikipedia*, *iTunes* form the fabric of their lives so any new innovation is quickly absorbed or rapidly discarded. Their ability to make instant 'like/dislike' judgements on new technologies must be particularly scary for software companies and information services providers. Unlike the early years I remember of desktop computing where we were fed software applications that barely worked, and users had to make do with poor screen layouts, sites that serve up 'information services' have to deliver instant gratification or face being black listed.

Graduates leaving University today aren't thinking about a job for life, even 5 years.

> **Research by *The Economist* in 2006 found that the median tenure for workers ages 55-64 in the United States was 9.3 years. For workers in the 25-43 age group, the median tenure was 2.9 years.[38]**

Young people with creative flair and knowledge skills might still wonder how they will pay back their student loans but the draw of a more free-wheeling life-style on their own terms is too great to give up.

> **There's not much slack in the global market for talent. The same report from *The Economist* found unemployment among American graduates was around 2%, and that's even before the baby-boomers have started to retire in earnest.**

A new social group is emerging in our society; partly by the way young, well educated people are being brought up. They think differently about *employment* and they look for new ways to sustain their culture, employ their social networks and enjoy economic freedom by levering their knowledge and creativity.

These are the knowledge bohemians.

The term bohemian arrived in Europe in the nineteenth century to describe the untraditional lifestyles of impoverished creatives – artists, poets and actors – in major European cities. They were seen to harbour antiestablishment views and lead unorthodox lives.

I use this term to describe the draft of the early 21st century because it has a great deal in common with their 19th century predecessors. Like the creatives of 19th century Paris and London, they are creative talents who feel disenfranchised by the 'establishment'. The establishment, made up of faceless corporations and middle-aged politicians, show contempt towards them by treating them as a 'transaction' or worse as 'the general public'. Neither description sits well with them. They think in a different way and they want to express themselves through their work. The medium they choose to use is the Internet. It provides them with a canvas for their work that the world can see. The way they think might not be something everyone can relate to. Regardless of the University or subject they chose, Gen Y individuals are being exposed to many different subject areas. They have more life choices than any generation preceding them. Having lightly touched so many interesting activities they're having problems picking just one and making it their life pursuit. They face peer pressure NOT to choose. And they're confused. This is eloquently captured in the verbatim excerpt below from an interview my Gen Y researcher had with a graduate friend, called Ross.

> Ross says: "Attitudes towards schooling have changed. In the past it had always been about learning practical and applicable skills and trades, whereas recently it's become more focused on knowledge and intelligence. I never learned a thing in school that really prepared me for life after it, not like my parents did anyway."
>
> "Hmm.. And what about apart from school?"
>
> Ross says: "In what sense?"
>
> "Maybe how in the parental generation it was like.. You do this degree, you leave Uni, you get this job, you retire, you die. Whereas 'we' are so enabled to do anything at all?"
>
> Ross says: "Oh, definitely, unless someone has a clear idea in their mind about exactly what they want to do, it all becomes utterly confusing. Back in the day, trades were tied directly into education and those qualifications, but now I think places are more reliant on people just having a degree, not neccessarily whether it's relevant to the job. It's so confusing."

As my researcher explained to me, "There are only four professions it's okay to commit to – medicine, education, engineering and charity work. Anything else is seriously un-cool. You can't possibly say 'I want to be an accountant', you'd be laughed out. More and more people are thinking 'I will give anything a try.' There is a peer pressure to be *free* with your future."

Knowledge bohemians don't feel the same pressure to join the rat race. They are happy to put the 9-to-5 gruel train on hold a little longer while they try out a variety of pursuits until the experiment itself becomes a career; a lifestyle of mixing 2, 3 or 4 interests at the same time until the income covers living costs.

Another reason for this reluctance to engage with the job market is that the young people of Gen Y don't see a role for themselves in society. When I grew up, like many of my peers, I saw a future for myself as the head of a nuclear family living in a pretty 4 bedroom house on the edge of a picturesque village with two children and a flashy car on the drive. Gen Y doesn't have that. Politicians and scientists keep reminding them that the planet has around 100 years left on its clock and with luck they won't see its end. Faced with that reality, small wonder why post graduates don't want to settle down and commit their life to a vocation that leads to a nuclear family living in a pretty cottage in a village somewhere. If you were given 5 years to live would YOU have still made the same life choices?

First and foremost a community 'individuals'

It's difficult to describe a genre of community without making it sound like every person in it fits the same mould, thinks and works in the same way.

This is not the case for knowledge bohemians. They're individuals who seek to assert their individuality on others through their collaborative communications and creative verve. They don't want to be part of a group or a cult. Their individuality matters to them. The Internet and its social networking platforms enable knowledge bohemians to have an audience that takes interest in what they say and do; and allows them to express their individuality in new distinctive new ways.

On the web, knowledge bohemians have a voice.

> **Sarah Blue is one of the talents of *Cambrian House*; a company I feature later. Sarah, an art school graduate with a**

passion for technology, is a well regarded expert speaker on the subject of 'ideas markets'. From the outset, she wanted to be a 'free to choose' knowledge worker. Sarah says, "My father worked for the same company for 40 years but that's not who I am. I left college with an Arts degree so I'm creative and it suits me to be doing 10 things at a time. Doing what I enjoy for 30% of the time and then fill the rest of the day with boring work is not something I could do. I like to take on a mix of 4 or 5 projects that keep me energized and that collectively offer enough income to provide reasonable income." CEO of Cambrian House, Shelley Kuipers, agrees, "Many people today want the opportunity and freedom to participate in a mix of projects and to decide for themselves how best to balance their work life and income streams." Highly employable creatives like Sarah see a distinct 'life-style and creativity' downside for working exclusively for one employer in a single job role.

Consummate digital networkers

Outsiders might think knowledge bohemians are isolated and work alone but in reality they're the most connected of people. They live their lives connected to the biggest community in the world – accessible on the web. Many develop their first relationships at college or University and through these early connections they build others. Never are they too far away from their associates who they meet in coffee shops, bars, and for some still on campus. For many knowledge bohemians, the campus lifestyle continues on into work life long after their years at University. It is extended by the employment of social networking tools so that peers are never too far away. How college students interact and gain mutual emotional support shapes the sort of life in the business world they want to lead.

Characteristics and cultural behaviours

As I mention in the introduction to this chapter, knowledge bohemians originate from Gen Y; the first generation to grow up with the web.

Instead of tumble down cafés, 21st century knowledge bohemians meet on the web and share a common bond as surfers. They want to be online and accessible. They think little of the consequences of sharing personal data. They haven't anything to hide. It's a cultural idiosyncrasy of their generation to accept the usage terms of the web. They know that corporations fund social networking tools by expecting to push advertising at them. They know it, but it doesn't concern them – it's part of *the deal*.

Cut from the Gen Y tree

From Gen Y, the knowledge bohemians have inherited into their culture a lexicon of language and a design code book that's been influenced heavily by R&B culture, Japanese tech culture, gaming and companies like Apple. These influencers are built into the way they communicate. With the websites and tools they use, *cool design and usability* beats functionality and site performance every time. And if dad starts using the same tool, no matter how good it is, it's not cool anymore.

As members of the 'hope-less generation' (this is how a Gen Y friend describes her *generation without hope*) they share a characteristically satirical humour that critiques a world going off the rails. And it's not cool to take yourself too seriously either.

The web is their birthright and they've got used to enjoying the deep emotional support of their web communities; people they don't always know in the real world. They know other surfers listen to them, value their opinion, share a desire to assert their personality in ways other bohemians can relate to. This creates a deep emotional support system they don't get from the traditional sources in the real world. Being online sets them free. It makes them feel part of a world that otherwise doesn't seem to understand them.

Gen Y doesn't connect in the *virtual world*. In their communities the two paradigms are conjugated. The people they meet on campus, in coffee shops, hotel lobbies and innovation centres they will also find online. Connections they make through the web might well to be associated with projects and activities, so there are sometimes opportunities to meet in the real world too!

Unlike Gen X people like me, Gen Y retains many more of its relationship connections; partly because of the tools at its disposal, and also because its more open, happier to share its contact information; much more comfortable with being online. This translates into *Facebook* contact lists in the hundreds! (If I think back to my personal address book, I'd be lucky to get to 50 including all my business contacts and my wife's extended family who I meet once every two years.) The dynamics of this step change in personal relationship ties means the opportunity to find out more about what's happening and who knows who is much greater that it has been for previous generations.

Part of the culture for young people of connecting on the web today is to give yourself a digital personality which could be as simple as giving yourself a new 'handle' or designing your very own 'avatar'. Avatars are your very own *virtual persona* used in the virtual world. I expect that if you don't spend too much time on the web you'd wonder why you need Avatars at all. But if, like Gen Y, you spend over half your life online, then it's pretty cool to have your own web personality you can hide behind and interact through.

Avators – your persona on the web

A Knowledge Bohemian's Life Support System

The thing that makes it possible for knowledge bohemians to thrive is the network that supports them. What makes this 'Life Support System' difficult to describe is its multilayered qualities and the fact that it isn't one entity. How it works is best told through an illustrative story.

> **Imagine that you're 24 years old and you've left university having graduated in computing. You're creative and you're looking to productize and bring to market the subject of your dissertation. You need lots of help and guidance but not to worry, there's a lot of support around you.**

You make contact with *Young Inventors International* (YII); a not-for-profit organization founded by Anne Swift, herself a young inventor and entrepreneur, who now dedicates much of her time in hooking up other young inventors to the support networks they need. A discussion with YII uncovers an opportunity to prototype your big idea with the aid of some contribution of time, lab space from the University and with some mentoring expertise from a local company. There's also an event coming up with the possibility of networking with some large corporate sponsors. Now you're thinking; do you really want a business or is there an opportunity to license the technology? Interesting, but next you need to make some instant cash and buy yourself some time to think.

Whilst online you find out that one of your college friends has just registered to be part of a project being run by one of the mobile phone companies to test one of their new designs. It's a couple of days during the next 6 weeks playing with their product and working out how to break it– but that's cool, you can fit that in. Maybe you've done too much thinking – time for a coffee break.

You trip down to the local Internet Café.

At the Café you run into Jeremy; a friend of a friend. He left University two years earlier but you've kept in touch occasionally via *Facebook*. Jeremy works for *Big Corporation* in their data centre. He tells you that *Big Corporation* is considering a new web project and they might need some extra capacity. It's right down your street because you've been using the same sort of software at University. Jeremy suggests that you take a look at their projects page and register your interest.

Home again. You hear your mobile go. It's Julia *twittering* again. She's spent the afternoon at a research focus group put on by a local market research company looking into new forms of viral marketing. Julia's *twitter* suggests that not only was it fun but she got paid $8.50 an hour for her time. She's even more delighted because they've asked her to go back and work on the project as part of their team.

There is no single source of emotional or practical support. This layer of emotional and financial support comes from a multitude of sources; the combination of social network relationships, professional and institutional groups, informal groups and associations that are established by others with similar challenges and interests etc. Businesses, governments and academic institutions are all creating new forms of advisory and investment mechanisms to spread risk and foster innovation.

While organizations continue to employ the majority of their knowledge workers on full-time contracts, new ways of harnessing the ideas of the masses and paying for their contributions are emerging. Shelly Kuipers is CEO of Cambrian House and a passionate enthusiast of 'crowdsourcing'.

> The term 'crowdsourcing' was created by Jeff Howe of Wired Magazine to describe 'the act of taking a job traditionally performed by a designated agent – usually an employee – and outsourcing it to an undefined, generally large group of people in the form of an open call.

I asked Shelley if she had any examples of crowdsourcing and other community based knowledge harvesting technologies that were proving themselves as income generating opportunities for professional knowledge workers.

"There are some really good examples like YouTest.com and istockphoto.com; business models that are providing people with real incomes on their own lifestyle terms. If you take the example of *Mob4Hire*, this organization offers mobile application testing to help mobile or cell application developers test mobile games and mobile applications. Using the crowd, the process will allow real people to test mobile applications in real field conditions. There are no employees as such. They acquire business and provide a brokering service work through a network of developers to get testing done faster than any other provider."

As Sarah Blue of Cambrian House adds, "People like me – professionals, creatives, other forms of knowledge workers – don't see a risk in not having a full time job with a single employer. I know that by running with a series of projects I all but remove any risk of not earning enough income, and as a creative thinker, I don't want to do the same thing all of the time. I need the variety and this comes from having the economic freedom to juggle multiple roles."

One thing you will notice about my example is that on no occasion is there an office or exclusive employer. The support network is much richer, much deeper and yet much more transparent. A key aspect of what makes survival for knowledge bohemians possible is the sheer size of their relationship networks and the layers of support that are relatively easily accessed if you're on the *inside* track.

The life support system of the knowledge bohemian is a network made up of a series of inter-relating but not connected *support platelets* made up of people, groups, associations, etc., that can help them. This support fabric changes over time. The sheer volume of inter-related support platelets means the probability of an individual finding no source of income at all is relatively small. But it is still possible for people to 'fall through' the system and onto hard times if they don't possess a suitable mix of skills.

The knowledge bohemian life support system is made up of interlinking support platelets they rely on to secure opportunities for income generation

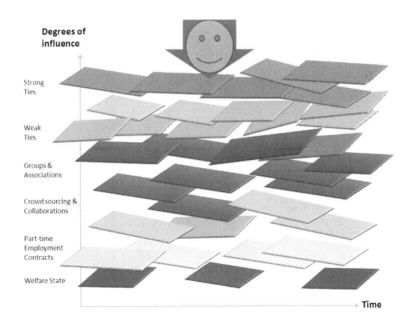

No two knowledge bohemians have access to the same support framework. It will vary according to their life circumstances; factors such as education, knowledge skills, location, social background, the size of their family, how well they retain and harvest their social network, how much time they spend socializing and making new connections and – the ultimate measure – their acquired social capital. They include:

Strong ties   These are the intimate relationships held with family and close peers; the primary source of references, endorsements, credentials, emotional support etc. Surprisingly Gen Y is less good at developing strong ties than previous generations. As one graduate puts it, "Any given person probably has 3 or 4 close friends they would ever dream of inviting for dinner and then has a *Facebook* list of others they pass in the corridor. Our generation knows more *about each other* but we don't *know* each other."

Weak ties   These are weaker ties born through 'who knows who' relationships that connect knowledge bohemians to life-workers, mentors and associates, corporate workers etc. Gen Y is good at retaining weak ties to peers using social media sites and is willing to share knowledge. In this 'you scratch my back and I'll scratch yours' community, it is considered socially acceptable to lever networks to make new introductions for income generating purposes. As one individual put it, "We're freer with our contact information. You might get someone approach you and you'd have a conversation like – 'Do you know Mary Brown? And you might say, 'Well I haven't actually spoken to her but I can give you her email.' Of course it's easier in the virtual world. In the real world I think you might feel really awkward!" Gen Y kids know that others will call on their weak ties to bridge to new relationships – and that's okay. There are numerically more relationships but they have less influence in guaranteeing to the knowledge bohemian a sustainable income.

These individuals feel less emotionally bound to help the requestor. The individual seeking new connections won't know these people as intimately or have so detailed an understanding of their character and day to day activities. Therefore they're not able to judge the value of their endorsements.

Crowd sourcing and collaborations	These are opt-in memberships to crowdsourcing websites and salaried collaborative communities that might include research projects, funded opinion pieces, ideas generation, product usability testing etc.
Groups and associations	These are opt-in memberships to self-organizing groups and institutional associations sponsored by individuals, business, academia, industry, governments, trades unions, professional bodies and trade associations. Finding employment is made more easily through the larger number of intermediary websites and groups. For example, many student unions have coordination departments and websites so that employers can promote their job opportunities to students. And there are skills-centric community sites like www.proz.com that provide another form of marketplace to connect demand to supply.
Part-time employment contracts	Knowledge bohemians rely on spending at least some of their time doing paid work, normally in the form of part-time contracts for business. As organizations become more aware of the resource pools available to them, they increasingly turn to the use of external resource pools to manage peaks and troughs in demand for labour.
Welfare state	The level of support provided by the welfare state for knowledge bohemians in most countries is very poor. If ultimately individuals are unable to find any sources of income then they can hope their government provides subsidies or unemployment benefits but the threshold is normally very low and accessing these resources – even where they do exist – can be difficult.

The life support system is presented in my diagram in tiers but, in reality, even those tiers are more vague and inner-leafing. A crowd-sourcing activity may result in a part-time job opportunity, or an employer might fund the formation of communities that produce outcomes interesting to them. Divisions between relationships, associations and income sources are blurring.

A key ingredient my illustration does not expose is the fact that relationships have different weightings. Some 'strong ties' have much more social capital and potential for supplying new ties to income generating opportunities than others. If you shared similar skills qualifications and competencies with a close friend (perhaps you went through college on the same course), then you might be interested in the associations they form, the income opportunities they identify, because you know your personal characteristics and skills match theirs.

Not all of the knowledge networking that originates on the World Wide Web stays *virtual*. It has become increasingly common for sites and third party networking providers to provide real-world opportunities to network (see Proz.com's *powwows, Twiistup and socialnetwork. meetup.com*). There are even sites like *meetup.com* that provide directories of groups. Many of these events, inspired by virtual social networking, are subject matter specific and provide an opportunity for people to meet like-minded people who share similar interests. I expect in the next few years we will see many new forms of real world social gatherings that bring people together on terra firma having met through their interests online.

Many knowledge bohemians with *so many* connections make a MARKET

One day there will be millions of knowledge bohemians. The scale of this community will itself create a market-place for skills and activities, products and services. Here are some characteristics of that market.

Workers are consumers too

New generations communicate across their social networks for pleasure and income. The same tools are employed for both. Knowledge bohemians assert their personality on the web. Their *ego-wall* describes who they are and this insight is used for both work and play to build ties. It forms part of their credentials, as does the breadth of their network.

Gen Y use knowledge of relationship ties in the same way that my dad's generation might have expected to meet someone on business and find out which golf course they frequent to further build social relationships. The divide between work and play becomes almost invisible.

In order for commercial organizations to promote their products and services to these very illusive communities they must play by the same rules. They have to disclose *their* individual space – the values of their brand, their social consciousness, their ecology commitments – and they must have personal endorsements from others in the network (who themselves must have sufficient social capital in *their* individual space). For this reason, many organizations now publish a *Facebook* page and *Twitter* messages; exposing their personality.

A new fluidity to the formation of knowledge markets

Innovation doesn't happen in knowledge markets in a straight line. Sometimes simple ideas result in products. Other times simple ideas, when shared with other organizations or associations might create *even bigger* ideas. More help might be needed from more third parties to mature big ideas into something saleable. Working with academia or commerce might help individuals to bring their ideas to the attention of 'others'. Those others might then acquire rights to the idea and redefine its purpose to make it appeal to a completely different buying community. At what point does this become a market? Within this value chain, knowledge is being discovered, assembled, enriched, shaped, formed into a 'something' and then that 'something' is exchanged through a number of hands. Each step in the process adds a little more value to the 'idea'. The intellectual property is the currency of this ideas exchange so knowing who owns it is vital.

New forms of federation

It's easy to understand how the formation of markets around 'ideas' creates an infinite number of unique combinations of associations between knowledge bohemians, academic institutions, commerce and governments leading to a high level of fluidity.

> **New types of federations are emerging on a daily basis made possible by social media and internet technologies. It reminds me of the early days of commerce when entrepreneurs and money men would sit around coffee tables and debate the**

formation of 'new enterprises' without the safety net of the legal framework that was formed by the Company's Act (and the creation of 'corporations'. These men were not following a well trodden path. To happen, an enterprise required money, innovation and an adventurous spirit but other than that there weren't any rules to mention on how companies should work or behave.

In an attempt to foster knowledge markets, governments are keen to encourage the formation of new forms of federation. Often they will do this by offering to make available investment funds to private equity groups on a 50:50 shared risk basis, or they will back academic programmes to spin out 'campus innovation' into the commercial world to deliver economic growth opportunities. Commercial organizations that seek to minimise their risk associated with research and development are already joining these new federations of knowledge markets to tap into innovation. Having a 10% interest in thirty possible innovation successes is more desirable than to have 100% interest in two or three.

New employment relationships

Within these fluid federations new employment relationships are forming. Knowledge bohemians must find their individual supply-chain of projects from a collection of income sources and these relationships become important. There are sites like *iStock-photo, Proz.com, Open.Ad* and *Experts Exchange* for practically any industry or discipline. In place of a full-time employment contract, knowledge bohemians might have a mix of part-time contracts, project work, grants, an *eBay* business, casual labour income, income from previous intellectual property sold. Every day, more graduates leave University and turn down the option of a lifetime role working for the same employer.

People on the OUTSIDE of corporations who find ways to get INSIDE

I stated in the last chapter that many Gen X life-workers originate from a career *on the inside* having come from full-time employment, and benefit from the credentials of having worked for a big name brand, maybe even in a significant role. They use their 'alumni' networks to *sweat out* new business opportunities, endorsements and references. In this way they live on the outside of the warm and comfortable surroundings of the corporate world but they have enough social network contacts to keep the door to their income stream firmly wedged open. Knowledge bohemians don't have these relationship advantages, or credentials, or wisdom – but they do have the enthusiasm of youth and a range of new social media tools and support mechanisms at their disposal. Knowledge bohemians don't have the same level of wisdom and experience as life-workers. They come from a completely different background and relate to a culture that probably started on a campus somewhere. Be that as it may, their talent, creativity and naïve willingness to jump in and try things is all part of what makes them special to corporations.

Wealth creation

Unlike their 19th century predecessors knowledge bohemians aren't expecting to live a life of virtual poverty. Their knowledge and creativity in a world short on talent and innovation comes highly prized on any terms. Corporations are prepared to engage with knowledge bohemians on whatever terms necessary to access their talent pool. This affords knowledge bohemians economic freedom and the potential to mix projects in a way that allows them to balance work projects with their other life commitments.

Why corporations need them

There are a number of roles that knowledge bohemians are playing for big business that make them valuable whilst providing the knowledge bohemians with the life-style they enjoy. One of them is to act as a gateway to the youth market; to be the guides that help corporations to understand how to engage young people who seem to think in a different way to them. But another big reason why corporations want to use them is the free-wheeling creativity and the new thinking they offer.

Every industry has its *systems*. Even advertising, which is seen as the ultimate creative industry by many, is littered with cultural norms, processes and policy manuals, risk mitigation and 'approved' and 'unapproved' technology tools.. New recruits quickly conform to these norms. I've spoken to managers and owners of London advertising and brand agencies who are vexed by the lack of fresh, raw creative talent in the people they recruit and worry when they find great talent how to avoid it becoming institutionalized. Known ways to approach problems that are known to work become the norm and if you steer too far away from 'the system' you risk scaring off corporate clients. But adhere to 'the system and creative, innovative people stop thinking *differently* and start thinking' *the same*. Suddenly, the characteristics that made this person special in an interview have been processed out and what's left is a shadow of what could have been. But how can employers hope to keep their people thinking outside the box when constantly battering them with process manuals? It's a big problem. One of the consequences of over exposure to enterprise logic is that people stop taking risks themselves. They follow 'the system'. They start producing work they expect will appeal to customers and internal sponsors because it's safely inside the box. Experimentation is cool but it costs money. The downside of learning is the cost of making mistakes and whilst businesses like innovation, they don't like the cost of experiments that don't work. They, the corporations, want others to do the experiments. They want to back many different horses in a small way, take a stake in a wider net of projects and benefit from the reward.

Knowledge bohemians are happy to experiment and play with new ideas and creations in their own time. They are paid for what they deliver. Corporations have the option to say no. It's a better deal for corporations and they know it. They gain access to a huge talent pool that stays fresh and thoughtful – hence the success of *OpenAd*.

Organic markets

Most successful knowledge markets like INNOCENTIVE (see later) are owned by businesses – i.e. where commercial organizations synthesize a market and provide the mechanisms to organize seekers and solvers, dictate contractual terms on how the market should operate, provide matching services, membership services, payment processing and administration services etc. to then ultimately profit from bringing buyers and sellers together. These companies today play an important role in fostering innovation and someone has to pay them.

But I'm not convinced this current 'owner managed' format will become the norm. Why should anyone own knowledge markets? When people started to share their poetry or entrepreneurial art in the past, did they have to subscribe to a market in order to do so? The next decade will see an explosion of social media communications technologies and lower cost ways of accessing free-to-air methods of sharing knowledge.

As this technology becomes more pervasive knowledge markets will organically form; engineered by individuals, not by corporations.

We are entering the bohemian years of knowledge exploration.

TECHNOLOGICAL INNOVATION

Technology will perform a significant enabling role making it easier for self-organizing people networks to form, operate, and for individuals and businesses to harvest their full potential.

We are seeing the *democratization* of computing.

Advancing from an era where corporations have enjoyed the very best that computing technology could offer, an exclusive club that smaller companies and individuals could not afford to join, innovations in computing will level the playing field of technology innovation.

Individuals, entrepreneurs and small businesses will be able to affordably exploit computing platforms, business processes and leading edge technologies superior to those global corporations use today.

We will experience a rampage of innovation.

New computing platforms and tools – made available through affordable pay-as-you-use information services – will encourage entrepreneurs and small companies to create a cacophony of new information services to serve individuals and loosely coupled federations.

9

Computers that *know you*

The simplest and yet hardest to grasp concept of being a human is *to be*.
In a world full of computer chips, portals and data-streams, sometimes it's difficult to hear the soul of a human beating behind the bytes of data. The single most important thing *Facebook* has done for the participative age is to help individuals realize they can describe themselves to the rest of the world.

A rich description of each individual is the fuel of the cloudspace.

As individuals engage in social networking activities, a profile develops of their relationship ties, interests, likes and dislikes. Progressively, this user activity profile becomes more complete with every conversation and document shared, with every project completed.

Were you to ask individuals to type everything they could think of about themselves into a computer few people would complete the task.

The cloudspace is different. It promises many rewards.

Instant gratification comes from the ability of the individual to assert their personality, and to make a statement to others that *they too* are now on the digital map and they *have a voice*.

More rewards come when friends and colleagues start to follow their thoughts (using instant messaging and micro-blogging technologies) and they can more easily share their thoughts with friends and colleagues.

A richer description of the needs of individuals means computing systems learn more about the discerning needs of each individual and network community. Instead of searching for documents, each document is catalogued and stored using self-learning index structures (created by mining user profile and ego-wall information such as interests, relationships, who people converse with etc.) that bring the documents out of hiding to the individual.

News that was once a gushing river of irrelevance is carefully directed through channels and into reservoirs formed around the key interest topics of each individual or network community.

Who dares to dream how sophisticated the ability of the cloudspace to serve our needs could become. One day perhaps you will be able to discuss serving suggestions with your *home computer* for your next meal in the knowledge that he already knows what you've eaten on previous evenings, what's left in the pantry and what your dietary requirements are for the week based on the level of energy you've consumed on activities.

The dark side

The ability of the cloudspace to *know you* is fundamental to its ability to serve. But it is a double-edged sword. Sharing the information that helps computers and systems to know what your needs are means that your digital profile exists as a digital record with the inevitable risk that unscrupulous people could lever its value in cyber crime, or that governments and corporations could engineer your 'disappearance' from the cloudspace. All manner of 'George Orwell' outcomes might be considered. This voluntary capturing of metainformation will lead to seismic growth in digital social interactivity around the world and place unimaginable demands on computing capacity; a scale we could never have contemplated before (serving up this capacity is where cloud computing comes in).

Passport to the digital space

With so many disconnected social networking sites, it's not easy to identify *you the individual* on the Internet today. Every social media site you visit today will ask for new information about you. They're not able to share a common digital passport to know who you are. Practically every application or system you use today has its own unique method of user identification. The information they hold about you isn't very rich and it's not very accurate because you don't keep it up to date. Why should you?

And that's a problem.

For social networking to really work each of us needs a way of being identified on all of the different sites that we interact with – and we need to be bothered to keep information about ourselves up to date.

What it boils down to is a sort of voluntary 'digital passport'; an identity tag and digital description of an individual; their experiences, skills, knowledge, specializations etc. captured in a single exchangeable file and recorded with a unique identification code so that individuals can painlessly maintain the information about them shared across the web by simply updating one table. It's not an easy problem to solve as there are (quite rightly) privacy issues to consider when doing something like this.

In the UK, a better way of identifying individuals has been big news over the last few years. Central Government and Civil Defence experts apparently believe that it will make us safer, while civil liberty groups take the view that it will be the last stone turned before we have computer identity chips embedded in our heads.

Companies face similar problems with user identification. Most organizations want to know who enters their office buildings, and who to allocate operating costs to – such as printing and photocopier expenses.

As we increase our use of the Internet and access more websites, the complexity of identity management becomes ever more troublesome for both information consumers and providers. I know in my own experience of using the web that I've probably subscribed to over 30 different sites and services by now. I've got no idea on half of them what information they hold about me, what email address I used when I subscribed (I've even got 4 or 5 of those!!) and if they asked me for a password or security identifier I'd be guessing.

Attempts by the software industry to produce a passport

Some vendors like *Facebook*, *Twitter* and *MySpace* are talking about making it easier to share member ID information but there are still issues to iron out. For example, what stops a person registering several aliases on different systems? It's not unreasonable for parents to continue to be concerned about the social networking activities of their children online. It's too easy today for people to exist on the Internet under a disguise. The problem of passports becomes more of an issue if social networks are to be used in a business (and knowledge market context) where it becomes contractually important for people, federations and institutions to know who they're dealing with and who they're paying for services. Absence of this information could create data security breaches, risk contractual concerns or ethical dilemmas. Even over the web, the fundamental starting point for any contract is to know who the parties are.

> **Microsoft has adopted a passport system intended to simplify online identification by providing a system that centralizes authentication and information sharing for users on the internet. The system stores user information such as addresses, ages, phone and credit card numbers and other**

personal details in a large central database. With one click, users can transfer their personal information to participating websites. But there are a lot of issues with this system and it's not likely to become a standard for Internet users any time soon. EU policy demands that users are informed and empowered to decide as to which data they want to provide and under which conditions these data will be processed by Microsoft or by the participating websites, something Microsoft Passport fails to do, and the United States Federal Trade Commission (FTC) ruled in 2002 that Microsoft made false security and privacy promises about Passport. Unfortunately, whilst it might be fundamentally flawed, there isn't another alternative to the Microsoft Passport system today.

There are too many unanswered questions about user identification on the web today. I can't see the present haphazard situation continuing for long but to resolve it is going to require an industry wide effort. Fortunately perhaps, the cloudspace is such an exclusive club (today there are less than 20 vendors offering cloud platforms and the top 4 or 5 vendors are so dominant) that it is probably much easier to force through an agreement on web passports which will ultimately benefit information consumers and vendors alike.

The open cloud manifesto (opencloudmanifesto.org) is an early attempt by cloud vendors to agree on a series of self-governance standards to help to resolve key issue of user identification but it's too soon to say how successful it will be. It will take the bigger players to get around a table to provide any realistic hope of a long term solution.

Why a 'common profile' matters

It's almost impossible to see social networking really becoming useful to business without a common user profile – a form of digital passport for the Web – to identify individuals; hard to imagine *trust* developing between parties without some level of assurety that you know who you're dealing with.

What could a passport do for you?

Certainly you would expect it to be used to profile yourself and your credentials and provide a mechanism to transfer this data to other sites so that you have a single version of the truth about you on the web and only one record to maintain. Having the ability to securely manage your personal web identity will mean that you can access sites you're registered with without always having to login – and if you want to join a new one then the authentication process becomes a one click routine. Exiting websites and cancelling subscriptions should be equally as painless. I'm sure we've all had situations when we've registered for a service and then forgotten what user identifier and password we used. Or perhaps the supplier sent a confirmation email detailing your secret User-ID and password that goes missing somewhere in your junk mail-box.

Another thing that's sadly missing today in 'web-world' is a means of logging the sites you've registered with. A log could show where your personal data exists (a snail trail as it were) so that users can easily control their personal web presence. If you're actively publishing content on the web over several years it's easy to fall into the trap of leaving old outdated blogs or articles lying around the Internet having forgotten or not registered they're still out there. Maintaining a *record of agreements* would also make working with web service providers a lot easier. Registering with sites today is a once only event and it's almost impossible to find contractual agreements on sites once you've progressed through the initial registration. When sites change their conditions of service, users in my experience normally don't get informed of the changes.

There are challenges for technologists to secure personal data in a single place. Any software application that's knitted together with *noughts and ones* of code can be similarly unpicked by unscrupulous coders with similarly adept skills. While encryption and security techniques are improving, responsibility for managing the digital identity of potentially millions of 'web people' is a mouth drying undertaking.

At some point it will happen.

Having some form of personal digital describer makes for an easier life when using a mixture of different online services, and for vendors it will make the growing market for web applications and services easier to manage and administer.

What's really important is to have a *single view* of YOU. Social media sites like *Facebook* and *MySpace* capture information about what matters most to an individual including their likes and dislikes, interests, how they want to present themselves on their *ego-wall* and the company they keep. Building this picture of YOU is what will fuel the growth of social networking and the cloudspace.

The digital passport builds a simple data description file that describes you on the social media sites scattered across the Internet – your 'social footprint' as it were.

As individuals we impart information about ourselves through every communication with others. We tell them what we like and what we don't like. We share interests. Social networking media picks all of this rich content up and can add it to your digital passport. What happens then is an about face in the way we work with information systems and services. Instead of always having to keep telling computers *who* we are and *what* we want – they already know.

That's *another* small revolution.

Of course, we have to *want to* volunteer the information first. And we're only going to volunteer the information if we get something in return (like finding new employment for example!).

And that's how the cloudspace forms. More and more people volunteering their personal information in order to enjoy in the rewards of being part of the cloud; telling 'it' who they are and what they want. In return, service providers can serve up the things that really matter to you, the individual.

It's a virtuous circle that everyone will love to hate.

10

The cloud

The 'cloud' is what technologists are calling it.

Cloud computing is an emerging computing model by which users can gain access to their preferred portfolio of information services from anywhere, through any connected device that uses an Internet browser.

> **'One third of all new IT investment will go on cloud-based technologies by 2013' – so says IT market analysts IDC. By 2012, they predict, customer spending on IT cloud services will grow almost threefold to $42 billion. The growth rate of cloud computing is expected to be over five times that of on-premise IT delivery and consumption models. That's a lot of money. So what is it precisely that the IT market pundits are expecting organizations to invest into and why? [39]**

The term cloud is used as a metaphor for the Internet to suggest a 'digital cloud' that's *everywhere* that can provide information services to web-connected users who are able to access their information resources from anywhere at any time of the day. The reality is far less nebulous. If you were to examine the computing platform that sits beneath the 'the cloud' and makes it possible, you would see a cluster of buildings the size of aircraft hangers brimming with air conditioning, security, and housing row after row of computer servers where resources can be dynamically provisioned and shared.

Critics of cloud computing stress the challenges that still lay before providers of the first generation of technology – security, scalability, multi-tenancy resource management issues – but I'm convinced none of these issues are show-stoppers. With such a big potential prize and with sponsorship for cloud computing platforms coming from some of the biggest names in the computer industry who know how critical data and platform security is to business information consumers. It's only a matter of time before the last remaining obstacles of cloud platforms are overcome. Technologists call this type of environment that serves many people from the same server platform 'multi-tenant' and it's a welcome departure from the *not-so* good old days. At one time, using computer systems meant buying one. Then technologists found themselves struggling to manage the peaks and troughs of user demand as more and more users were insisting on more and more applications; with each and every application needing to be hosted somewhere. IT departments, instead of focusing on organizational improvement, found themselves spending more of their time worrying about the massive infrastructure of networks, servers, data stores etc. and worrying about which part of this complex architecture might be hit by a peak in user demand, a power failure or punitive attack of a disenfranchised former employee. Instead of our best computer scientists advancing computer science, they found themselves the watch guards of the computer stacks corporations had built to run their businesses.

But that's a picture of a world that's changing.

The cloud is great news for the little guy; it offers an unprecedented opportunity for entrepreneurs, small companies – even individuals. Only a select group of cloud-wielding Internet giants have until now had the resources to harness huge masses of information and build businesses upon it. Our words, pictures, clicks, and searches are the raw material for this industry. But it has been largely a one-way street. Humanity emits the data, and a handful of companies—the likes of *Google*, *Yahoo* or *Amazon* – transform the information into insights and opportunities for advertising and services revenues.

The cloud has levelled the playing field for most data-intensive forms of computing. You see, if you're a small business with a big idea, usually you don't have the cash to scale up your computing platform if the idea takes off. Ideas that capture the imagination of thousands, potentially millions, of people can quickly run out of steam when a website falls over.

Here's a story I really love that was written up as a cover story for Business Week by Stephen Baker in 2007. It describes an extremely clued up graduate called Christophe Bisciglia, a 27-year-old senior software engineer with long wavy hair, who joined *Google* and found a company that embraced big ideas and serial innovation.[40]

> *Google* has a policy of giving its people a play time (they call it their '20% time') representing 20% of their billable time (wow) to experiment and work on projects of their own choice. Bisciglia's idea was to use his 20% time to glue together the processing and storage power of lots of little PCs to create one great big computing environment that could be used as an R&D platform to encourage undergrads to think like *Google*rs and 'dream on a vastly larger scale'. As writer Stephen Baker describes in his article, Bisciglia's idea grew into a network made of hundreds of thousands, or by some estimates 1 million, cheap server storing staggering amounts of data. The platform could ferret out answers to billions of queries in a fraction of a second. Unlike many traditional supercomputers, this system would never age. When individual pieces die, usually after about three years, engineers pluck them out and replace them with new, faster boxes. This means the cloud regenerates as it grows, almost like a living thing. What started as an idea to encourage *Googlers* to dream big resulted in a compelling strategy for cloud computing.

With its ability to share and rapidly scale resources, effortlessly manage hardware component replacement and tackle all of the complex multi-hosting issues, Basciglias' project had all the hallmarks of a step change in computer science. It attracted the attention not just of *Google* who funded the project, but of technology partners like *IBM* and a watching industry. Was this the birth-place of 'the cloud?'

I expect there were tens, perhaps hundreds of people moving to this perspective of the future of computing. But I'd be happy if Bisciglia gets the credit. It's good sometimes to see a lanky, long-haired nerdy guy change the world – even when they're on the payroll of a corporation!

What's in the cloud?

The cloud space is made up of lots of data that creates the virtual space where *information consumerism* occurs; a cloud of data that information consumers are able to access from anywhere in the world on-demand provided they have access to the Internet. It's not possible to 'see' this mountain of data, so technologists imagine this mass of bytes as a big cloud that hovers overhead.

Measures of binary data storage:
1024 Bytes = 1 Kilobyte
1024 Kilobytes = 1 Megabyte
1024 Megabytes = 1 Gigabyte
1024 Gigabytes = 1 Terabyte
1024 Terabytes = 1 Petabyte
1024 Petabytes = 1 Exabyte
1024 Exabytes = 1 Zettabyte
1024 Zettabyte = 1 Zottabyte
1024 Zottabyte = 1 Brontobyte – 1 followed by 27 zeroes

The technology innovations that make the cloudspace exist in the first place are impressive and should not be overlooked which is why I devote this chapter to them. The cloudspace displaces the need for PCs that offer a little bit of hardware, a little bit of storage, a little bit of operation system, a little bit of processing and a sprinkling of software applications.

But it would be easy to concentrate on the 'bricks-and-mortar' aspects of what makes the cloudspace exist – the great air conditioned warehouses brimming with heavy duty computer servers and the advanced software operating systems, data security infrastructures and software applications etc. – and overlook what *the cloud* means for society and business. Think about *the cloud* more in terms of what it does rather than what it is. It provides a new space for individuals to assert their personality, to come together to learn, seek entertainment, invent, evolve ideas and live. It democratizes access to information for future generations. Greater access brings with it more freedom and more risks.

The irony for me is that on a summers' day when I was young one of my favoured pastimes to lie down in a grassy meadow and make shapes out of the white fluffy cumulus nimbus clouds. Now I help others to visualize their own clouds.

The making of the cloud

Cloud computing didn't just happen.

The IT industry has been moving further towards more virtual, open and extensible computing infrastructures since the 1980's. The starting point was the concept of *Grid Computing* that emerged as a means to applying large numbers of systems to a single problem. The lessons learnt from these endeavours fed into approaches towards *Utility Computing* in the 1990's. *Utility computing* offered clusters of computers as virtual platforms for computing based on a metered business model. Innovations by major technology companies like *Microsoft, Hewlett Packard, Hitachi, IBM* and *Fujitsu Siemens* have made significant strides in harnessing large farms of computers to provide information services to end users who need only a web-connected portal to access all of the computing they need. The outcome is that – from large corporations to individuals – all computer users can reliably access trusted information systems on demand and pay for their services as they use them.

To consumers of cloud applications much of the technical jargon and detail I cover in this section hides beneath easy-to-use web portals that show no hint of IT complexity. Think of how you use applications like *Googlemaps* and blogging tools that use point-and-click user interfaces to perform tasks whenever there's any risk of IT skills being needed. To users, *cloud computing* is something that makes using information and collaboration with other people just happen. The next generation of computer users, our children, won't think in terms of operating systems, applications and databases, they will use new information services' that are every bit as easy and intuitive to use as *Googlemaps*.

Most individuals and organizations that use computer systems don't really want to be responsible for managing their personal infrastructure of networks and servers, so the idea of procuring information services from a cloud appeals to a great many people; hence the high level of demand anticipated for the technology.

The idea sounds so compelling that you'd have to ask why it's taken so long for the IT industry to come up with it. The answer to that question has a lot to do with three key factors:

1. The IT market has been profitable for the leading players for many years and I expect many vendors have been happy to continue with existing business models that have proven to work.
2. A series of key innovations have emerged over the last few years

to make cloud computing possible (which I cover in this chapter).

3. Demand for cloud computing is still weak because information consumerism is new to all of us and had these services been available years before, I doubt the market would have been ready for them and there's still an argument that the technology is ahead of its demand curve.

The main benefits of cloud computing for organizations that have traditionally employed on-premises systems include:

- The ability to focus on core business without the distractions of managing computer and networks infrastructures.
- Cost savings from commissioning that result from significantly reducing the time taken to introduce technologies and innovations, by reducing labour costs associated with the design, procurement and building of hardware and software platforms.
- Avoiding human error in the configuration of security, networks and software configuring process.
- Organizations need only pay only for the services they use as they use them and with most service providers there is no up-front commitment. Rarely do vendors insist on complex contracts or commitments. Through the ethos of pay-as-you-use, commercial contracts aim to be straight-forward and most vendors will allow users to sign up with limited details and a credit card.
- Data security. It's of prime concern to providers and they will adopt the highest standards of data security and management that few end user organizations could afford to implement.
- Enabling software technologies that vendors include or support through third party relationships are extremely versatile. This flexibility means that users can effectively build any application they want to and retain control over the resources they consume. Much of the software that supports IT systems required for data archival and management, security, load balancing, integration etc. is provided by hosting vendors.
- Cloud computing platforms are hugely scalable compared to traditional on-premises platforms. The vendors who offer cloud computing utilize huge computing resources supported by networking and telecommunications infrastructures that ensure they're available for use 100% of the time and have the bandwidth

to support whatever capacity demands are placed on them. They offer dependable computing for business critical systems – a key concern to computer users large or small.

- Acquired expertise. Cloud vendors are experts in computing who possess the necessary skills to professionally manage robust and secure hosting platforms. The costs of acquiring all of these skills would be prohibitive to most organizations but with this business model, these costs are distributed across revenues from many thousands of users who benefit from their expertise but pay only for a tiny fraction of their upkeep.
- Peaks and troughs of usage are taken care of by the enormity of the computing platforms. Vendors are able to absorb the spikes of usage but continue to only pay for what they use.

Cloud enabling software

The technologies that support cloud computing are complex.

To avoid this book from becoming a technical manual that only computer geeks would find interesting (that is, if they didn't already know more than me!) I've categorized the umbrella technologies and innovations that have gone to create the cloud into three broad categories and kept descriptions brief.

If you want to find out more about the technologies behind the cloud then I'd recommend you visit the vendor websites I include in the glossary.

The three main categories of cloud computing technology are:

1. The virtualized hardware and operating systems platforms
2. Platform administration services
3. Application design and deployment services

1. Virtualized hardware and operating systems

Providers of cloud computing technology platforms operate huge data centres that enable multiple groups or individuals to share computing resources. In days gone by every application was required to exist on its own server. The idea behind virtualization of computing platforms is that software applications consume as much processing power, memory and storage as it needs and that the computing platform offers suitable scalability to grow with demand. This sounds reasonably straight-forward but it has represented a hug challenge to the computer industry. For example, poorly designed software applications can bleed memory capacity dry. If you've ever experienced the performance of your laptop slowing down due to an application consuming more than its fair share of resources, then imagine the consequences of this scaled up to the proportions of information services being consumed by millions of businesses and people who share the same servers.

2. Platform administration services

The companies that provide information services via the cloud demand a range of facilities to enable them to administer their software applications such as the ability to manage security privileges, make decisions on how data is held and archived, automate uploads and information feeds etc. All of these demands must be met by the cloud computing platform providers – i.e. the collection of information services demanded by *information service providers*.

3. Application design and deployment services

Tools must be provided to enable the applications created to serve information consumers. Traditionally, developing software applications has demanded coding or scripting skills but today information services are being created using simpler software tools that mean non-technical authors can design their applications without needing to be computer experts.

Key players that made the cloud happen

Who are the key players in cloud computing?

I expect that some of the companies will be familiar to you while others you probably haven't heard of before. Some might come as a surprise.

Amazon

Amazon is a company many people don't associate with computing.

Amazon has leveraged the global computing infrastructure that is the backbone of its $15 billion *Amazon*.com retail and transactional enterprise business. On this huge computing infrastructure *Amazon* hosts its *Amazon Web Services* (AWS) business that launched in 2006. *Amazon* was one of the first players in the cloud computing market and benefitted from its technology investments directed toward scalability, reliability, and secure distributed computing infrastructure that has been honed for over 13 years. Through its experiences, *AWS* knows that it can provide a suite of elastic IT infrastructure services for even the largest of companies.

Microsoft

Microsoft has quietly been developing its cloud infrastructure but hasn't yet actively promoted its services in the same way as *Amazon*. *Windows Azure* is *Microsoft*'s cloud services operating system that serves as the development, service hosting, and service management environment. *Windows Azure* provides support for on-demand Web applications and services on the Internet in *Microsoft* data centres. It offers functional components to support business applications, manage data storage, host, scale and administer relationships with developers. As the leading global software manufacturer, *Microsoft* benefits from the broad acceptance of its technology across large and small companies. Interestingly, the components of the Azure Services Platform can be used by local applications running on a variety of systems, including various flavours of Windows, mobile devices, and others. Those components include:

- A Windows-based environment for running applications and storing data on servers in *Microsoft* data centres.

- A suite of infrastructure services to cloud-based and local applications.

- The provision of data services in the cloud based on Microsoft's SQL Server database.

- A component that provides access to data from *Microsoft's Live* applications that also allows synchronizing of data across desktops and devices, finding and downloading applications, and more.

Microsoft has apparently invested more than $8 billion in cloud computing technologies in recent years and *Microsoft Research* operates a 'Cloud Computing Futures Group' to research new innovations.

Google

In a similar way to *Amazon, Google* has been able to leverage much of its hosting expertise and R&D to rapidly transition to cloud provisioning. Common to all vendors at this time, the focus of their offer is to serve software service providers. The thrust of *Google*'s development has been its *Google App Engine* which is an applications design and deployment platform that empowers developers to easily build, maintain and scale applications using *Google*'s infrastructure. Developers benefit from a plethora of ready-to-use building blocks like *Googlemaps, Gmail* and *Google*'s own database, applications integration and orchestration tools.

IBM

One of the best known names in computing, *IBM* has arguably led innovative thought in the area of server virtualization. The company is a supplier to *Amazon Web Services* and *Google*, positioning itself as a trusted supplier of the infrastructure technology that supports cloud computing (*IBM* licenses its software to run in the *Amazon Elastic Cloud Computing* environment including using its databases *IBM DB2 Express* and *Informix Dynamic Server*, and portal design and configuration technologies *WebSphere Portal, Lotus Web Content Management*, and *WebSphere sMash* software).

Adoption challenges for corporations

I mentioned earlier that the technologies supporting cloud computing are complex and the technology is very young. Therefore there are still many grey areas that concern IT professionals who are considering porting their core business applications from on-premises systems.

No two clouds are the same

The first dilemma is that clouds aren't strictly open. They are owned by private sector companies who have developed platforms to their own specifications (even though most will attempt to employ de facto industry standards where possible), so they are proprietary. There are peculiarities between systems that can create lock-ins. For example, when data is stored more often than not proprietary Application Programming Interfaces (API's) are employed. Given that every cloud is different, deciding which one to use is not a purely economic decision.

Retaining a 'static IP' address for applications

An internet Protocol (IP) address is the address on a network of where an application is located. For most businesses, IP addresses need to be 'static' so that users, potentially customers and suppliers, can log into applications (like websites) over the internet. Not all cloud computing vendors guarantee a static IP address. For most business this feature is essential, yet the challenge of administration for millions of users is substantial for cloud vendors.

Interacting with the cloud

There are a lot of processes that on-premises IT people need to perform to maintain their applications and these interactions need to be supported by cloud computing providers. But supporting all of these tasks without having to get on the phone with a sales person, or submit a help ticket sounds easier than it is – as anyone knows who has worked with an outsourced hosted server provider to support core business applications.

Data management and integration

An issue facing cloud computing vendors is which database technology to employ that would meet the discerning aspirations of such a wide variety of user types. Relational databases are the primary technology used to manage large amounts of structured data. They build relationships between subjects and then manage them. For example, you might organize contacts by their country location. Data management is more effective if a list of countries is saved in a separate table and can be referenced by each contact record. This 'relationship' is defined normally when the database is created. But creating and managing databases is beyond the skills of most non IT people.

Unfortunately there is no common and openly available database – they're all slightly different and most demand a sizable upfront capital outlay. Cloud vendors appreciate that data management is a potential show stopper and so they're innovating in this area. *Amazon* uses its own *SimpleDB* database; a web service providing the core database functions of data indexing and querying, while *Google* has *BigTable* which they describe as 'a distributed storage system for managing structured data that is designed to scale to a very largesize: petabytes of data across thousands of commodity servers'. The problem for potential cloud users is once they've committed these technical architecture differences make it hard to leave either cloud: because neither *SimpleDB* nor *BigTable* is available anywhere else. But this issue is no different to the problems corporations have today with their commitments to large software houses like *SAP* or *Oracle* they depend on for core business systems. This allows companies like *Oracle* to dispassionately increase their software maintenance fees year on year in the knowledge that their customers have little choice but to accept cost increases.

Building, editing and managing applications

Today there are few common standards in the software tools and techniques that people use to create business applications. What makes matters more challenging is the move towards individuals serving themselves with applications. Cloud vendors have yet to provide the millions of non-technical IT users that want to use hosted applications served on-demand with useful tools to shape their information environments.

Automatic scaling of applications

You might think that cloud computing vendors offer an ability to automatically scale applications – but they don't. This is primarily because of the complexities of databases (scaling databases is not easy) and the fact that there are many load balancing and user constraint issues that are difficult for vendors to factor in. The result is that the ideal of 'remote support' of applications that can infinitely scale is not quite a reality.

Limited 'back doors' for developers

No matter how clever they might be cloud computer vendors can't think of everything a developer might need or want to do. So the cloud needs to be editable and extensible by developers – an administrative account of some sort that empowers developers to shape and mould their clouds to their specific needs. By definition, cloud computers must be built on top of some sort of virtualization technology, so the developer never has a "root" directory to the cloud, only a "root" directory to their own part of the cloud.

The cloud 'space'

Cloud computing has some interesting angles to it: Will large corporations migrate their IT systems to the cloud? Or if they don't will smaller companies benefit from new innovations at a faster pace than the big boys who have invested millions in IT? For technologists cloud computing represents the ultimate power-play super-computer; a near limitless data storage space powered by banks of processors. For the individual, entrepreneur or small business, cloud computing means they can access information services affordably and have the potential to scale their big idea on a global scale. But the 'cloud' will move into the fabric of society not for what it is but for what it does. It provides the massive scaling potential that new applications of a global scale need to grow and to thrive. It opens up new possibilities that haven't existed before.

The cloud is a *huge* computing platform; but what is this capacity to be used for – word processing? That would be a waste of a step-change in computing. I believe the legacy of the cloud will be remembered for the biggest of all applications ever conceived – the *cloudspace*.

The cloud is the gigantic computing platform needed to house the *cloudspace*: the inter-active digital life space of the planet made up of metainformation that will describe our relationships, passions, emotions and frailties – our humanity. It enables data to be captured because almost everyone on the planet will be connected to it and use it on a daily basis. It creates a new layer of social metainformation that only cloud computing could make possible.

Consider the data volume implications of sustaining the cloudspace. Every 'node' needs to be recorded. In addition to acknowledging the data volume implications of the number of nodes there must be metainformation to manage the number of connections between the nodes, and then there's the metainformation about likes and dislikes, strengths of ties, associations, historical records of activities etc. The cloud will open up a huge reservoir of computing that can be filled by social metainformation captured through the interactivity of the cloudspace – gathered, organized and then re-used. You still won't be able to see it but, like stars across the sky, you will know that next time you look at your web browser the cloudspace will be there to shine its light on you.

Welcome to the 21st century and era of the cloudspace.

11

Enterprise information consumerism

Enterprise information consumerism describes people who consume information in business. They're the beneficiaries of a mind-set change in the way that computing works; evolving away from platforms and applications to personalizable information services. These 'knowledge workers' expect the same level of access and ease of use from their business systems that they enjoy as consumers at home with their iPhone, iPod and social media sites like *MSN*, *MySpace* and *Facebook*. None of these products require a training course or user manual. The onward expansion of the knowledge economy is placing huge pressures on information technology in business to keep up. IT departments are pressured to respond to growing demands for new applications that the knowledge workers need to satisfy their changing information needs.

Addressing the 'long-tail'

It's no surprise that the displacement of IT budgets is weighted in favour of big core software applications that ensure business continuity. A common core of business applications, like Oracle and SAP Enterprise Resource Planning software, support core processes and the information needs of the majority of workers. These applications contain a significant amount of logic and formalize processes that need to be meticulously managed to adhere to governance protocols. Implementations of these solutions are led by IT rather than Line-of-Business heads because of technical complexities that need to be qualified to get procurements right.

Increasingly, organizations are coming to realize that their more creative knowledge workers are poorly served by traditional IT systems. These people – who are responsible for innovation, sales growth and the empowerment of cross-organizational teams – represent smaller groups of users (often no more than one or two people per situation) who demand a much broader range of information services. The information they require is often held in disparate data sources that somehow need to be brought together. Using traditional software development practices and tools, internal IT teams are unable to affordably resource such large numbers of user requests for 'micro-systems'. This has become known as the 'long-tail of applications' (see how the diagram below stretches out to the right because of small numbers of users demanding a larger number of applications to serve their needs). Development projects of this sort are led by Line-of-Business managers who might still require sustainable and robust IT solutions even if the information is for themselves or a small project team. In many cases, rapid prototyping is essential to obtain clarity over new situations. Many of the solutions are likely only to be useful for a short period of time to answer a new business situation that might ultimately be resolved or overcome.

Diagram illustrating the 'long-tail' of user information requirements

Strategic, Core Business
- Governance and risk outweigh speed and flexibility
- Construction is IT lead, LOB influenced
- 'Platform' preferred over agility
- Advantaged by agile development approach

IT custodial, but LOB Controlled
- Code-free design approach increases speed and flexibility while maintaining high level of governance.
- Construction is IT lead, LOB directed
- Rapid prototyping is desirable

Tactical, Opportunistic
- Implementation speed and flexibility is critical
- Construction is LOB specified
- Often combines internal and external content.

Number of users per application

Number of applications

Business mashup software

Creating and deploying business applications and new information services has until recently required teams of software programmers and specialist applications.

But not today. The building blocks used to create new information services are ready-made for non programmers to 'mash' together. The software industry has responded to this 'long-tail' of demand for new applications by designing new software tools engineered to create portal based applications. This genre of applications is sometimes called *Business Mashup software*, other times *situational applications software*. This new genre of software gives business people the tools they need to adapt to change, develop new insights and act on new business opportunities. Examples include Encanvas, Coghead, JackBe, Microsoft Popfly, Serena Business Mashups, Kapow and *IBM* WebSphere sMash. These applications offer organizations a way to rapidly adapt to changing business needs. These tools mashup existing and new sources of data with re-usable 'building blocks' knowledge workers can use by themselves to 'serve up' the information they need.

I liken the transition from software development tools to business mashup tools to the impact Meccano and LEGO had on children's toys. Before these innovative toys gave children the ability to create their own cars, boats and planes, the only way children could fire their imagination was to carve toys out of wood or purchase a ready-made toy. Following the launch of these 'building-block' style toys children were able to create their own designs. Business mashup software removes the need for scripting or programming skills.

> According to one thought-leader on *situational applications*, *Luba Cherbakov* of *IBM*, the term describes "…an application built to address a particular situation, problem, or challenge. The development life cycle of these types of applications is quite different from the traditional IT-developed solutions. Situational applications are usually built by knowledge workers who perform iterative developments often measured in days or weeks, not months or years. As the requirements of a small team using the application change, the situational application often continues to evolve to accommodate these changes. But, significant changes in requirements may lead to an abandonment of the used application altogether; in some cases it's just easier to develop a new one than to update the one in use." [41]
>
> In a 2008 survey conducted by IBM, a majority of CEOs rated their organization's ability to manage change 22% lower than their expected need for change.

Business mashup software:

- Unlocks innovation and the creativity in their business

- Helps organizations to collaborate with industry partners to achieve shared business outcomes

- Helps organizations to respond to rapidly changing market situations and therefore need to uncover business insights more speedily; often relying on a blend of information that exists within and beyond the enterprise fire-wall

- Helps IT teams to reduce their long-tail of applications development. Business mashup software provides a new form of rapid development capability to reduce the cost and risk of applications development for the majority of knowledge worker applications. Iterative design ethos and integrated tools present more agile ways to manage development projects that dramatically cut the cost of publishing new information services.

- Builds applications that exploit data without requiring aging systems to be replaced or upgraded.

In January 2007, an Economist Intelligence Unit survey revealed that mashups were the most popular traditional web 2.0 technology in the enterprise, with 64% of companies saying they already use or planned to use mashups within the next 2 years. And in 2008, a report by IT industry analysts Forrester Research found that mashup usage is growing rapidly. According to their research the enterprise mashups software market is expected to generate global revenues of $700 Million by 2013 (Forrester defines mashups as "custom applications that combine multiple, disparate data sources into something new and unique").[42]

From applications to information services

Shrink-wrapped software applications have traditionally been the lowest risk option when purchasing business software because they offer pre-shaped business processes expected to install *templated* best practise. But there's a problem. Large organizations run *so many* processes they can't afford to buy a shrink-wrapped solution in response to every single demand. For example, it's not untypical for a local government authority to operate over 150 different discrete software applications to support the operations of their 16 to 20 different service lines. In addition to common core support services like finance, customer services, human resource management, facilities management and executive services, each department will expect to procure its own collection of business applications to manage their processes.

Software vendors employ a mix of third party building blocks and home-made code that results in applications adopting a peculiar interface users must get used to and 'different engines' under the bonnet. The IT teams of procuring organizations are left having to get packages to work with each other that were never intended to. Worse still, they must deal with software vendors who have no commercial interest in opening up their systems to others.

A software application is nothing more than a collection of information services aligned to achieving a process outcome.

Almost any activity relating to the capture, management, analysis, manipulation, organization and workflow of content can be described as an *information service*. In the world of corporate IT the abstraction of information services from applications is a mini revolution. Business mashup software makes it affordable for IT teams to create new solutions for knowledge workers without having to procure shrink-wrapped software applications. Case examples published by business mashup software vendors suggests it takes something like 40% to 60% less time to create new applications using business mashup software compared to traditional applications development methods and tools. Using business mashup software requires less technical skills and fewer IT people so the total cost of deployments is reduced substantially. Business mashup software means new applications can be developed on-demand and potentially marks the end of the road for shrink-wrapped software that companies would previously have purchased.

The death of enterprise portals?

Today, when IT teams deploy portal applications, they have to design them so that everyone in a department or workgroup has the ability to use them. Business mashups change that. Users can serve themselves with as many personalized portals as they need and every portal can be different, yet this doesn't place any extra burden on IT teams because administrators are provided with tools to simplify the task of managing the data accessibility, security and user administration. For knowledge workers, it means they no longer have to use the lowest common denominator of portal site, designed to please everyone. Some IT pundits suggest that business mashup software will ultimately replace enterprise portal tools like *Microsoft Sharepoint, SAP Portal* and *IBM WebSphere* that businesses use today. This is because business mashup software produce portals requiring less user training that are easier to maintain and precisely fit the needs of any given situation.

Enterprise portals also suffer from being designed by IT people for 'the business.' Users inherit a new toy to play with that they didn't ask for holding content that quickly goes out-of-date, becoming irrelevant. In 2000, one retail bank told me their intranet was used mostly by staff to sell cars to one another! As Martin Vasey, one of the UK's leading enterprise knowledge management gurus will tell you, 'You can't do knowledge management *to people*, you have to do it *for people*.'

Information Services Software

I stated that business applications are nothing more than a collection of information services. Take the example of a Customer Relationship Management (CRM) software application used to manage customer relationships in business. It will contain data entry forms to capture information, reporting tools to analyze it, visualization tools to make sense of it. Each of these sub-components could be described as an *information service*.

With business mashup tools, knowledge workers have the ability to work with their own building blocks to create 'applications'. Serving up these 'applications' to web browsers requires a new form of computing architecture that I call an *Information Services Exchange* because the technology acts like a big telephone exchange to manage the relationship between users, groups, portals and the information services collections (should I say *applications*?). These new computing platforms must support the life-cycle of design, deployment and operational administration of information services. A typical Information Services Exchange is made up of two parts as exampled by the architecture of Encanvas software as illustrated in the diagram overleaf.

Illustration of a simple Enterprise Information Services Computing Architecture

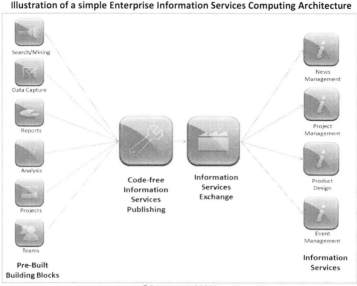

©Encanvas Ltd 2009.

The first component is the portal design application.

This desktop or web-based software enables knowledge workers to employ pre-built building blocks (sometimes called 'widgets') to create new portals of their own design to serve up their selection of information services. To prevent designers from getting overwhelmed, the design environment doesn't expose any script or code. Instead a 'What-You-See-Is-What-You-Get' (W-Y-S-I-W-Y-G) facility provides a design view of the final portal application users will see. Software used to build information services needs to be immensely dexterous whilst still satisfying the expectations of IT teams.

The second component is the deployment platform.

Once designed, an *information service* is published to a web server-based application that manages the interaction of users and groups to portals and the information service they consume.

Challenges facing early adopters

Whilst information services *based* computing sounds ideal, adoption of this approach is not without its challenges. I summarize them here.

User Administration

User identity management is typically poor in organizations, with systems using alternative authentication methods. And because it's poor, user administration becomes difficult for IT teams to manage.

Every person that works for a business has a tax code, employee number and unique email address. In most corporations, workers also have a contactless identity card to access buildings and use photocopiers. Yet, with all of this technology, most organizations have no single view of an employee.

The most popular mechanism to gain a single view of 'the user' is the 'Active Directory' from Microsoft®. Active Directory (AD) stores objects such as users, associated emails and passwords in a database. Used predominantly in Windows operating environments, it allows administrators to assign security policies and manage user associations with network resources and applications. Unfortunately, not all software employs Active Directory as a mechanism to log into content and resources so a great deal can go on in the enterprise that is not on the radar of the IT team. Information services solutions aim to overcome the obstacles of managing identity by inter-operating with AD and providing administration tools that make it easy for IT administrators to govern user identities and their associations with groups, web sites and content.

User Group Administration

The next challenge is how to organize users into User Groups. Individuals could potentially participate in 'tens' of user groups relating to projects, interest groups and communities they're involved with. It's important that users can create and govern their participation in User Groups for themselves. But there also has to be regulation and control; particularly when it comes to the sort of content users are given authority to access as it might be privileged or confidential.

Data Security, Management and Governance

There are two big issues with data – how to avoid losing it and how to make it easy to find. Both issues are joined at the hip.

Imagine how much data exists in an enterprise. Not just the content securely held in core business systems, but all of the other stuff held on laptop hard-disks, USB drives, electronic document and content management systems, blogs, paper documents, mobile phones! Business analysts believe that something like 60% of business content is held in the 'informal office', outside of the control of IT governance.

But how do you control such vast amounts of data? If you can, it makes sense to have one big database holding all of your data and digital content. This way, data is held in one place making it easier to organize and prevent several versions of the same content existing in alternative locations.

This 'single version of the truth' mantra has been behind the success of the German software company *SAP*. Their Enterprise Resource Planning (ERP) software brought together customer, product, accounting, human resources, production and logistics data together in a single database. The challenge for IT teams is that organizational demands for data are constantly changing and very often data is shared (sometimes even held) by third parties. Attempting to hold every single bit of data in one vast database has proven to be an almost impossible dream.

IT leader must meet the demands of information consumers without data management spinning out of control

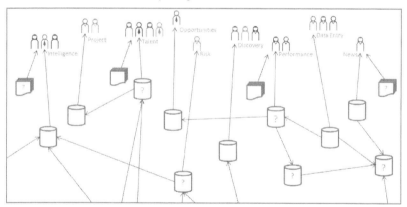

New information services platforms like Encanvas tackle the problems of data management and governance by adopting a stringent governance model. Data that can be held in a single database *is*. Data owners are charged with identifying the fields and tables that hold sensitive information. Each field is tagged with an authorization level that determines who can access it. User requests to use data are logging and presented back to administrators through their governance consoles. Wherever it is held, data is made secure and referenceable.

The application components used to achieve this are:

1. A **Web Services Library** that organizes assemblies of structured data into a library that can be re-used and managed (just like books in a library).
2. A **Digital Content System** to ensure that all unstructured forms of content – documents, videos, images etc. are brought together in a single administration system.
3. A **Data Governance Directory** that enables administrators to assign access rights to data tables so that usage may be prohibited according to the authority of the user. With a Data Governance system like Encanvas *Ring-of-Steel (RoS)* administrators can track and be pre-warned about potential data breaches and security threats across their corporate information services architecture.

With these new technologies, the ability of IT teams to manage their data is vastly improved but while organizations continue to employ software applications that sit outside the governance of Active Directory, even down to popular files like spreadsheets created by desktop tools such as Microsoft Excel, there will always be back-doors to enterprise data that provide unscrupulous people with access to sensitive information.

Web 2.0

Thanks to recent advances in web technologies the user-experience now offered through web browsers is every bit as good as the rich user interface desktop software users have grown accustomed to.

These innovations, together with low-cost of market entry and scaling of applications enabled by the cloudspace, have given small software companies the opportunity to go-to-market with a plethora of new information services. It's heralded as the 'Web 2.0' revolution: a second generation of prolific web development where small software companies introducing many new and interesting ways to work with information and provide services that appeal to individuals and business.

Web 2.0 isn't really revolutionary, but it's true that new agile web technologies bring better ways to share, communicate and present small software start-ups with the ability to rapidly enter the web services market: Web 2.0 means they can employ their ideas, innovation and mashup technologies to introduce new ways of working with information and then serving them up on the cloudspace. They provide the richness of choice that information consumers are now demanding. Individuals can today vote with their feet by choosing the best applications and information services they like and share them painlessly with their friends, colleagues and online communities through the social networking media. The cloudspace provides a home and opportunity for the prolific adoption of these ideas.

Attitudes will be slow to change

While new information services technologies offer a compelling return-on-investment, it doesn't mean that big business will adopt them with open arms. The software industry has worked the same way for years and, consequently, it has an instilled mind-set that will be hard to change (I mean REALLY, REALLY hard). If the computers stop in most businesses today, so too does business. Corporate IT teams are under enormous pressure to protect the computer servers and networks that ensure business continuity. This understandably creates a cautious, risk averse behaviour that prohibits innovation and the curiosity to try out new technologies that 'might' be useful.

According to Martin Vasey, a thought-leader in corporate knowledge management who has spent most of his career working in large corporations alongside IT colleagues, attitudes towards new technologies, already cautious, have become even more so. He says, "I see IT people, even the younger ones, getting more like content police. You can understand it. They have the responsibility to prevent intellectual property seepage, data breaches, IT terrorism and theft. That's a lot of responsibility on young shoulders. There have been too many cases in the press of what happens when IT lets its guard down. Generally I think IT teams feel they have enough technology around them with the tools they've bought already to deliver the core processes that organizations depend on. The innovations in IT are outpacing the level of change businesses can cope with. IT teams are a huge filter to new innovation so there must be enormous enthusiasm for an emerging technology before they will consider it."

Even some of the brightest minds of Silicon Valley get caught out sometimes on the slow take-up of new ideas in enterprise computing and the reluctance of decision makers to try something new. Just recently, William Coleman, a well-known figure in *The Valley* came unstuck with his latest venture in the cloud computing space because of the reluctance of enterprise clients to try something new. In a statement published by Forbes.com he said, "I thought I could give companies something radical that had a proven return on investment, and they would be willing to change all their companies' computer policies and procedures to get that."

There was nothing wrong with his idea. Coleman's plan was to steal a march on the competition by offering cheap computing via the cloud that would result in a new market price for computing infrastructure that bigger IT companies like HP and *IBM* would not be able to compete with. Needless to say, the *mind-set* of enterprise IT buyers eventually killed the idea. A few years from now no doubt someone else will do precisely the same thing and will look like a genius!

Information served to the 'social office'

When IT people talk about their *users* it always sounds like data traffickers sharing ideas on how to keep their addicts *taking*.

In the 1970's the pick-up place where *users* went to get their fix of data was the data centre. In the 1990's, information addicts enjoyed the comfort of *home delivery* as the data traffickers started serving data to desktop personal computers. Addicts would take as much good data IT traffickers were prepared to give them and they were happy to pay for it. It was a good time to be a data trafficker working in IT during the 1990's but in the early 2000's *users* were afforded mobility with their laptops and keeping them on a tight leash was becoming more troublesome. Worse still, the *users* were finding new suppliers of the information they wanted that was outside of the control of the data traffickers. By 2010 their monopoly of supply will be over.

For the enterprise, the value of data has always been associated with the big number crunching processes: The quality of a computing system has been measured by its up-time and response speeds. An orientation towards business continuity has encouraged IT people to think about new requirements for IT in terms of *new software applications* that must somehow be made to fit on top of their enterprise computing *platform*. This *platform-centricity* means that new innovations thrash about to get a foot-hold on the enterprise computing mountain unless they can demonstrate their ability to embrace incumbent technology components.

Enterprise information consumerism forces organizations to turn their attention towards the needs of *people*.

Workers have become information consumers demanding better information services to perform their roles

In the brave new world of information consumerism, the *people are the network*.

When business people speak about sharing information across their network these days they're probably not talking about PCs, servers and the cable that bind disparate systems together. They're most likely talking about people networks.

The *person* has replaced *systems* as the focus of information value.

Information services software, social networking and micro-blogging tools are transforming the office workplace. Attitudes towards use of *instant messaging* and *on-the-hoof* information sharing are bleeding into the enterprise on a wave of information consumerism.

Mix the *technology innovations* and *information consumer attitudes* with the *new shape of knowledge markets* and we see all of the ingredients in place for a major step-change in the office workplace.

Collaboration is moving from behind the ring-fenced world of IT into the new social office workplace and users want to take their data with them.

12

The real organogram

The world of business is so far away from harnessing social networking because *social networks* are invisible to the naked eye.

If only business leaders could glimpse for a moment how much knowledge (and how many relationships with other businesses) their workforce has access to they would be jumping up and down on their boardroom chairs.

Social network analysis tools are emerging to expose social networks and help people to make sense of them. These are tools that visualize social networks and expose the ties between contacts.

In the 1930s, a psychologist called Dr. Jacob Levi Moreno came up with the concept of a 'sociogram', a cluster of points social scientists call 'nodes' connected by straight lines that denoted relationships. It was the first formal attempt to map out relationships within a network of people. Moreno's sociogram became a powerful tool for identifying social leaders, outsiders, and what he called the 'sociometric star' – i.e. the person to whom all others are connected.[43]

There are two main genres of software tools used to expose social networks. Some provide *drawing pin and connector* tools to enable users to draw their sociogram (sociogram design tools), while others visualize data that already exists (social network analysis and visualization software) like the relationships found on email, *Facebook* and *MySpace*. This type of software mines data and then graphs it in a sociogram-style map. With these modern computer visualization software tools it will shortly be possible for every enterprise – large or small – to expose the relationships that exist between their workers.

Mapping the social enterprise

Since the birth of corporations, how management teams *understand* their workforce and organize it has been guided by 'organogram' illustrations that bear no reflection to the real world. Using organograms to model the operational excellence of an enterprise is like trying to command an army of men using toy soldiers on a chess board!

Business leaders aren't stupid. They know organograms aren't a good way of describing an enterprise. Matters of creativity, ingenuity, wisdom and enthusiasm don't fit well into the boxes and lines of the organogram.

While managers know that organograms are a poor management tool, in a world of mechanization and processes, they have served their purpose to explain to Jimmy or Jemima their personal roles in the pecking order, which cog they're to replace in the machine, and very little has been done to attempt to displace them.

Employers expect to fit new employees into their business processes like cogs in a machine; to then discard any other skills, relationships or attributes recruits might bring.

Employers satisfy themselves when the needs of *processes* are met by their recruitment activity and, without any clear economic argument to cherish the talents of their workforce, they dismiss the emotional needs of *workers* that go unheard.

Feeling unloved, and miss-understood, workers put in their 50% of required effort and go home feeling emotionally underwhelmed.

Since the beginning of corporations, organizational modelling has been based on a one dimensional organogram of the enterprise

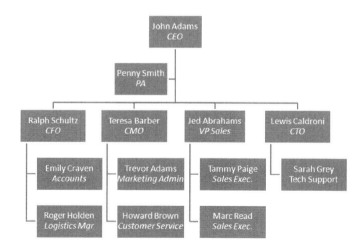

Managing an army of workers with such basic tools compromises command and control performance. Without the advantages of being able to mine terabytes of social networking metainformation, the generals and corporals of the enterprise must work blind-folded; arbitrarily appointing workers to roles and projects based on scant knowledge of each individual's qualities and previous performance.

The 'real organogram'

There is a growing realization in the business world that social networking structures represent the *real organogram* of an organization; often conflicting with organograms that illustrate function-based divisional and departmental structures. Knowledge of the role, position and status of workers within the social fabric of an enterprise is being seen to be essential to the success of any organization in the latter part of the 2000s.

Obtaining a *real-world* view of how organizations really work is becoming all the more important to business leaders because they know the make-up of their workforce has become ever more complex due to the rise in flexi-working, cross-industry collaborations and the influx of *life workers* and *knowledge bohemians.*

This social map of the enterprise is invisible to the naked eye and yet holds the key to future operational excellence and a step-change in knowledge worker productivity.

New types of workers and work behaviours are emerging setting new challenges for command and control, business process orchestration and organizational design

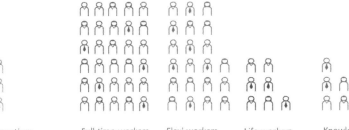

Executives	Full-time workers	Flexi-workers	Life-workers	Knowledge bohemians
Executives spend more of their time managing projects that exploit pools of resources and information beyond the enterprise	Full-time workers expect to harness the web, richer information sources and their social networks	Encouraged by Government legislation, workers are demanding more flexible working arrangements	Large numbers of workers are electing to leave the workplace to improve their work : life balance by becoming self-employed knowledge workers	Many post-graduates are finding new ways to employ their creativity and expertise to serve business

This new mix of workers places fresh demands on the way

organizations and systems are designed. There are practical security concerns given that some people aren't employed by the organization they serve anymore and won't be found in the company address book. So far as the organization is concerned they're assigned the same status as *visitors* (how many company car parks have parking spaces labelled for life-workers?). But this new and important part of the workforce will need to access network resources; they need to communicate and share data that is *formally* considered company confidential but they *practically* need to discharge their roles. New workers and worker behaviours demand that people can roam and work remotely. This has been exasperated recently by EU law enacted to support the rights of people to seek flexible working arrangements.

> **In the European Union, parents with children under 16 are being given the legal right to request flexi-working from their employer. This has been extended in 2009 from the original flexi-working legislation enacted in 2003 that covered parents having children under six. To example this; in the UK, around 6 million employees have the legal right to request flexible working arrangements but over 14 million employees, including part-time workers, actually work flexibly.[44] It's expected that something like a quarter of employees will be flexi-working by 2012.**

It's a great idea to let people work from home if they can but there can be technical challenges. For example, how does the business organize telephone communications to forward calls? How can meetings take place with remote workers? How is letter post distributed? And how are workers given access to the business systems they use in their offices?

It's no longer possible to assume everyone that delivers outcomes for an organization is a full-time employee. How does the CEO organize a meeting of 'the organization' when 40% of the workforce isn't found in the company directory? From a command and control perspective, how can an organization hope to instil appropriate *norms or behaviour*, positive *customer service attitudes* and effective *health and safety* and *quality assurance* policies without fundamentally understanding how the organization works?

Generals need a *real organogram*.

Formalizing human-centric processes

To achieve operational excellence in the 21st century, management disciplines must adapt and find better ways to organize the social network structures that support the human-centric processes that go unnoticed in business.

What I'm talking about are all the hand-cranked activities that people *make work* in business – the water cooler conversations, the email traffic that alerts people to issues, the 'go-to-guy' who knows everything about your biggest customer, the mentor that volunteers time to help greenhorns out of the jams they get into and the techie guy that always finds a way out when there's a dead-end technical problem.

Even in large organizations, it's surprising how much *hand-cranking* of processes goes on. See what happens when a big tender opportunity hits a business. It's rare for the knowledge needed to complete a complex tender opportunity to exist within the sales department. Marketing 'runners' are normally sent round the organization to find out who's able to answer the information requirements. They need to eke out: Who knows about the legal framework? Who knows 'if feature-x' is industry compliant. So much of this information is hidden in tiny pools of knowledge around the organization.

Human-centric processes rely on social networks

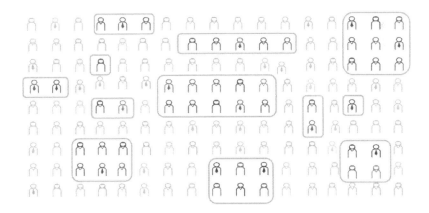

Here's a quick story to example this point:

In the .COM era I found myself working for a software company that had been on a heavy acquisitions trail. I was appointed to the team given responsibility for turning these disparate operations into a coherent and hopefully profitable organization. Having searched through the wreckage the project team discovered many of the acquired companies were small operations that had previously been managed by 'hands-on' directors. As soon as the directors were given their bag of cash they'd run to the hills. These people who *lived* these businesses for years took with them the knowledge of their client relationships, of how their businesses worked and an instinctive appreciation of how they were able to create value that customers were prepared to pay for. All that remained were fancy titles on the stationery, small pockets of good people and bits of software code that didn't fit together no matter how creative we tried to be.

Organizations that formalize information flows that cut across office social networks enjoy enormous cost reductions by cutting the amount of time wasted through parallel conversations. I don't think there's a person in business that hasn't been touched by poor formalized information flows at some point.

Say you were searching out information on a competitive product to publish some competitive arguments in a tender response. You talk to the sales and marketing people in your office that might know something about the competitor. Then you contact HQ marketing to see if they know anything more before you get down to writing your own document. You obtain a few responses that you can piece together. So you publish your new content that describes why your product is so much better than your competitors. The tender response goes out. A week later you receive a call from the *Channels Department*; a relatively new team at HQ. The lady on the phone sounds irritated and asks why you've produced this content because it's her job to do it and she's already authored a document that describes what the competitive arguments are! You shrug your shoulders. Who knew?

Enterprise Content Management Systems attempt to solve this type of information sharing problem but they don't work and never will. The way these systems work is to catalogue content into logically indexed boxes of content. That's a great idea in principle but how in practise are workers to know what boxes of content exist and what's in them? Today's content management systems don't embed knowledge sharing into the social fabric of the organization. All that normally happens is that content gets electronically hoarded into a *better* information structure that makes it more likely a person can find what they're looking for once they've got their head around the taxonomy (indexing structure) of the site. And users have to be very, very patient.

Content Management Systems require people to publish content in a formal way; to make sure versions of documents are properly controlled and that the quality of information remains relevant and useful. Publishing to content management systems is time consuming and normally requires workers to go through a triage of checks that adds more tasks to the way they work (for example, you might publish a document in MS Word and save it on your hard-drive and then have to publish it again to the Content Management System). These extra steps mean that many people don't bother to keep content up-to-date and soon return to the *informal social network of the office* as a more reliable way to find the answers they're looking for.

Organizations need to formalize information flows across people networks to optimize performance and keep information secure

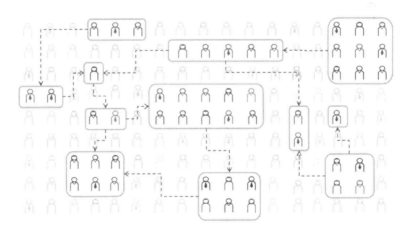

Knowledge sharing and collaboration has been a bottomless pit of IT expense for 20 years or more; so convincing business people to spend more on it is a hard sell. Leaders are understandably sceptical as to whether any better way exists to organization human-centric information flow. So anyone selling a new technology or approach has got a lot of convincing to do. For this reason, new technologies that expose and make sense of the social networks of the enterprise are better off if they yield *new value*.

Leveraging the 'little-black books' of the workforce

One exciting *new value* area is the opportunity to enable the organization to tap into the *little black book* of its employees; to leverage their relationship ties to find the best talent for projects across their business and – better still – to enable the organization to access new sales and partnership opportunities by leveraging relationship ties of its workforce; ties that extend beyond the enterprise.

Just imagine how many useful contacts are known to the workforce of an organization employing 10,000. Within just 2 degrees of separation it's likely that the 'who knows who' relationship ties of this many people will connect the organization to *practically every other organization* in their region.

> **Think about a situation where you want to make an introduction to a company but you don't know anybody that works for them. Could it be that someone you know has a relationship with an employee, or partner, or supplier of the company you're trying to make an introduction to? How would you know? Perhaps, with social network visualization software it will be possible to trace the threads of networks of all of the people you know, they know etc. until the grid extends to your target audience. Software will ultimately make these invisible social networks visible by graphing the lines that join up the dots.**

The graphing of social networks within an organization's 'biosphere' is not new: Visible Path (www.visiblepath.com) is an early example of such discovery software. While the technology needed for individuals and organizations to harness relationship ties isn't quite there yet, and there is no clear market leading approach, it won't be long before small and large organizations can expose and make sense of the associations that exist between their people; the nodes on the network.

Organizations seek to harness relationship ties

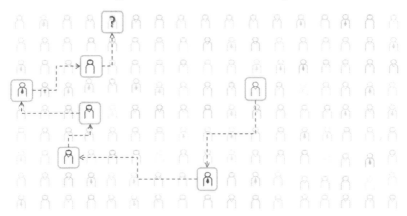

With effective tools to make sense of their social networks users, businesses could quickly understand just how broad their networks are and where they need to invest in developing new relationships by acquiring the *right people with the right connections.*

In search of talent

In chapter 12 I accused employers of recruiting employees to replace cogs in the enterprise machine, to serve the business processes that power business continuity, and through this indiscriminate approach to recruitment they access a tiny part of what workers are actually capable of. I will often ask employees how much of their talents and skills they believe their employers are wasting. It's not unusual for generous employees to suggest that figure is around 30%; a more realistic figure is 50%.

And the reasons?

"They don't know what I do."

"I have no idea what they're actually expecting of me."

"My job role is 'x' but I know more about 'y' than anyone else in the company."

"They're not aware I exist."

"I'm constantly being asked to do things that I know are a waste of time and won't help the business but they won't listen to me."

"The information I need to get my work done isn't available."

"I can't be bothered and the management team does nothing to <u>make</u> me bother."

To place this into a productivity context, what it means is an enterprise of 10,000 employees employs 2,500 more capacity than it's using, or benefitting from. It would be economically more efficient to give employees 1 day in 5 off if they agree to share their ideas and adopt better ways of to exploit their *true* potential!

The absence of a *real organogram* to the enterprise – and with no means of capturing rich metainformation on what makes each individual special; what they're truly capable of – means that management teams aren't equipped to make best use of their talent pools.

The make-up of the 21st century enterprise workforce presents more opportunities for organizations to harness talent and relationship ties that reach beyond the corporate fire-wall. The richness of these resources is invisible to blindfolded business leaders.

The mantra of *operational excellence*, that so many business advisors have praised for decades, is so obviously a myth to millions of workers who every day find themselves surrounded by generals and corporals living in denial of how their organization really works.

Organizations seek to harness talent to tease out creativity and knowledge

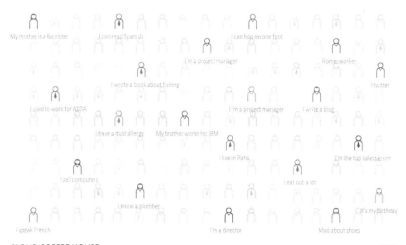

Too much data, not enough information

Social networks carry lots of data and scale very quickly to thousands of nodes and connections. The potential size of social networks means that computing the relationships, even before any attempt is made to visually present them, is a mammoth task – but this, after all, is what cloud computing was born to do!

Social networks are multi-dimensional. People want to make sense of relationships in different ways – perhaps by categorizing the types of contacts or geographical locations. Presenting so many 'perspectives' across so many 'layers' of data is not easy on a typical computer screen. To become useful, users need to be able to zoom in and out like they do with geo-spatial maps today. But unlike digital geo-spatial maps there is no instantly familiar *physical aspect* to social networks that humans can use as a basis to make sense of what they're looking at. Therefore, inventors of new visualization tools have to create new forms of user interface and this will inevitably take time and investment to get right.

One of the most useful layers of metainformation that isn't captured today is the *strength of ties* between people.

We all have contacts that are dear to us and other acquaintances we barely know. Social networkers need to make sense of their own relationships to really exploit weak ties. To do this requires technology to lend a helping hand to compute strength of ties based on frequency of contact, relevancy of association, the age of the data – and whatever hints and tips about strengths of ties that the content of messages bring.

It's still not possible today for me as an individual to make sense of my relationships and *their* relationships in a way that I can understand. Most of the visualization tools I've seen so far are more like the tools a consultant would use to make sense of organizational behaviour rather than a living and breathing day-to-day mechanism that business people can use to manage their relationships. This software doesn't represent a *real system* that you could instantly get to work with and benefit from.

If these tools were available today it would be much easier for business people to organize customer relationships and focus on their more profitable relationships. Users could apply revenue and resourcing models against their relationship maps to understand how the two worlds of *business* and *relationships* interplay.

For businesses, understanding who the *super networkers* are in their organizations could provide an indication of how much individuals contribute to the information flows that *grease the gears* of their enterprise that today no one can see.

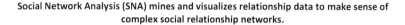

Social Network Analysis (SNA) mines and visualizes relationship data to make sense of complex social relationship networks.

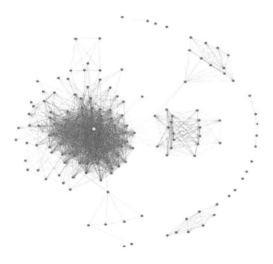

New challenges, new technologies

If you want to explore what's out there today you could take a look at *Commetrix, DyNet, EgoNet, inflow, MetaSight* and *NetMiner.*

None of these tools currently deliver the type of easy-to-use platform that would enable a normal Jo or Joanna to make sense of their networks – or companies for that matter – but the computing challenges of social network analysis are considerable.

In the example on the previous page, nodes are presented according to their relationship with the most prolific networker. Other visualizations might display <u>your</u> ego-centric network, or group nodes by topic, expose key business processes and how people contribute to them.

The future for visualization software is rosy. With the increasing level of standardization of computer operating systems and platforms it's becoming much easier to create new forms of visualization and make these tools available to the masses via the computing power and scale of the cloudscape.

The technology behind social network visualization software is in its infancy but, given that it promises so much value to businesses, I don't think it will be long before we're all able to employ visualization tools to make sense of our email address books and other systems that carry information on relationship ties.

13

The social office workplace

The social office is the *new workspace* of the 21st century enterprise. It is a browser-based computing environment that embraces ego-centric social networking technologies and behaviours.

A workplace that connects people globally

The new make-up of a 21st century workforce with its life-workers, flexi-staff, knowledge bohemians and globally dispersed organizations makes it hard to sit around the same table anymore and have a meeting. Middle managers complain how the air miles to 'HQ' are grinding them down. To get some respite they want to work from home. The workplace has transitioned from a physical place to something virtual. Knowledge workers spend more time with their favoured tools, Microsoft Outlook and Blackberry's, than their spouses.

Say 'workplace' and most knowledge workers imagine an office. But a workplace is literally a *place where people work*.

For modern knowledge workers, the *web browser* has become a portal to their workplace. Whilst there are several different forms of web browser clients – *Google Chrome, Microsoft Internet Explorer, Opera, Mozilla Firefox* – they all serve a common purpose; to provide a window to the World Wide Web (and now the cloudspace). Web-served applications no longer demand the resources of a desktop PC or laptop to use them. They don't insist on hard-disks or special software. Any browsing device will do. Armed with a simple laptop, mobile or PDA, knowledge workers can visit their workplace while seated in their hot-desk, garden, home-office or favourite coffee bar safe in the knowledge that their data is protected, their documents are recoverable, and they will only need to pay for the services they consume without the hassle of buying computers, software or maintenance contracts. The *browser* connects people around the globe to the cloudspace: a workplace big enough to support an entire planet of knowledge workers. But the past decade has proven that workers connected only through data-streams don't experience the same emotional support that daily interaction with colleagues and peers brings. This virtual workplace environment is unable to promise the traditional forms of interactivity that people have come to expect from the office environments they're used to. The *society* of the enterprise is surely lost?

All of this is true, and yet the office workplace is changing anyway. Corporations are shrinking their office foot-prints to trim operating budgets. In doing so, they're also responding to changing work patterns as workers spend more time away from the office. Today a new generation of workers is arriving at the office workplace and they have a different view on where they want to work.

Make-up of a social office workplace

The *social office workplace* is a browser-based computing environment that provides knowledge workers with the work-tools and information services they need to discharge their roles. It encourages individuals to assert their personality and show others what they can do. Mimicking the cultural behaviours of social media sites, the social office workplace encourages people to leverage their relationship ties.

These new 'virtual workplaces' bring the *ego-wall* and *micro-blogging* conversational tools of social media together to deliver the fast paced communications environment that new generations like. These features are united with more traditional collaboration and personal organizer tools. This hybrid mix of technology combines to produce a browser-based workplace that does not attempt to replicate how real-world offices work today – because software vendors know that future generations of knowledge workers will want to work in a different way. While solutions vary from one supplier to the next, each finds a way of servicing the emotional needs of workers by supporting conversation and collaboration in ways that appeal to new generations.

Typical components include:

- Browser-based portal site user interface
- A means of managing users, permissions and people networks
- Tools to manage and exploit relationship-ties
- Ego-wall – enables users to volunteer information on themselves
- Micro-blogging and conversations (advanced systems might include voting and crowdsourcing)
- Customization and tailoring tools (to enhance user experience)
- Integration with email, calendar/diary and desktop software
- Dashboard and activities management tools
- Collaborating web meeting and online conference tools
- Document / file sharing and organization
- Information services and news feeds
- Meeting room and facilities booking

Knowing me, knowing you

What makes the social office different to traditional office productivity software is its *ego-centricity*. We've never told computer systems before about our personal preferences, likes and needs, so they haven't known how to *serve us*. The social office workplace harvests vast amounts of metainformation it captures from user profiles, conversations, activities relationship ties, stated likes and dislikes, tag clouds and projects.

From this metainformation, the social office is able to build a profile of each user. Social office tools interrogate the profile of an individual and, from this insight, organize content in ways that will make sense to the individual. The more complete the metainformation acquired through daily interactions, the more accurate sorting and filtering engines become. It means that instead of having to go looking for information, content is selected and catalogued according to the profile of the individual (the information you want comes looking for you!).

Documents and other forms of knowledge can be associated with people networks, projects, even conversation threads. To find documents and content, workers refer to the conversation, people network or project they've been involved with.

Support of social processes

The social office is designed to support *social processes* within a virtual workspace. Social processes are activities that take place over time that increase the strength of ties between people. They contribute enormously to the effectiveness of an enterprise. Failing to support social processes leads to breakdowns in communications and poor work-group productivity.

Take business meetings for example. Meetings follow a common formula that is by now well understood: The purpose of the meeting should already be known, participants enter a room and present themselves to each other, and then matters at hand are discussed and outcomes agreed. What sounds a reasonably straight-forward exercise can keep people tied up for hours. It raises the question why do meetings drag on for so long?

Part of the answer lies in poor organization; another in the acts of social courtesy; like arranging for refreshments and waiting for others to make their opinions known. With any meeting, participants will be building their relationship ties, determine whether the outcomes are achievable and if contributors will actually do what they say they will. Virtual meeting rooms that attempt to bring people together over the web have failed to provide suitable vehicles to support these social processes. The methods and technologies needed to provide *virtual support* of social processes are slowing emerging, improving in quality, and becoming more affordable: Video conferencing technologies are becoming more life-like and reliable, so people can see one another and judge reactions based on the facial responses they see. Real-time collaboration, desk sharing and voting systems are becoming more accessible and easier to use; information publishing tools are improving in quality and providing richer visualization and charting that helps people to share content and make sense of it more easily.

The *social office* supports *social processes* and makes the experience of working with colleagues across the web more intimate and involving.

Generational shifts in communicating

While my mother writes letters to her utility suppliers, I make a call or send an email. My children send text messages to their friends. Attitudes towards modes of communication change between generations. Generation Y and Z live in a world of instant messages – *twittering, MSN* messaging, texting. From generation to generation the pace of communications is getting progressively faster while content is slimming from structured documents to conversations. The tone of voice of written material – even in business – has moved from formality to relaxed 'text-speak'.

I doubt it was any more than 10 years ago, sometime in the mid 1990's, that I had my first experience of email. When everyone started to use email, the volumes of formal internal memoranda and letter correspondence circulating the workplace took a swallow-dive. Suddenly, the majority of communications could be met by sending an email, and copying it to anyone else who needed to be kept in the loop.

From those days of innocence, email has become an uncontrolled tyrant that rampages its streams of poorly censored content throughout the enterprise and beyond. Within these information flows are hidden business-critical processes – customer liaisons, confidential internal company documents, contracts and forms – yet control over email has remained unfettered due to concerns over privacy. For some strange reason, when email appeared in the enterprise to replace the organization's systems of communication it was seen to belong to the *individual*, not the organization. Opening someone else's email was like cutting open envelopes to their private correspondence.

The richest information source of the enterprise – a treasure chest of knowledge, relationship understanding, information flows etc. found in a company's email server and repository of email data – is off limits to the organization it serves. The organization is not wanted or expected to tamper with this repository of messages. What we learn from email is that communications and relationship matters are *personal*. If workers want to volunteer information on their contacts and communications that's up to them but they can't be made to do so.

The tools people use to communicate in business are *still* changing.

Email and the humble telephone are finding new competition from the messaging and micro-blogging technologies of the social net. New ways of communicating are being tested live in organizations around the world – like sharing ideas and problems by broadcasting questions to a work-team via instantly broadcast 'twitter' style messaging.

> **Google** has recently announced the imminent launch of **Google Wave**. This is a new form of conversation technology that employs textual conversation on a web-site that

participants in the conversation can all see. Unlike email where you send a message from 'person A' to 'person B' and might copy in persons 'C' and 'D' for reference, with *Google Wave*, the person who starts a conversation can invite as many people as they like to the 'same web-page' where they share their instant conversation. Participants get to see what someone is typing as it's written, so participants feel entirely engaged. They can also share documents, photographs and links across their conversations. Once a conversation is completed it is saved and all of the coMmunications can be tagged so that they can be referenced later.

Similarly, *Encanvas Squork* is a secure business conversation technology designed specifically for business people who want to keep their conversations private between individuals or groups. Like *Google Wave*, *Encanvas Squork* enables the person who starts a conversation to bring other contacts into a conversation. Invited people view the 'same web-page' and can share textual conversations instantly. It highlights which people are online and even lets users share their ideas over the web. Any attached files or documents are automatically saved and recorded in a conversation history so over time users build up a complete history of their collaborative activities. *Encanvas Squork* differs from *Google Wave* in the way it allows users to create their own secure groups across which they can share intellectual property securely. It can also be deployed by organizations internally so they can have total control over content shared through business conversations.

Web 2.0 companies like *Noodle*, *blueKiwi* and *SocialCast* provide other forms of social office communication software designed with businessses in mind. These companies are benefiting from millions of investment dollars from venture capitalists fuelled by the hype curve of social media technologies. Their products mimic many of the communications features found in consumer social media tools – like blogs, wikis, twitters and personal walls.

These new forms of instant conversation technology have advantages over email:

- When people email one another they must keep replying to the same message in order to build up a conversation history. Should people create a new email on the same story they fragment discussions.

- It's not easy to organize emails by conversation topic or network.

- Email doesn't automatically save attached files and documents into a common folder archive so finding them later is difficult. Attachments can only be found by trawling through email history which can be time consuming.

- It's not possible to add tag clouds to emails on most email servers so recovering conversations and content is made more difficult.

- It's not possible to bring people into a conversation. Often, people who should be involved in a conversation miss out.

A big loser in this new era of *online real-time chatter* is the trusty *printed document* which used to enjoy a seat at the top table of business communications, but not anymore. People find it easier to ask a question and get it answered while it's in their heads. Use of email and instant messaging changes worker behaviours. Lean office management consultants report that they have seen office worker behaviours transform over the last 5 years as workers move away from a segmentation of their working day into rationalized *time-slots* such as 'correspondence time', 'meeting time' and 'think time' (etc.) into a *constant blur* of email messaging activity that threatens to puncture through activities at any moment.

This real-time *instant response culture* actively discourages the use of formal documents. Instead, messages are short and take on the form of 'textual conversations' (falling somewhere between email and texting vocabulary) with absolutely no tolerance for the traditional formalities of letter writing.

> The volume of hard-copy printed documents produced by office laser and inkjet printers is going into a steep decline. Younger generations (i.e. Generation Y and Generation Z) are happy to read documents onscreen and use digital document stores that give them immediate access to files. Users trust they can recover their filed documents in a digital format should they ever need to.

Corporate IT teams are finding it tough to deny business stakeholders access to the social networking tools they already use at home. *The sorts of tools that Generation Z would like to use* are seeping into the corporate office.

During my research for this book I had the opportunity to speak to Jamison Roof, technology lead for User Centric Design of PA Consulting Global Systems Integration and Solutions Group and I asked him for his thoughts on how corporate IT teams are responding to pressures for new communications forms and social media tools.

"Access to information has becoming more ubiquitous and business people are much more aware of what's possible than they were 5 years ago. Yes there are still issues when it comes to introducing new ways of working but business managers are under great pressures to harness the potential of their teams to drive out more productivity and exploit resources. Even in larger organizations, when these small teams of 6 to 12 people come up against an information black-hole – perhaps because IT is not exactly in-line with user needs – I'm finding the business heads are pushing to try new innovations to solve these small specific problems. On occasions when these emerging technologies prove themselves, meet the core hygiene factors or IT and deliver value quickly to the business, IT leaders won't normally stand in the way. There's no doubt, when push comes to shove, that business outcomes are worth more than neatly designed IT platforms even to IT leaders. But it would be fair to say IT people do see a lot of the down-sides of these tools in terms of the security threats they might introduce, their reliability and the operating overhead they might leave behind."

In search of solutions acceptable to the business and their own fastidious security and reliability expectations, IT leaders are steering business sponsors towards 'corporatized' copycat versions of the instant messaging and social networking tools of the consumer world.

Driven by generational shifts in modes of communication, the age of the document is gone, the era of email is dying and a period of instant conversation is emerging.

Personalized news services

Knowledge is being devalued because it's always there. Click on a browser and knowledge is there waiting for you on the Web 24-hours a day. Why bother learning or trying to remember anything? The trouble over the past decade has been too much information and not enough insight. Many thousands of people today make their living by 'filtering' and turning information into insight so corporations can process the answers that matter to them.

Users expect their social office workplace to overcome the need for human informediaries by pro-actively bringing worthy news to their attention; to draw their attention to useful relationships, useful insight, alerts, new connections and new opportunities.

Technologies like RSS feed systems (employed by blog sites and Internet publishers today to update subscribers on news) are likely to become ever more integral to online social networking.

News and subject-matter specific aggregator technologies (only available to the world's largest corporations today because of their high price tags) will shortly be available through the social office. These technologies intelligently gather information on particular stories and function as *robotic digital informediaries*; sifting through content on our behalf to work out what's useful. Instead of having to rummage through pages of 'stuff', the metainformation we volunteer will help enable the cloudspace to summarize articles that find their way into our personal digital knowledge banks.

New ways of working with documents

The role of documents – and what we understand a document to be – is changing. People today visualize documents to be printed on paper. They are seen as *containers* of content, *transports* of content. But digital documents are changing that perception. It's now possible for people to collaborate on the creation of 'a document' working from different locations. Content is edited and enriched time and again by different people working on areas of the same document. The document itself becomes 'the place' where content is contained (you have to imagine a document like a web page that works like a bulletin board where people can change aspects of the content).

Sharing of ideas and intellectual property through the online real-time presentation of digital content is also becoming possible with technologies like Adobe's LiveCycle Rights Management Enterprise Server. As these new forms of 'document sharing' technology become mainstream, it becomes increasingly difficult to see a document as a 'transport' or stand-alone container.

When users start to collaborate on content in this way it introduces many new challenges to organizations in terms of how intellectual property is protected. The focus of IT data security moves away from securing the *container of data* to the *data* itself. It may be that in future, organizations will seek to adopt technology that can manage intellectual property contained within paragraphs and subsections of a document. This becomes particularly relevant if different agencies are contributing 'paragraphs' of intellectual property to the same document.

The use of documents as a content container for long-term storage is also changing. As a computer user today I manually save my content as 'documents'. Later, when I need them, I hope (pray) I will find them again somewhere on my hard-drive. It's easy for me to forget how a document was stored. So often the content is reproduced again, as I work on the logic that the time it would take to recover the document could be better spent re-drafting. I'm sure it's not only me that does this.

Use of the web is encouraging people to experiment and find better ways of cataloguing information. One of the more recent developments has been the greater use of bookmarks and tag clouds to pull out from documents words and phrases that people find helpful as references to find documents.

tag clouds make it easier for people to find content held in unstructured documents

The cloudspace automates the formation of tag clouds by comparing document content with frequently used words and terms found in your correspondence, conversations, relationships and special interest topics. This insight can be applied by the cloudspace to pull out tags from features and articles that carry a high propensity of subjects you're interested in. Perhaps one day personal digital newspapers that work this way will catch on too!

I'm sure documents, as containers of thoughts and knowledge, won't die out for at least a generation but, as with news-feeds. It is likely that the majority of content will transform to less formal conversations. The social office will fulfil the role of the *informediary* and organize documents for us. Instead of manually filing documents, information services will take our ideas, passions, content experiences, relationship ties etc. and use this as a foundation to automatically build cataloguing taxonomies that will order our thoughts and documents.

The technology needed to enable this already exists today. What is missing is the knowledge of 'us'.

Business mashup software and the social office

For businesses awash with data, enterprise portals hold great promise but don't have the means to deliver.

For this reason, the mashup portal technologies I introduce in Chapter 11 are set to become an integral component of the social office workplace. They provide information workers with the ability to *serve themselves* with portals that *bridge across* disparate data repositories to extract additional value from corporate information assets.

Traditional enterprise platforms like Content Management Systems and enterprise portals are unable to learn from behavioural metainformation on the individual – because it isn't volunteered. They can only present a common place to go for office workers through dumbed down portals designed to be *good enough* for everyone. Content sits isolated from conversations, activities and behaviours of the workforce and quickly loses its relevance. Enterprise portals are also considered part of the *enterprise computing platform* that falls under the administration of IT because creating portals of this sort today demands skilled IT people.

How the social office workplace breaks down barriers

Many organizations suffer from 'siloism', where the operational silos of the enterprise (departments and divisions) create cultural divides in the work-force that disrupt social and business processes leading to sub-optimal business performance. The social office breaks down barriers between people and departments by making it possible for workers to share thoughts and ideas painlessly. The virtual workplace feels very connected because of instant messaging that allows questions and ideas to be 'pinged' around people networks rapidly without causing a major overhead on people's time or network band-width.

Innovate from the bottom up

The social office creates a communications hub where anyone can float an idea. Business leaders can use this new communications capability to tap into a rich pool of ideas and innovation without creating formal 'organizational structures'. I'm thinking particularly about 'champions teams' who are people picked out of their departments as champions for change programmes. This type of cross-organizational structure sounds a great way on paper to share ideas but it often leads to new silos forming that distract management capacity away from priorities that matter most. It also means that contributing people suddenly find they have 2, 3 or 4 bosses and find it impossible to satisfy all of them.

Crowd engagement through crowdsourcing and voting systems help business leaders to tap into the ideas pool of their extended workforce. For change managers and improvement programmers a richer knowledge of the social relationships of the office help to identify the 'well-poisoners' and 'champions' of the workforce who are people high in energy who tend to be the stronger influencers and therefore need to be kept on-side.

Learn differently

Improved communications and greater transparency in the activities of project teams across the enterprise gives workers the opportunity to understand *how* and *why* they, in their job role, contribute to a process. This sponsors more curiosity in the workforce that results in more *single loop learning* (where people find a better way of performing a specific task) and *double loop learning* where workers are able to come up with completely new solutions and alternative methods that solve the requirement a better way. Social office tools will often incorporate open notice-boards, ideas walls and voting systems to harvest ideas and suggestions.

A vocabulary to formalize social networks

Social office workplace needs individuals to have the capacity to share their networks and transport them. But there is no *vocabulary* we can use to describe social networks to others to enable this type of information to be easily absorbed and shared.

It's not possible today to write down on a piece of paper what your personal network of relationship ties looks like. This makes it impossible for people to easily organize their relationships, or share them with others. Language is a vital ingredient to sharing knowledge. The new era of social networking metainformation must have its own vocabulary if social network data is to be made transportable and non-technical people are to share their network metainformation.

I don't believe the open social networks of consumer-land like *Facebook* – and to some extent tools like *LinkedIn* – are going to work in a business world that fears innovation leakage and data breaches, and is (probably quite rightly) repulsed by the notion of any system that isn't regulated and administered by someone operating on behalf of the business it serves. Sometimes, making money in business comes from who brings an idea to market first. Remember, the guy that brought the invention of the telephone to market second made no money from it! Knowledge is precious to businesses and it has to be protected.

Organizations want to mirror the advantages of social networking in the consumer space but they need solutions implemented in a different way. In my opinion, a step-change in the levels of adoption of business social networking will only occur when a more robust level of governance can be applied.

There has to be a way of *gating* networks so that owners and participants are very much aware who owns the knowledge and what the purpose, interests and outcomes of any network might be. The role of networks must be made obvious and who owns intellectual rights must be established from the outset before members commit themselves and feel betrayed. In some forms of network, members will also need to know how they will be rewarded for participation and maybe even how they will be paid.

Some 'social networks' aren't <u>social</u> anymore

It's inappropriate to call these gated social relationship structures 'social networks' when the purpose of the network has nothing to do with *being social*. A better description of this sort of structure is a 'situational network' because people networks are brought together to solve a commonly shared problem that responds to a *new situation*.

These *situational networks* must operate within a governance framework that makes them eligible to be considered by managers as a useful delivery vehicle for projects. It begs the question what impact they will have on organizational design when managers can use situational networks to harness people from outside of their organizations in order to contribute towards projects that traditionally would have been assigned to full-time employees.

There's another big question that needs answering.

As situational networks flourish, will organizations attempt to organize them into knowledge markets (like INNOCENTIVE has successfully manage to achieve) or will they become *self-organizing*? Whilst INNOCENTIVE has proven that it is possible to balance organizational and member needs and to achieve a critical mass of seekers and solvers sufficient to make a market for knowledge work, I believe self-organizing networks are likely to evolve by themselves.

I use the term 'ego-centric' to describe a social network that starts with YOU, the individual. YOU select the people you want to have in your network. YOU choose the parameters of how the network will operate and the terms of reference. People networks are natively ego-centric. We all think about relationships from our own context. Even if I were to establish a new business enterprise, I would be starting with me and thinking 'who else should I include?'

Ego-centric, gating and *easily described* situational networks hold the key to the quickening application of social network structure in business organizations.

Through their ego-centricity, situational networks provide a mechanism to bring value to individuals without imposing dominating *big brother* structures. They expose the individuality of workers and won't disregard 60% of the talents of an individual due to a poorly worded job description written by a supervisor who was unaware of the talents of his staff; they will recognize the need for formality and regulation; the need for clearly defined ownership over intellectual property and most of all, they will become an intrinsic component in organizational design and behaviour. Why? Because they can be assigned accountability for delivery of measurable outcomes.

But how do you design a vocabulary that enables the common man to describe an ego-centric, gate-able, situational network?

Inspired by this challenge, in 2006 I had a go at creating a social network description language to enable one person to describe their social networks to another. It was an occasion that led me to jump out of bed at 2pm one cold January morning and declare to my wife when she came around that I'd had an epiphany. But like most things, after a coffee and a shower, my big idea turned into just a bit of well applied common sense. It does however remain as a useful common-sense way to describe gated situational network structures.

I call this description of a situational network a 'people-grid'.

Here's how it works.

People-grids are social relationship structures articulated by using a series of symbols to describe each characteristic of a situational network.

Situational networks are ego-centric so they always start with an owner and then describe others members and the rest-of-the-world.

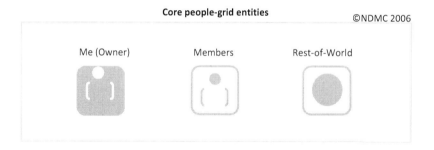

Core people-grid entities ©NDMC 2006

Me (Owner)   Members   Rest-of-World

In my computer-based version of this language, the definition of any individual's skills and capabilities in a people-grid are determined by a 'passport' description. Every individual must possess a passport in order to join a grid. The originator of a people-grid is automatically assigned the role of owner, although ownership can always be changed once created. A series of visualization icons denote other entities and associations in a network.

©NDMC 2006

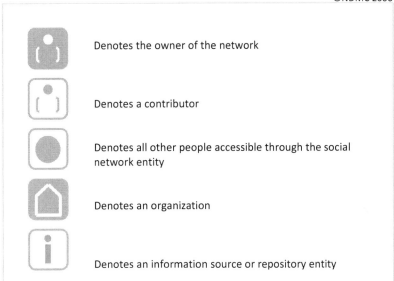

Denotes the owner of the network

Denotes a contributor

Denotes all other people accessible through the social network entity

Denotes an organization

Denotes an information source or repository entity

To then organize contacts into hierarchies within the people-grid a series of *operators* are applied as shown below.

People-grid operator characters ©NDMC 2006

⸴	Separates levels of seniority between nodes.
⸴	Separates the people-grid from the 'rest of world'
( )	Denotes a gated people-grid (i.e. data is secured within the portal space and any intellectual property generated becomes the property of the owner or organization – whichever is closest to the left-hand margin).

Colours are used to show people vectors like language skills, interests, projects, associations etc. Icons are dragged into a platen area where commas are used to separate different levels of seniority. *Gates* (brackets) are used to denote a closed network. In such cases intellectual property and data rules may be assigned to the network to resolve ownership issues.

People-grids might belong to an individual, organization or community. Therefore, degrees of 'openness' and terms of access and use will vary. To give a crude example of how the people-grid language works, let's say you want to create a people-grid for a new project with yourself as the owner, a project team of three people and a third tier of two other less senior people. The people-grid would be presented as follows:

Illustrative example of a simple people-grid

©NDMC 2006

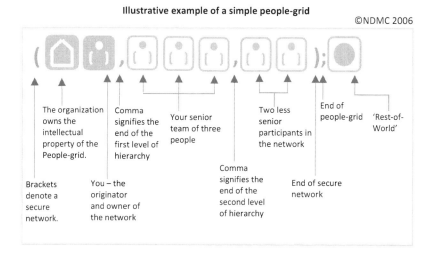

The organization owns the intellectual property of the People-grid.	Comma signifies the end of the first level of hierarchy

Your senior team of three people

Two less senior participants in the network

End of people-grid

'Rest-of-World'

Brackets denote a secure network.

You – the originator and owner of the network

Comma signifies the end of the second level of hierarchy

End of secure network

In future, I expect approaches like people-grids will make it easier for individuals to create their networks and share those network descriptions with others. For the individuals that form them, and organizations that seek to exploit them, people-grids could codify and *formalize* the *nature of relationships* between themselves and other individuals operating within self-regulated communities to assist individuals and organizations in managing and exploiting relationships more effectively.

A symbology-based language system like people-grid *qualifies key attributes of relationships* between individuals within a community; set down in a repeatable specification and graphical model that is easy to understand and share.

For individuals, the benefits of using a common vocabulary are to:

- Manage social networks more easily; and within this structure formalize the maintenance and use of contact information.

- Access and build relationships with a broader community of individuals with common interests and skills.

- Simplify the sharing of social network metadata.

For organizations, the benefits of people-grids are to:

- Employ social network structures to deliver project outcomes because they describe ownership of intellectual property and the contributions made by individuals.

- Make sense of social networks by establishing a common, shareable vocabulary.

- Increase the volume and completeness of social network data by enabling individuals to contribute their social network information as part of their day job.

Like a mad scientist I tested this symbology based language on my teenage daughter and having explained the principles of the mark-up language I asked her to describe her friendships at school to me by writing down the relationships using the vocabulary I had created (she managed the task with ease which gave me great encouragement!). Now I'm not suggesting this language form will ever become widely adopted but it serves to example how innovation in social networking might progress.

Until the emergence of Balanced Scorecard as a method for describing business strategy there was no formal method that business managers, leaders and consultants could use to articulate strategy on a piece of paper that others could understand. As Balanced Scorecard became broadly accepted as an effective way of articulating strategy, the level of professionalism in the activity of business strategy planning increased ten-fold.

I'm confident that once it becomes simpler for people to describe and share situational network structures, people will start to recognize the value that can be derived through gated social networks and start applying them to organize the activities of groups and teams to achieve finite outcomes.

Situational network portals

A gated *situational network* creates a definable user hierarchy.

IT people can use these structures to determine user privileges around a web portal. It's not unreasonable to believe that one day, web portals will be orchestrated around gated social network structures.

All of the information services participants of a situational network want to use can be mashed-up exclusively for the purpose. Information relating to a project and the applications developed to capture insight and make sense of it can all be generated expressly to respond to a new situation and discarded when no longer required.

With business mashup software, creating a new portal space to support the needs of a situational network won't require programming or scripting skills. A collection of wizards and code-free authoring techniques will take care of that.

I still expect the complexity of creating and building databases will continue to be something that experts will need to lend a hand in to support. Whilst specifying databases has become increasingly simpler with technology tools, understanding how databases are best architected in order to properly manage and make the best use of data remains a black art.

The social office and the customer

In the next 5 to 10 years, having dominated the enterprise, I expect social networking workspaces will extend their reach to embrace customers too. This will enable businesses to engage customers in a more informal tone-of-voice using instant communications – to make them feel part of the business they've just bought from.

When this happens I expect the printed business document can finally enjoy its long overdue retirement.

14

A market for knowledge workers

As they always have, employers must secure the people resources needed to drive an efficient and agile business.

But today, employers are faced with new resourcing challenges. How organizations turn whatever they do into customer value (their business models) is changing frequently. This means organizations must adapt skills portfolios time and again to align internal capabilities to the needs of their ever changing business models.

Employment law makes this adjustment costly.

> In the late 1990's, the global electronics company, Canon, found a reduction in demand for its single function copier and fax machines was met with corresponding growth in customer requirements for multi-function devices. Suddenly they needed fewer hardware engineers and more software quality assurance experts. As a Japanese company, the idea of laying people off is truly a last resort and as the result, thousands of engineers were retrained. That might have been okay in the 1990's, but in the 2000's such a dynamic step-change would probably not be economically viable for most corporations.

The alternative for employers to putting highly skilled knowledge workers on the payroll – and thereby creating rigidity of workforce supply – is to seek out knowledge competencies from online markets. The cloudspace, with its affordability, scalability and 24-hours a day availability, provides a perfect landscape for knowledge markets to organically form and grow, very different to hosted knowledge markets of today, run by companies and funded by industry and academia; normally for a single purpose.

Knowledge markets – where *seekers of knowledge* and *solvers* (who have the know-how to deliver value) can meet – aren't mainstream. They're not trusted as useful components in organizational design.

If our generation is going to solve *Drucker's challenge*[45] (i.e. "to increase the productivity of KNOWLEDGE WORK and the KNOWLEDGE WORKER"), the pace of growth in the popularity and use of knowledge markets will have to increase substantially. For this to occur we'll need to see a step-change in the way knowledge markets are perceived and ultimately used. This transformation demands a new *mind-set* driven by *commercial* necessity, and *enabled by technology*. The global war for talent will be the economic stimulus that will cause businesses to think and work differently. We can expect technology, and the innovations of the social office, to play an equal role in making knowledge markets useful, accessible and affordable.

Creating a knowledge market isn't easy

Orchestrating a market for knowledge is something few people have managed to get right; it's a complicated blend of commercial and technical challenges.

To attract a critical mass of buyers and sellers, knowledge markets must be highly visible and appeal to all-comers, set and manage expectations, develop contract structures, simplify administration and contracts, agree contributions etc. If they're to *become* mainstream there has to be a place where *seekers* and *solvers* can expect find one another. There needs to be a volume of demand for knowledge and an on-tap supply of providers.

Detailed overleaf are a few examples of the many different types of knowledge markets that are emerging.

INNOCENTIVE Inc.

INNOCENTIVE's knowledge market brings together companies that post problems ('seekers') for scientists and engineers around the world to solve ('solvers'). An e-business venture by Eli Lilly and Co., INNOCENTIVE connects scientists and science-based companies online to collaborate on complex scientific challenges. It resulted from a fundamental and business critical challenge; how to resource the right skills at the right time for research and development at Eli Lilly, one of the world's largest pharmaceuticals companies. Like many scientific research industries, pharmaceutical research organizations face the constant challenge that demand for new drugs changes over time as new problems and new opportunities emerge through advances in medicine. Balancing demand by retaining employees on full-time contracts is difficult when organizations are required by market dynamics to be more agile and fleet of foot. INNOCENTIVE today involves 125,000 registered scientists worldwide who work for companies including Eli Lilly, Dow Chemical, Solvay, Janssen and many non-profit entities. The business has created a marketplace that removes the barriers of distance, specialization and organization from the sciences, facilitating global collaboration and driving scientific discovery. Seeker organizations that post their challenges on the INNOCENTIVE web site will offer registered 'solvers' financial awards for the best solutions while all identities are kept completely confidential and secure, and INNOCENTIVE manages the entire Intellectual property management process. Other organizations have attempted to adopt this same model of knowledge markets.

Cambrian House

Cambrian House shepherd the creativity of the masses towards solving problems and innovation through their crowdsourcing thought leadership and Chaordix technology platform.

> **In the first instance, crowdsourcing sites look like message boards that enable people to publish and vote on the best ideas across a crowd, but unlike traditional voting systems that are ultimately a shallow popularity contest susceptible to bias (because it's easy for groups to vote up ideas and *game the system*, crowdsourcing technology strips out bias, and mines both explicit behaviour (what people say and how they vote) and implicit behaviour (what people read and really do).**
>
> **This results in unbiased ranking of the ideas economically most-likely-to-succeed.**

Unlike many software companies that start life coding in a back-room, the team at Cambrian House developed their methods and technology through their personal experiences of growing an online crowdsourcing community. As Shelley Kuipers, CEO of Cambrian House explains:

"We started Cambrian House three years ago. We wanted to create a community to discover new businesses and technology ideas. In building the community we employed methods that have since come to be described as 'crowdsourcing'. Our community attracted 50,000+ members and resulted in over 7,000 ideas being submitted. We couldn't support all of those ideas, so we set about distilling to a few awesome ones. More than anything else we gathered 3-years of experiences. Our business is focused on leveraging our technology platform and the expertise we've gathered through our experiences of community based crowdsourcing."

Methods of capturing ideas like crowdsourcing are new to most organizations and there are adoption challenges due to the lack of understanding of the critical success factors and ultimate rewards. As Shelley Kuipers describes, "We work a lot with oil and gas companies. They don't often understand this mode of thinking. They can find it challenging to adopt unorthodox ways of engaging with customers in more involving ways through communities. There's a shortage of understanding of what's required within businesses. What leaders know is they're not looking for technology alone. They're saying, 'We have lots of technology widgets but we need knowhow to make our communities work. Even getting to that point requires strong leadership.' While there are many different technology tools out there, when considering a community-based platform, organizations require coaching on how to build the social fabric, to understand what makes people want to invest time in a community and they want providers to consider the structural issues such as acknowledging the differences between 'function A' and 'function B' and to appreciate whether people are like-minded... There are a lot of 'people issues' to consider. Our role is to be the guardian of embryonic communities to help them to form, mature and thrive."

Other companies engaged in the application of crowdsourcing technologies include *IdeaScale*, *CrowdSpirit*, *FellowForce* and *IdeaBlob*.

Approaches like crowdsourcing have proven to shorten time to market for new products, uncover methods of cut costs and find new ways to improve service levels. All of the companies engaged in the crowdsourcing genre of knowledge markets incorporate some element of voting and reward for the best ideas. As with social networking sites, achieving the critical mass of participants is the make or break issue. The focus of this technology is to source ideas and feedback from a broad community but many of these models suffer from a lack of structure around contracts and the absence of any guaranteed level of income. So while these initiatives are very interesting it's questionable whether they will dramatically influence the future of commerce.

Experts Exchange

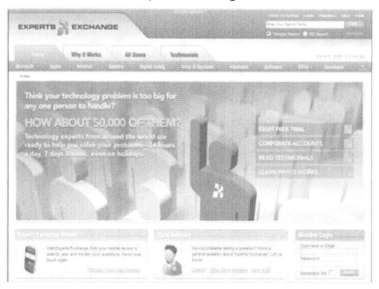

Like INNOCENTIVE, Experts Exchange is an online platform specializing in the field of IT solve technical problems. Over 251,116 expert members have collaborated to create a searchable knowledge base of over 15,951,090 postings of previously answered questions.

Enquirers ask a question and if other members elect to answer the question they are awarded points that go towards payment of their membership. The result is a self-regulating market to source knowledge from an expert community where members are encouraged to help answer problems for other members. Solutions are captured in an online knowledge bank that grows and grows to become progressively more valuable.

The performance of the knowledge market is impressive with questions normally receiving custom responses in less than 30 minutes. In operation since 1996, the knowledge bank now offers over 2 million useful answers to technology questions.

Openad.net

A slightly different market formula is promoted by *OpenAd* who operate in the creative advertising industry.

The company brings together client organizations (seekers) looking for advertising innovation and creatives (solvers). Solvers are either self-employed people or individuals who work for smaller companies that lack the brand reach to serve large advertisers. *OpenAd* describes itself as the world's first online marketplace for buying and selling advertising, marketing and design ideas accessing over 11,500 creatives in 125 countries. Clients who have already used the service include MTV, Lastminute.com, EMAP and the Make Poverty History Campaign. *OpenAd* works through heavy moderation and provides online wizards and tools to assist Buyers and Creatives in coming together and sharing concepts. For example there is a Sample Pitch wizard to help Buyers describe their requirements in sufficient detail to enable suppliers to pitch. Both Buyers and Creatives must endure a formal application process but once registered they can share access to a growing market space. Creatives from smaller organizations (or even individuals) can tap into new business opportunities that they would scarcely have had a chance to bid for. Opportunities are qualified and presented by the *OpenAd* portal. Creatives set the prices of their ideas. They can choose to use *OpenAd*'s Standard Pricing system or calculate prices themselves. Buyers can set prices for ideas submitted to pitches but if they don't want to, then the Creatives who reply to the pitch set their own.

Proz.com

Another form of market is presented by **www.proz.com**. *Proz* is a market-place that provides an international home for knowledge workers who want to exploit their language skills.

Proz focuses on providing a network for its members to find new employment and access relevant resources for their work. It doesn't operate a Seeker/Solver model but instead has a directory that puts buyers in contact with sellers.

Proz makes its revenues through membership subscriptions and therefore has to ensure it offers suitable value for the membership fee. The organization extends its services to members beyond the online market to include conferences and events, contests, training sessions, quick polls and forums. As a moderated web site, members can contact other professionals for advice when translating difficult terms. The site also displays the location of members on geospatial maps so that clients can find local people.

Recently *Proz* has added administrative tools such as online invoice creation so that members can send their own personalized invoices. *Proz* means that an entire community of language workers does not need an office or employer to earn its income.

Kluster

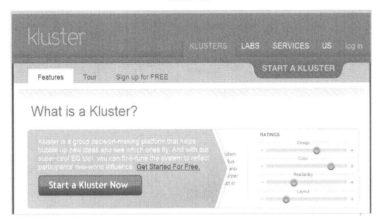

On a number of occasions while researching this book I've encountered a web-site or business model that has felt completely alien to me. Coming across Kluster was one of those experiences.

Kluster describes itself as a group decision-making platform that helps bubble up new ideas and see which ones fly. The foundation of the website is a voting platform to encourage crowd participation in creating and validating ideas. Its business model is to produce and support community-directed businesses where the revenue from these businesses is shared with the people who influence their growth. It's a novel approach that fits well into the cultural world of knowledge bohemians who like to juggle between projects.

Utility based computing provides affordable access to knowledge markets

Many software applications fail to reach their required critical mass of user adoption because they're simply too expensive.

The computer industry's traditional approach has been to charge for tools and capabilities rather than outcomes and services. The majority of applications are shrink-wrapped and users purchase licenses in advance for the right to use them. This has meant many early adopters of IT have found themselves the guinea pigs of unproven technology that later shows limited economic value. This charging approach has suited the software industry. Software designed for business can be extremely expensive to develop. Historically, when launching innovative new technologies, enterprise software vendors would focus sales efforts on the largest enterprises first to quickly achieve early-stage revenues before their innovations trickled through the market down to less affluent mid-sized and smaller companies. This meant smaller enterprises found they were constantly being forced to fit their businesses into oversized off-the-shelf 'technology clothes'. Sage, the UK software company, is one of the few notable exceptions to this rule. They successfully broke this mould and designed their software specifically for small to medium sized businesses from the outset.

'Utility computing' is a relatively new charging model. It describes a situation where buyers pay for the information services they consume – as they would for any other utility such as power and water. Gradually, utility based charging models are coming to the fore. They offer better value because potential buyers can try out services and see if they like them without facing a large upfront cost. They can also switch off services if they no longer find them useful. This approach suits the buying culture of information consumers who work on the assumption that *software platforms* should be free and they should only pay for the information services they consume, as they consume them.

Cloud computing vendors overlook the expectation of charging for the bricks and mortar of their platforms. Instead they look towards the customer value the information services their platforms can bring to information consumers. This is a long-term and high risk game with big ticket infrastructure and technology investments required upfront. For their reward, vendors expect to charge many millions of information consumers a small pay-as-you-use fee for the information services they support as they're consumed. This approach means that individuals, small businesses and corporations can equally exploit the same quality of information services – and do it affordably. A corner shop business can enjoy the same standards of performance, security and functionality that corporations 1000 times their size would struggle to afford were they to build their IT systems internally.

As far back as 2006, *Google* talking about offering a full range of services to individuals including web hosting, desktop applications (like a wordprocessor and spreadsheet), search, mapping, web-space and email for $10 a year. When they suggested this, the software industry took a gulp of air!

Instrumentation to make connections and identify opportunities

In any market place it's important that traders know where to setup their stall and buyers know where to shop. This has been a big problem for vendors trying to get knowledge markets off-the-ground. Achieving the critical mass of buyers and sellers needed to create a market has required mammoth marketing and advertising budgets to reach out to people.

But social networking in the cloudspace potentially overcomes this issue. What we are seeing on sites like *LinkedIn*, is the organic formation of communities and groups with common interests. I hear you say 'but that's nothing new, *eBay* has being doing that for years and yet their groups area has never really taken off'. True. But what makes the *LinkedIn* environment work better is that the site orchestrates notification messages to inform you that *your friend or colleague*, with whom you might share a common bond or interest, has just joined 'x' or 'y' group.

The natural response I have whenever this happens is to think 'Ah, that's interesting. Why have they joined that group?' Then what I will probably do is go and take a look at the group and see if it's for me. Now, just imagine what happens when you have situational networks springing up all over the place and you're living in an era when it's common-place to make money from participation in knowledge markets. Imagine too that you wake up every morning with a string of new messages giving you information about new opportunities from markets that you already frequent and see notifications about people you've worked with before who have just jumped into a couple of new markets.

Suddenly, we're not talking about some distant URL or web-site you've never heard of before. We're not talking *either* about you having to go through an exhaustive routine of filling out forms and working out how to navigate curious page structures before you can join a new market. What I'm describing is a fabric of social networking that assumes participation and adopts common mechanisms and tools that everyone uses every day.

The cloudspace becomes a knowledge WORKPLACE.

Money, contracts and outcomes

I don't want to make too much fuss about it because it's almost a non-issue, but any market must have an administrative and contractual framework that members understand in order for it to flow.

Knowledge markets operate just like any other marketplace.

To thrive, any market needs lots of buyers and lots of sellers and knowledge markets are no different. The big challenge is always to get parties together in the same place at the right time. Having managed this small feat it's then important that people who seek knowledge can put forward an offer and present their terms to potential contributors. Project sponsors must also be able to articulate the outcome they expect to achieve and it should be possible for knowledge contributors to explain how they can contribute towards the outcome and whether their contribution fully or partially meets objectives.

Then, there must be an easy way of paying for services.

Technology can lend a hand in all of these areas. It's no big deal. Markets don't have to be complicated. Provided that the rules are clear, and both entry and exit are relatively frictionless, a trading environment can be painlessly created.

In my experience markets work best when there's a high degree of choice and the opportunity for negotiation.

> **For a small period of time my parents used to have a haberdashery stall on a market. Many of the products they sold were clearly marked with an offer price. Other materials were charged by the meter. There was never really any formalized contract structure. They didn't ask customers to sign a document before they started trading. My parents would pay a small amount for a 'pitch'. They figured out that by going to the same market halls and taking the same pitch, passing trade would remember them and go to their stall whenever they needed anything to do with haberdashery. Why should knowledge markets be any different?**

The cloudspace will create a similarly fluid and open trading environment as the one I describe above. Traders in projects can appear and disappear as they see fit (why attend a market if you've nothing to sell?).

It's not unreasonable to expect people who use a market to pay for a 'pitch'. Neither is it unreasonable to expect that seekers and solvers will be able to find one another in a frictionless way through the social networking activities of the cloudspace. Contracts and outcomes I expect will require a light-weight hand of governance but regulations on the actions of companies are already highly regulated so I expect there won't be a need for extraordinary controls on knowledge market trade. Finally, when it comes to the final delivery of goods and payments I expect cloudspace-borne knowledge markets will adopt existing Internet mechanisms for trading goods for money and making payments (services offered by companies like *Amazon*, Ebay and PayPal spring to mind).

I don't see any of these issues resulting in huge technology challenges that haven't already been overcome somewhere on the Wibbly-Wobbly-Web. Cloud social networking will progressively form a landscape to bring buyers and sellers of knowledge together. Knowledge markets will form.

'Build it and *they will come*' as my dad would say.

IMPACT OF THE CLOUD

How will the cloudspace spread its influence across society and the business world?

History has a habit of repeating itself. The future of our society, patterns of behaviour – and of how business and communications infrastructures will in future serve society – will closely resemble a page from our past.

15

The coffee house

c.1700 (anonymous painting, The British Museum)

So far in this book I've described the rise of social networking, of *cloud* computing and the *cloudspace*; a digital cloud of social metainformation residing in a hugely scalable, always-on, affordably accessible computing platform. With its *access-to-all* ethos, *pay-as-you-consume* economics and *always-on* operational dynamics, the *cloudspace* will become a meeting place and an integral part of our society's social landscape in much the same way as the coffee houses of the 17th and 18th century were to a progressive English middle class. It will become a *'cloud coffee house'*.

The *cloud coffee house* becomes the meeting place of the 21st century world; for social networking that leads to the organic formation of groups for both business and pleasurable pursuits, and ultimately the organic formation of more institutionalized knowledge markets.

This chapter illustrates the progression of the cloudspace into the *cloud coffee house* through the story of the London coffee houses.

Origins

The rise of social networks feels new but our society has been here before. In a time before corporations, when an enterprise was anything a gentleman with money wanted to invest in, the place where these gentlemen would meet was the coffee house.

Coffee houses first appeared in London in the early 17th century and lasted as the place of social interaction and of doing business for well over a century. Their arrival occurred when England was bristling with innovation and landed gentry had bags of money swelling their pockets. For much of their day, gentlemen would sit at their favoured table in their preferred coffee house conducting their business. It's believed a Turkish immigrant called Pasqua Rosee opened the first coffee house in St. Michael's Alley, Cornhill, London in 1652. He was thought to have been brought to London by a merchant named Daniel Edwards. So the story goes, Edwards so impressed his friends with this tasty brew that he allowed his servant to open the city's first coffee house. The venture grew so successful that, within a matter of months, coffee houses sprang up throughout the city.

Social networks find an affordable home

Social networks of the 17th century found *their* home in coffee houses. They offered a relatively low cost to enter comfortable place to be for the majority of the day where the increasingly literate middle-classes could socialize. Through the economic model adopted by cloudspace providers the *cloud coffee house* is today offering similarly affordable entry costs. Like the owners of the London coffee houses, cloud computing vendors and a supporting cast of software vendors are seeking to offer new services that will appeal to *patrons* and attract others to their sites.

Unlike the social media sites of today that rely on advertising, London coffee houses charged a penny for administration. Having paid a penny, any appropriately dressed man could sip a coffee, read the newsletters of the day or enter into conversation with other patrons. From simple beginnings, London coffee houses quickly became the centre of social life.

In the digital age we have grown accustomed to paying for services. We pay up to £30 every month for mobile broadband access and a similar amount for digital television channels. We will all have to pay for the cloudspace – but it won't compare to the high premiums we have paid for shrink-wrapped software and telecoms services in the past.

Organic formation of groups and markets

The cloud coffee house will encourage the formation of federations and knowledge markets. A portfolio of information services will grow over time to serve the requirements of these new 'people networks' that will prescribe what services are needed.

In earlier chapters I mentioned that communities of 21st century digital social networks will ultimately select the most appropriate social media site that best serve the needs of their social networks. When we look at the different websites for social networking – *Facebook*, *LinkedIn*, *Xing*, *MySpace*, *Microsoft Live* etc. – we are beginning to see patronage of social networks favour the 'coffee house' that *suits* their social group and their interests. In future, will we see one of the social media platforms becoming the place to go for political commentary, and another taking the lead for students, another for members of the armed forces, another for investors in stock markets?

> This migration of patronage towards sites *chosen by groups and communities* also happened in the 17th century. London coffee houses quickly came to be identified with particular groups in society. They served as a meeting place for a particular occupation, interest group, or type of specialized activity, although patronage was somewhat determined by location. Coffee houses such as Jonathan's, Lloyd's or Garraway's, located in the area around the Royal Exchange, were, for example, the gathering places for businessmen of the city, and those such as the St. James and Cocoa-Tree, located in Westminster, were frequented by politicians. Many of the coffee houses near St. Paul's Cathedral were the choice of intellectuals and clergymen who gathered to discuss theology and philosophy.

A place for business

Business takes place where business people are located.

The cloudspace will become the place where people of the 21st century conduct their business because it's where they are.

No longer will individuals expect to commute into their offices. Under pressure from Governments to encourage flexible working, employers will support workers who want to exploit the low cost communications and knowledge sharing environment offered by the cloudspace. Workers will prefer the intimacy of their homes and communities – being close to their families – over the costly commute to corporate offices.

> **Businessmen of 17th century London found the intimate atmosphere of the London coffee houses more pleasant than the Royal Exchange or nearby taverns and soon businessmen were keeping regular hours at their preferred coffee house. By 1666, the year of the fire of London, the square mile surrounding the Exchange had the highest concentration of coffee houses in London. Irritated by the noise made by people trading stocks and shares – the 'stock-jobbers' – in 1697 the merchants had them removed from the Royal Exchange. London's Stock Exchange continued to operate from coffee houses for seventy-six years until 1773 when it was moved to quarters behind the Royal Exchange.**

Events like the enactment of flexi-working legislation, 'green' policies to reduce commuting behaviours, risk of pandemic – these are our 21st century equivalents to the 1697 eviction of the stock-jobbers; events that encourage changes in attitudes and ways of working that encourage the use of the cloudspace as the place of work.

Having grown accustomed to workers 'existing' in the cloudspace, the axis of business behaviours will shift. Organizations will start to question why they operate their own internal processes when 'good practice' is seen to exist in the cloudspace. The richness of the metainformation managed and held in the cloudspace, the vast market of creativity and expertise – these factors will make the cloudspace more informed and useful to business than internally funded resources.

Software companies will be able to grow quickly with the patronage of cloudspace communities. Their information services will become 'best of breed' through the investment resources they can tap into, and this will make corporations that use internally funded software tools quickly feel like second class citizens.

By not having to finance their IT infrastructures, software applications or full-time employees, organizations embracing the cloudspace will gain a competitive advantage through increased agility to always fit their most profitable markets.

The cloudspace will spark the creation of new *commercial structures*. New cross-industry organizational associations will form as organizations who share common objectives to deliver their 'customer value' find they can work more efficiently by sharing information and resources through the cloudspace (examples might include *health and social service organizations* working together to deliver patient care; and *utilities, their civil engineering sub-contractors and highways authorities* who must work together to maintain congestion-free transport networks.

> **Many of England's best known financial institutions grew out coffee houses. When the stock-jobbers left the Royal Exchange they invading the favoured haunts of the 'maritime crowd'. So the maritime crowd moved across to the coffee house of Edward Lloyd at 16, Lombard Street. By 1727, the business of underwriting ships and cargoes had moved from the floor of the Royal Exchange to Lloyd's coffee house. It remained until 1771 when a society was formed among the shipping underwriters who frequented Lloyd's – Lloyds of London. In the same way that 'campus culture' enabled academia, finance and innovation to come together to place *silicon valley* as the cental hub of the computer industry, the coffee house years played a huge role in establishing London as the global centre of the financial services industry. The expulsion of stock-jobbers from the Royal Exchange forced various segments of London's business community to come together and develop their own specialized institutions. The city's coffee rooms provided the social networking fabric upon which institutions were built.**

A hub for communications

Having become a regular meeting place for so many people, the cloud coffee house will create a market for informediary organizations serving the specific information needs of individuals and groups.

> In another parallel to our 21st century equivalent, an important development of London coffee houses was the emergence of a communications infrastructure. Many coffee houses functioned as reading rooms for the attending gentlemen who treated them like a home from home. The cost of newspapers and pamphlets was included in the admission charge. At this time, when the country's postal system was in its infancy and journalism hadn't found its feet, coffee houses became the centre of communications; the place where newsletters and gazettes were distributed. Any major news story, gossip, battle or political upheaval, would be posted through runners sent round the coffee houses. Bulletins announcing sales and auctions, sailings and hangings covered the notice boards providing targeted information to patrons. This newswire infrastructure diseminated the ideas that became the topics for discussion in the forum of the coffee house. Like blogs and social media sites of the 21st century, patrons would seek the opinions of peers on the propriety and efficacy of any enterprise or venture they were considering.

I expect that we will see many more advances in the harvesting of knowledge made possible by the use of *digital passports* that describe our likes and dislikes, our interests and work roles.

News services will bridge across the communities in the cloudspace offering services we're prepared to pay for. Newswires will become a hybrid of gossip, interest stories, job opportunities and advertising targeted towards specific audiences – like newspapers do today but with much more targeted content to their readership as individuals and communities of interest. Professional and industry associations are likely to play a role as sponsors for these information services which will make services more tuned (and acceptable) to the needs of business organizations; who have traditionally shunned access to externally sourced news services that attempt to breath-through their corporate fire-walls and into their offices. Expect to see the profiling of online communities in the cloudspace used more and more by information service providers to align their content to the interests of discerning online communities.

> London coffee houses became so identified with specific groups and interests that *The Tatler*, an early London newspaper, printed stories under coffee house headings. Many of the articles published in newspapers were written by the early columnists who frequented the coffee houses. Like bloggers the difference between readers and authors was hard to see. In the first newspaper published in 1709, Sir Richard Steele wrote: "All accounts of Gallantry, Pleasure, and Entertainment shall be under the Article of White's Chocolate-house; Poetry, under that of Will's Coffee house; Learning, under the title of Graecian; Foreign and Domestick News, you will have from St. James' Coffee house."

The power of patronage

Online communities grow more rapidly when notable people frequent them; people like celebrities, successful business people and thought-leading 'supreme bloggers' whose prose make content interesting. Consider the impact Barack Obama had on *Facebook* and *MySpace* during his presidential campaign, and the potential impact that teen idols can have on social networking sites when they start to engage with others. Celebrities and people of notoriety can to some extent govern the direction of content and debate. Perhaps we will see emerge social media equivalents to today's powerful media moguls like Rupert Murdoch who could bring value to members by offering their own unique perspectives on news content. This idea has its foundation in the history of coffee houses. A small number of 17th century coffee houses achieved a boost in status due to the notoriety of their patrons.

> John Dryden was 'blogger in residence' at Will's Coffee house. Dryden's commentry shaped public taste and inspired writers of prose by raising a debate on the latest poem or play. Dryden had a huge reputation and his twittering grew a huge

following. With it the reputation of Will's also grew. Some of England's most famous men of letters, including Pepys and Pope, frequented the coffee house. In addition to serious discussions on topics of literature, the 'bloggers' of Will's turned their talents to cheeky *YouTube* style libels, so visitors to Will's could be assured of great entertainment.

Similarly, Button's coffee house, also in Russell Street, Covent Garden, grew in popularity because of the patronage of writer Joseph Addison. In about 1713, he established Daniel Button as the proprietor of the coffee house and like a 'super blogger', Addison's blog featured in the pages of *The Tatler, The Spectator* and *The Guardian*. These newspapers were read widely by coffee house patrons, and provided a rich blend of topics for discussion on standards of public taste fuelled by Addison's perspectives.

Managing user behaviours

Today, sceptics of social networking sites are quick to point fingers at the poor control that sites like *YouTube* and *Facebook* have over the behaviour of their members. Pundits criticize Internet Service Providers (ISP's) for disclosing *their* personal information to public authorities in support of home defence initiatives when they do, and criticize them for withholding information on *others* when they don't. When people sign up to social networking sites they are sometimes critical of the terms they must sign up to. But Gen Y and Gen Z accept 'the deal' of losing some of their personal rights and liberties in exchange for having access to information services they would otherwise be unable to afford. When *Google* takes photographs of our streets, Gen Y and Gen Z don't make a big deal of it because they want the benefits of online maps. Users of the cloudspace accept that there is a general code-of- conduct they must sign up to.

Patrons of coffee houses agreed to conform to the posted "Rules and Orders of the Coffee House," where 'every man was an equal and none need give his place to a *finer* man'. Those caught swearing had to forfeit twelve pence, and the man who started a quarrel 'shall give each man a dish t'atone the sin' and lovers were forbidden 'in corners to mourn'.

It would be interesting to see cloudspace providers handing out on-the-spot fines for inappropriate behaviour! *YouTube* would no doubt be a very different place if members thought their images might result in a penalty fine.

Politics and government

The Barack Obama presidential campaign proved the importance of social media sites in 21st century politics.

Since his election President Obama has continued to publish his thoughts through digital media including his campaign blog site change.gov and the recently launched recovery.gov blog site aimed at delivering the highest level of transparency. To enable citizens to create their own mashup websites the administration intends to make available a portfolio of information feeds and website components that can be assembled to consume governmental information updates. The administration has stated it plans to embrace crowdsourcing to gauge feedback on the popularity of initiatives. We have yet to see politics in Europe move to embrace similar standards of transparency and engagement. When people will vote in their millions every Saturday night for their favourite artists on television shows like *Pop Idol*, it appears absurd to voters when they can't express their opinions in a similar way on key issues that affect them like taxation policy, education and trade agreements. Political parties and political systems can do more to engage citizens through digital social media.

The opportunity exists for politics to rediscover itself through the cloudspace by embracing its potential as a collaborative and engaging meeting place. For more than a decade in the UK we have seen central government attempt to engage public opinion through formalized meetings and traditional market research vehicles that attract a disproportionate number of older citizens with time on their hands who already engage in politics and all but ignore the opinions of the young.

Today, President Barack Obama's administration is floating its political commentary across practically every social networking media tool available today. I think it more likely in future that some social media sites will excel over others in their ability to carry political commentary to those people who still find politics interesting.

> The political parties of 18th century Britain, the Whigs and the Tories, had their own favoured coffee houses. The Tories frequented the Cocoa-Tree while the Whigs went to the St. James. While coffee houses were open to anyone who spent a penny it would have raised a mighty raucus were a Whig to attend the Cocoa-Tree or a Tory the St. James. In 1724 if you wanted to meet politicians you walked into a coffee house.

For centuries, politicians have held the purity of democracy in one hand and pressed the other in the face of the *man on the street*.

Political constitutions run scared of placing real decision making in the hands of 'poorly educated folk.' In the United Kingdom during the 1980's, liberal and social democratic political reformers failed to get proportional representation on the political agenda; so UK citizens today continue to vote for the unknown name of a *candidate* representing a major political party who promises if elected to represent his constituency in a manner enshrined in an election manifesto that has no legal or moral binding.

Even the founding fathers of the American Constitution were concerned about the influence the common man might have on their fledgling democracy. They designed a voting system that meant a voter chose an *Electoral College* candidate of their choice; an educated chap who could be trusted with better judgement to vote in the right way just in case the uneducated masses made really bad decisions. To this day in US national elections the electorate vote for Electoral College candidates *who vote on their behalf* and not politicians directly.

The world of politics is becoming a smaller place, particularly for politicians who will have to accept a shift of social attitudes towards more hands-on participation in decision making. This 24-hour political engagement extends beyond local and national boundaries to regional political debates that span continents. Politics is no longer a *local* issue. The people of China can touch the people of the United States through the cloudspace. When one part of the world hurts another sheds a tear.

Future generations around the world who live in democracies will come to expect, even demand, the higher levels of transparency that President Obama has introduced at every stage of the political process – elections, voting on key decisions, constituency representation and principled matters of social conscience.

With the technology available today there is no practical reason why individuals can't vote on key decisions for themselves.

Representatives of *the people* can expect a future of surgeries held online through social media sites that are always accessible so that citizens can express their opinions with political representatives directly. Crowdsourcing technologies mean that political representatives can attend debates armed with the 'will of the people' and able to feed back their progress in real-time to interested citizens. Politicians will find themselves held much more to account. The cloud coffee house exerts huge pressure on systems of political representation to become more transparent and accountable to the social consciousness of a connected global world.

Gaming and entertainment

Gaming, gambling and entertainment is as much a part of 21st century social culture today – with its PlayStations, digital streaming video and online Bingo – as it was in an era when *Whist* was the game of choice.

The cloudspace provides greater opportunities for people to engage in gaming and other forms of entertainment. Groups of individuals with common interests will find others who share their interests more easily to play games. They will be able to engage in gaming wherever they are; games that extend around the globe. The best gamers on a global stage will no doubt one day be celebrities. In-game advertising is growing already and is set to be a major industry.

Procurement of entertainment will change radically as groups of people with common interests harness their buying power to drive bargaining with providers. Already, digital entertainment companies like Sky and Virgin Media are working hard to 'package' their offerings into personalized choice selections that consumers might want to buy – sports, crime drama, history and documentaries, children's programmes etc – but imagine what happens if an international Manchester United football fan community forms in the cloud coffee house and someone comes up with the idea of negotiating a season contract for always available digital media viewing rights.

This type of demand driven negotiating is likely to change the dynamics of the entertainments market, producing a smaller number of huge international information services providers who are able to negotiate contracts with discerning groups of individuals who share a common passion.

Whilst many of the London coffee houses found favour with politicians, poets and businessmen, there were others whose speciality was to serve more hedonistic elements of London society. From the birth of the coffee houses until well into the nineteenth century, gambling was the national pasttime among leisured classes; many of whom lost fortunes at the tables. Coffee houses served as a meeting place. Among the most famous was White's Chocolate House. White's was increasingly identified with gaming for the most fashionable gentlemen of the city. It was destroyed in April 1773 by fire but was rebuilt and later reopened as White's Club; one of the first London coffee houses to become a club. The transformation of White's to a private club marked the beginning of other such transformations; a factor in the declining numbers of coffee houses at the end of the eighteenth century. In an effort to maintain an ever more exclusive clientèle, famous coffee houses following the lead of White's and began allowing admission only through membership. It wasn't long before coffee was replaced on menus by more robust alternatives, but these establishments (White's, St. James, Boodles, Grahams and the Cocoa-Tree) continued in their new form at the centre of regency society for many more years.

A place for extremists and revolutionaries

The cloudspace gives politicians something new to worry about; the birth of a global social consciousness; a global meeting place that no single government can control.

The London coffee house provided a place for society to meet; even people with criminal intentions. They were used by highwaymen and robbers as a place to meet and gather intelligence. Outlaws would discuss worthy objects for their efforts; perhaps the *gentleman by the window* in *White's* who had done well at cards, or *the elderly man leaving Lloyd's* who had done well at business this last year. Even for the lawless, the coffee house was the centre of life.

Governments will dread the possibility of the cloudspace becoming a melting pot of extremism, carrying uncensored social commentary to billions of people; words with the potential to spark revolution.

> In its early years, Jonathan's coffee house was known more for its revolutionaries. Catholic patrons were suspected of plotting to overthrow protestantism in the 1641 'popish scare' and for sparking the 1696 assassination plot again William III. Patrons were also accused of being central to the events of the 'South Seas Bubble day' of 1719-1720, an early forerunner to the Wall Street crash, when intense speculation in *The South Sea Company's* shares brought ruin to many private investors.

Like Jonathan's coffee house, the cloud coffee house will provide a meeting place for extremists and revolutionaries as well as businessmen and gamers. Even though society is made up of a mix of good and bad people, society ultimately benefits from having a soapbox where people can say what they think. John F Kennedy said, 'those who make peaceful revolution impossible will make violent revolution inevitable'.

In the beginning the rules and orders of the cloudspace will probably be shaped by the acceptable behavioural standards of patrons and the cloudspace providers themselves.

Will people always be free to say what they think in the cloud coffee house? Will it lead to the final battle for freedom of speech, or will governments act together to create international regulation to silence the man in the street in the interests of society?

I hope not. Thomas Jefferson said that *every generation* needs a new revolution. And not all revolutions turn out to be a bad thing.

Society has been known to celebrate revolutions when they are no longer seen as dangerous and their events lead to social reform and a rebalancing of power (think of the Boston tea party, the storming of the Bastille et al).

Death of a social networking institution

Coffee houses began to disappear from the streets of London in the early 19th century. Their demise came partly because the British East India Company was importing tea which overtook coffee as the nation's most popular brew, but it was also because a significant number of more regimented institutional structures appeared.

Coffee houses brought London society together. They provided a place for trade, innovation, entrepreneurialism, journalism, gaming and political debate to prosper. From this 'lightly organized' social melting pot, people were able to meet others who shared their interests. The coffee houses became branded locations that signposted where individuals could go to find like-minded people when they wanted to trade, debate, or gamble.

These informal, self-governing, social structures were to become more efficient, more formalized:

Buyers and sellers could find one another and markets were made.

Soon loosely coupled communities of interest turned into groups.

Groups and federations turned into institutions.

For those people engaged in business it was institutions like Lloyd's of London and the London Stock Exchange that rose up, for those whose passions were more oriented towards gaming and society it was the new gentlemen's clubs, many of which still exist in London to this day.

> **London coffee houses played an important role in every aspect of London society in the late 17th and early 18th century (the 'Augustan Age'). With more time on their hands the growing, better educated middle class developed a taste for education and for news. Journalism boomed and a proliferation of newspapers and periodicals soon became popular. Poets and writers of the age won economic freedom from their patrons to become independent professionals – the life workers of the era! The middle class were writing and reading and the identity of the readers and the authors of knowledge became blurred. It was the *participative age* of the 19th century.**

Will the *cloud coffee house* sustain for decades to come? It's very difficult to see through to the other side of the cloudspace and imagine anything that could displace the digital meeting place of the world. I expect that the cloudspace will spawn a number of its very own coffee houses and these too will grow to become more formalized as their predecessors ultimately did to create new markets for knowledge and maybe even the next *Lloyd's* or the *London Stock Exchange*.

For the sake of our children, we might hope the cloudspace installs a new level of federation that overlooks differences in religion and culture to deliver the global compassion and cooperation that is vital to the survival of the planet. A global social consciousness may be what's needed to act as the ultimate regulator over the unrelenting addiction to power of politicians and of greed found in pockets of the human race.

The collaborative environment of the cloud coffee house might just be the thing to spark human ingenuity and surface the solutions our race needs to escape the looming environmental disaster our planet faces.

The social instincts of humans to meet and share ideas might one day be the single thing that saves our race from its own self destruction.

A FIFTY-FOLD INCREASE IN KNOWLEDGE WORKING

The cloudspace will deliver a fifty-fold increase in knowledge work and knowledge worker productivity to redefine organizational design

A more fluid organizational structure will become commonplace.

Innovation will be shared.

Organizations will manage federations and their outcomes, not projects.

To achieve more flexibility and harness discrete resources, organizations will require technologies and operating protocols that formalize contributions and outcomes of work teams and knowledge markets.

As Peter Drucker suggests, the productivity of knowledge work and knowledge working will become a key economic differential.[45]

16

The cloud and the new post-modern era

Considered by many to be the founding father of today's management consulting industry, Peter Drucker had a talent for picturing the events that were happening in his time and anticipating what might happen in the very near and next era. He made the following statement in his book called 'Landmarks of tomorrow' that he wrote in 1959 which to all intents and purposes to me sounded like a challenge to our generation, so for as long as I can remember I've always called it Druckers' challenge:

> **"The most important, and indeed the truly unique, contribution of management in the 20th century was the fifty-fold increase in the productivity of the MANUAL WORKER in manufacturing. The most important contribution management needs to make in the 21st century is similarly to increase the productivity of KNOWLEDGE WORK and the KNOWLEDGE WORKER."** [45]

He made this observation in 1959 – before *The Internet,* Broadband, the digital age, the march of individualism, of *MSN, Facebook, MySpace,* social networks and cloud computing. I get the impression Peter Drucker wasn't the sort of person who made life easy for people by offering up answers to their business problems; he wanted people to invest themselves into a problem. And so it is in this case. For the business leaders and management consultants of the 21st century business world, Drucker suggested that:

[45] "...the new organizing capacity has by-passed the age-old fixed positions of individualism and collectivism alike, and is giving a new vision of the nature of individual and of society and of the bond between them."

Druckers' vision would today be described as *individualism*, the *participative age* and *social networking* – the new connections ('bonds' as Drucker puts it) that result from this new relationship between people, society and the world of business. That's what this book is about.

Drucker did pretty well to spot this from things going on in 1959. Sometimes events do take a little while longer than we think they will to take hold. Perhaps Drucker was noticing the imbalance in the treatment of the workforce by employers of the 1950's and recognized that it was a sustainable means of achieving productivity. Who knows.

When Drucker originally came up with his vision of the key challenge facing 21st century business world he spoke in terms of a report on the new 'post-modern' world, stating that the society of his age had "imperceptibly moved out of the Modern Age and into a new, as yet nameless, era."

Through Druckers' eyes the world of business was deluding itself that it was (in golfing parlance) *hitting the green with every shot* when in fact business leaders were seeing their world through a distorted 'old world view' that might have made sense a few years before but didn't any more. Drucker's big message to business leaders was in essence 'wake up and get real if you don't want to feel the pain of the decisions you're thinking about making'.

With a sense of déjà vu, the world of business finds itself at similar cross-roads; a new post-modern age. The cloudspace changes things – and for the first time in our history the instruments are in place to answer the challenge that Peter Drucker set our generations.

All that is needed to make it happen is the faith and courage of a few people to believe in the possibilities of the ultimate vision.

The cloudspace has the potential to produce a fifty-fold increase in the productivity of the knowledge worker in knowledge work. In this chapter I explain the *'mechanics of how'* through a series of guiding principles.

THE POST-MODERN PRINCIPLES OF KNOWLEDGE WORKING

Here I summarize the events that must happen in order for organizations to achieve a fifty-fold increase in *knowledge work* and *knowledge worker* productivity

1. The cloudspace creates a market for knowledge working
2. The cloudspace becomes a place to work
3. A social office supports social processes
4. A new component of organizational design emerges to formalize gated social networks in the enterprise
5. Virtual teams share project outcomes
6. Organizations learn to value wisdom and harness their social networks to promote talent
7. On-demand resourcing re-models the enterprise
8. Organizations re-define knowledge worker productivity

THE CLOUDSPACE CREATES A MARKET FOR KNOWLEDGE WORKING (PRINCIPLE 1)

A new knowledge workforce

In the *participative age* people will assert their opinions and personality on others because *they* want to matter. This very different attitude and perspective on life carries into the workplace. It means that workers are no longer prepared to kowtow to employers and behave like dutiful sheep. Sure, they want to work – and they want to commit themselves to their employers – but not in the form of a career marriage with one employer.

Their *commitment* is measured in outcomes and rewards but far less through an emotional attachment to the longevity of the organization that pays for their services.

Workers no longer 'pledge allegiance to the flag of the corporation' every morning. This shift in attitudes means that young people expect to spend no more than 2.5 years of their life with any single employer.

Instead they become life-workers at the earliest opportunity, or choose not to engage in a career at all but instead continue a campus life-style as knowledge bohemians.

Flattening of labour markets

Transitions to the workforce will create new labour market dynamics.

> **According to Koncept Analytics, the total worldwide recruitment market is valued at over US$420 billion and has grown at an average 12% per annum during the last decade.[46] Being the informediary between employers and job seekers today is a profitable business. Unless you've ever had the challenge of trying to recruit staff you'd wonder how it's possible people can make so much money from putting two people in the same room. I know from bitter experience that recruiting people today is costly. As an employer you know perfectly well that there are hundreds of people out there who are perfectly suited to the vacancy you've got but trying to get a message through to them isn't easy.**

The cloudspace makes job markets work differently.

Visit www.xing.com and you will see a thriving jobs section concealed within a business social networking site that lists a series of opportunities for people to get involved with.

Many individuals, the growing masses of *life workers* and *knowledge bohemians,* will look to the cloudspace to find new work opportunities. Thousands of specialized knowledge workers will be seeking problems to solve as independent professionals.

As corporations start to question why they employ people on full-time contracts when highly specialist and experienced casual workers are available to work as needed (a resource that can be switched on and off like a tap), employment of knowledge worker professionals will just grow and grow. The cloudspace will give employers more choice and a vast pool of potential workers at their beck and call. The sheer numbers of project based work opportunities made available through the cloudspace will be vast compared to what we're used to.

The geographic location of workers will matter less. Proportionately more workers will be available to employers because they can work efficiently whilst still being remote. They will be able to meet online, capture and submit data, share ideas and research online. Digital passports and published ego-walls will make it easier for individuals to broadcast their specialist skills to prospective employers and this will make it easier for technology to lend a hand to connect seekers to solvers; thereby flattening the employment market. If you're an employer, you won't just wait for CV's to pop through the door, you will be able to post a requirement for a role on the cloudspace for skilled people to reply to.

With the flattening of the job market, the granularity of skills made available will increase in depth. Rather than designers, employers will be able to specify precisely what *sort* of designer they seek.

Employers will use the richer insights on individuals and their track record of projects, their ego-walls, knowledge of their contributions to previous projects etc. to assess credentials.

New forms of *job opportunity informediaries* will emerge to provide vetting and sifting services, and offer advice on which respondents to projects represent the best cultural fit and capacity to deliver – for both the project team and organization.

New knowledge federations

The global war for talent and high costs of research and development will cause businesses to explore how they can tap into new, more economic knowledge resources. Employers will seek to explore new possibilities to resource their in-house projects.

Seeking to capture their share of the economic growth potential of knowledge markets, governments will invest in telecommunications infrastructures, install social welfare structures to create flexicurity for independent knowledge worker professionals and finance new forms of federations that encourage the proliferation of knowledge work in their territories. Corporations will aim to lower their research and development and operating costs by employing knowledge workers from outside of their organizations. This will cause a growth in the demand for knowledge markets.

Cross industry federations will emerge to underpin the cloudspace and fill in areas where *virtual* collaborative systems underperform. Organizations like Young Inventors International (YII), with sponsorship from academia and industry, will grow in importance as companies seek to harness the *lower-cost innovation* provided by individual knowledge bohemians and small independent research and development teams.

An always on and affordable computing environment

The cloud will provide an always-on, affordable computing platform to source useful information services that free individuals and groups from the limitations of shrink-wrapped applications and computing platforms that are unable to scale. Individuals will have the ability to interact painlessly with colleagues and connect to the knowledge markets that offer them economic freedom to escape the life-style constraints of full-time employment.

Information services for the individual

Growth in the popularity of Web 2.0 software services will democratize IT and give individuals, entrepreneurs and small organizations access to the same powerful data processing and visualization tools that global corporations use. Cloud computing will speed up the pace of innovation in the software industry by offering smaller companies the ability to rapidly scale their ideas and reach a global market of information consumers who are more prepared to try out new innovations.

Thriving social networks

The user experience of the cloudspace will be like visiting your very own gentlemen's club. All of the other people you know will be there, accessible to you from this portal. The groups and associations that you have, friends and family, work projects etc. will be organized *by you*, to suit your individual needs as an individual.

Use of social networking vocabulary (like the people-grid language) will enable you to quickly create new, secured, project team and group portal sites that bridge across information sources.

The cloudspace will support a number of different social networking media choices and business social networking sites like *Xing* and *LinkedIn* will alert users to interest group activities and new contacts.

Infinite federations and opportunities

Knowledge workers will create their own networks and federations through evolution of the cloudspace and over time form more institutionalized structures (in the same way the London coffee houses produced Lloyd's, the London Stock Exchange and the Private Clubs).

Talent becomes more accessible

Access to ideas and innovation through the cloudspace will be more accessible turning the role of the internal employees of corporations into project 'specifiers'. Use of internal research and development resources will decline.

THE CLOUD BECOMES PLACE TO WORK (PRINCIPLE 2)

In the 21st century, the cloudspace becomes the place where individuals will work and play in equal measure.

It will act as a digital informediary that interrogates the digital passports of individuals and serves up relevant content. It will facilitate introductions between individuals and their communities because it will know where *everyone fits* in the cloudspace. Unlike a mobile phone or laptop, it won't be something workers switch on at the start their working day and turn off at night – because it will always be on.

The cloudspace never goes to sleep.

Thankfully, people won't be putting on their *digital overcoats* and leaping into their screens any day soon to become *virtual people*. The cloudspace is *what* workers will see on their *browser*. They won't need a computer as such because the processing of data and its presentation, will be delivered by the cloud computing platform. With a simple browser as their tool, whether it's on a portable device, mobile phone or embedded in a coffee table, knowledge workers will have the means to access the people, information systems and other facilities they need to do their work.

Virtual social networking will result in *real-world* networking. This behaviour will encourage entrepreneurs to invest in new types of meeting places that will grow in local communities; new forms of 'coffee houses' that blend refreshments and a nice place to meet with desk hoteling and business centre functions.

A blurring of work and home life

Where people physically work is already changing and the cloudspace will increase the pace of change. Many knowledge workers today commute to work, complete a full day at their desk – taking 20-minutes for a snack for lunch probably while they're at their keyboards – and then commute back home to a concrete dormitory in the suburbs. Still, there are marked differences between the phases of the day.

An increasing number of people this century will see distinctions in the phases of their day *blur*. People are more likely to be working on *a variety* of income generating projects and blend these activities with picking up Henry from the schoolyard and snatching a ready-meal. The contributions people get paid for will be measured by the project portals of the cloudspace that will set the outcomes individuals are tasked to achieve. People who are paid for what they *produce* rather than the time they spend producing it will fix their own clocking-off times. The work-day pattern adjusts to a more diffused work and home life.

Through the always online cloudspace the *knowledge workers of our society* who can function remotely – people who perform their role on the telephone, write things, mark papers, design, solve computer problems, consultants, advisors, inventors – will have the opportunity to attend whichever federated office centre is closest to them or work from home. 'Hoteling' (Providing members of staff with office desk space on an as-needed basis through a booking system on similar grounds to hotel rooms) will become increasingly popular and it's likely that we will see physical office space providers and hoteliers start to target communities of users in the cloudspace to sell their hospitality spaces and bring the virtual meeting room back down to ground level.

> **According to research conducted by the CoreNet Global Research Center 10-25% of workstations (in the US and some European countries) are expected to be part of workspace environments by 2010.** [47]

A SOCIAL OFFICE SUPPORTS SOCIAL PROCESSES (PRINCIPLE 3)

A social office workplace

Adoption of social media technologies in the office, such as ego-walls and micro-blogging will change the culture of communications towards conversational dialogue. Documents and email will be demoted in their importance. The meta-information acquired through social office workplace will be exploited to create a rich profile of each individual's topic interests. This insight will be used to automate the creation of tag clouds employed to organize content and filter news and business opportunities. Information, news and documents will be trawled as needed from the World Wide Web to the desk of the knowledge worker.

Remote working that supports social processes

The quality of web collaboration tools will improve to enable virtual workers to overcome the social process barriers that have dogged traditional online collaboration tools. New methods of conversational technologies will emerge that change meeting behaviours.

A NEW COMPONENT OF ORGANIZATIONAL DESIGN EMERGES TO FORMALIZE GATED SOCIAL NETWORKS IN THE ENTERPRISE (PRINCIPLE 4)

The adoption of vocabulary and tools to describe social networks (e.g. like the people-grid language) will cause relationship ties to *come onto the radar* of senior managers of organizations.

The simplified formation of 'gated' networks will make it possible for organizations to harness independent knowledge workers to deliver projects with tangible and measurable outcomes.

Confidence in the robustness and value of gated social networks to deliver business critical projects will encourage their increased propensity of use by large organizations as an alternative to in-house teams.

VIRTUAL TEAMS SHARE PROJECT OUTCOMES (PRINCIPLE 5)

Virtual teams will share project outcomes

Organizations will adopt new organizational design methods and emerging workplace technologies that orient the reward schemes of situational 'gated' networks towards shared outcomes.

> One of the most difficult challenges for businesses over the coming years will be to solve the problem of how to get people who work more virtually on projects to share responsibility for delivering outcomes. Research conducted by Eric Trist of the Tavistock Institute for Social Research that I quote on page 73 point to the fact that people who are

targeted to make very specific contributions to a project will normally only deliver the minimum expected. What's needed is a group of people who emotionally share in achieving the outcome.

I still think we're on a sharp learning curve when it comes to understanding how to get virtual collaboration working properly but we're now on the right track and technologies like video conferencing and micro-blogging tools that engender more informal conversation are a big part of breaking down distance barriers.

In my first book 'Agilization' I spend a chapter talking about the importance of alignment in business; the need for individuals to understand why their contribution matters and how it contributes to the strategic outcomes of businesses. In my opinion, poor alignment between people activities and strategic outcomes is the biggest cause of inefficiencies in the enterprise. So many people sit at their desks working hard on things that just don't really matter. And it's not because they don't want to contribute to the success of their employers, they just don't know how.

In the next decade, expect to see creative solutions to this challenge.

ORGANIZATIONS LEARN TO VALUE WISDOM AND HARNESS THEIR SOCIAL NETWORKS TO PROMOTE TALENT (PRINCIPLE 6)

The importance of measuring leadership and wisdom

The performance of work teams and productivity of knowledge worker will only achieve substantial improvements if account is taken for the social processes that operate within collaborating teams.

The role of people who are excellent communicators and astute decision makers – the generals and corporals – remains critical to operational effectiveness. Often, these are the people in an organization who have developed the greatest wisdom. But it would be a huge assumption to believe that it's always the case. Wisdom is important to organizations because making the right decision in business often has much to do with the context of the decision and understanding potential consequences – learnt through experience.

> Consider the decision made by Winston Churchill in June 1940 to sink the main battle group of the French Fleet as it lay in the Port of Oran in Turkey. Churchill had received assurances from the French Admiral Darlan that the French Fleet would never fall into Axis hands. Yet Churchill knew that had the Germans been successful in capturing the fleet, Great Britain would never have sustained its fight for freedom and democracy. Without this context I'm sure history would have portayed Churchill as a war criminal, not a hero.

Recording the performance of situational networks

When projects run their course and situational networks are closing down I expect it will fall on the owner of the network to perform a 'closing down' routine to account for the contributions made by individuals, the performance of the project, the usefulness of the information systems and data sources, and the effectiveness of the team.

Knowledge relating to the activities that occurred on a previous projects – the pools of information resources that were tapped, the paper trails that followed, the people spoken to, relationships forged – all of these attributes will be held 'in memory' in the cloudspace so that experiences can be re-channelled and insights re-used.

These qualities will no doubt start to influence the social capital measurement of each of us. Others will start to consider us for roles, not simply based on the names of big companies we used to work for, but richer data captured from the networks we've participated in and what other colleagues said about our performance on previous project; our level of wisdom and leadership.

ON DEMAND RESOURCING RE-MODELS THE ENTERPRISE (PRINCIPLE 7)

Confidence in the supply of quality knowledge skills through an open market, and of the effectiveness of *gated situational networks* as a manageable and measurable component of organizational design, will lead to more organizations adopting on demand resourcing model as a matter of course (i.e. having identified a new situation or project, network owners will advertise for roles through the cloudspace and recruit talent as required). The impact of this approach will be to reduce the proportion of employees retained on full-time contracts. As enterprises cut the numbers of people employed on full-time contracts, this will further swell the ranks of knowledge professionals available for employment via the cloudspace which will increase confidence of organizations in the availability of resources.

When a point of critical mass emerges in this transformation it will be uneconomic to resource innovation by any other means.

ORGANIZATIONS RE-DEFINE KNOWLEDGE WORKER PRODUCTIVITY (PRINCIPLE 8)

Of the principles I summarize in this section (all of which are important), the most influential on the productivity of knowledge workers and knowledge work are:

1. The discovery of the real organogram of the enterprise

2. A knowledge market that flattens the labour market, brings a critical mass of 'seekers' and 'solvers' together

3. The invention of situational gated network vocabulary that individuals can use to describe their networks and formalize their regulation

4. The invention of a social office workplace that binds a virtual workforce together, captures metainformation on individuals and their activities within the situational network

Discovery of the real organogram of the enterprise

To make sense of the human-centric organization demands that metainformation is captured – about the people, their relationships, skills and habits – and can then be visually interpreted in ways that managers can understand. The former requires voluntary effort from workers; it is a by-product of their social networking activities from which they must derive a reward, while the latter requires highly sophisticated technology and significant data processing capacity.

Only when the way the relationships and social processes of the organization are understood can they be effectively orchestrated.

A knowledge market that flattens the labour market, brings a critical mass of 'seekers' and 'solvers' together

Business leaders will need to be confident that sufficient volume and quality of knowledge worker 'raw material' is available in the cloudspace before on demand resourcing will be considered as an organizational design mechanism. In equal measure they will have to have confidence in the operational effectiveness and productivity of situational networks to deliver measurable business outcomes if these resources are to be seen to be a really useful alternative to internally sourced employees.

The invention of situational 'gated' networks (and vocabulary) that individuals can use to describe their networks and formalize their regulation

The huge influence made by situational 'gated' networks as a component of organizational design lies in their ability to formalize the role and activities of a group of individuals charged with solving a problem.

A situational network offers an organizational design element that exists only for as long as it's needed; it can be understood by the participants in the network and the organization; its actions can be aligned to strategic goals; its people can be rewarded by the shared achievement of outcomes.

Through the adoption of situational networks, organizations can measure the contributions of individuals that make up the network, and also the outcomes of the network itself – even when the contributors are independent knowledge workers. The fact that networks are clearly owned (and intellectual property can be controlled) means that organizations can trust their use.

The invention of a social office workplace that binds a virtual workforce together, captures metainformation on individuals and their activities within the situational network

In most organizations today the productivity of knowledge workers is not properly measured. (How do you measure the productivity of someone who uses a spreadsheet?). In today's organization, the email server is the heart of organizational behaviour and performance: It alone holds the rich metainformation on relationship ties, key interest topics, use of content, effectiveness of communications, wisdom. And yet it is off-limits to the organization. Without it, no affordable mechanism exists to monitor the productivity of the knowledge workforce.

With its ability to unobtrusively gather metainformation on the day-to-day activities, communications and performance outcomes of knowledge workers, the social office workspace becomes the mechanism that makes knowledge worker productivity accountable. Adoption of better information tools for communication collaboration, analysis and visualization will remove the need for workers to spend much of their day repurposing documents, filing others, writing emails and responding to emails making them ever more unproductive.

Unlike email, the social office workspace is not off-limits to the enterprise. Managers and leaders of organizations have an opportunity to acquire a real-world view of how the human-centric processes of their enterprise operate. Having come into the light, astute business leaders will know how to harness the full talents of their real organograms and release the 50% of additional knowledge worker productivity that lies immediately within their reach.

If organizational leaders are courageous and able to put in place these measures they will have made their most important, and indeed the truly unique, contribution to the 21st century world of business.

THE CLOUD AND SOCIETY

The cloudspace will protect the human race from power, corruption and greed.

The voice of the common man (and woman) will travel further and have more influence.

Individuals will have the opportunity and powers to do bigger things for humanity.

No single government will be able to control the human consciousness of the cloudspace.

Business will exploit and operate within the cloudspace but on terms dictated by individuals and the self-organizing federations they form.

17

The birth right of new generations

Druckers' hidden challenge

Peter Drucker saw the business world through a wide lens that captured in its vista the society that framed it. This made his commentary so much more poignant and insightful. In the *same* visionary document Drucker authored in 1959 to introduce his challenge to 21st century business champions, a second less obvious challenge was directed to leaders of the Free World. Under the title 'The Work to Be Done' Drucker states:

> "This is the crisis of the Free World – a crisis of vision and understanding of leadership and realism. We are in mortal danger not because we are weak but because we misdirect our strength to fight over yesterday's battles and to repeat yesterday's slogans." [45]

What was Drucker getting at? The essence of his thoughts are captured in a single paragraph where he states:

> "In a time of change and challenge, new vision and new danger, new frontiers and permanent crisis, suffering and achievement, in a time of overlap such as ours, the individual is both all-powerless and all-powerful. He is powerless, however exalted his station, if he believes that he can impose his will, that he can command the tides of history. He is all-powerful, no matter how lowly, if he knows himself to be responsible."

Even if it wasn't his intention to do so, Drucker is describing the essence of *individualism*, the *participative age* – and *the cloudspace.*

Our children show us the way

Not knowing *another way,* and yet to be shackled by the covenants of previous generations or rule of law, the children of the world are brought together through the World Wide Web. They feel the sense of freedom; freedom to communicate with anyone they want to; interact with others at any time of the day; feel grown up because others on the social net trust them. Through these interactions they assert their personality. They volunteer information about themselves on their ego-walls and slowly a picture builds of this massing social network – the people, their interests, likes and dislikes, their relationships. These thoughts and opinions can't be influenced or contained by politicians, or misrepresented by journalists because there are too many of them. It creates a global social consciousness.

The largest computer the world has ever seen

The *cloud* provides the perfect place – the only place with sufficient capacity – to hold the social consciousness of 7 billion people.

The conscience of the World

The cloudspace grows to form a virtual cloud that surrounds our world that we can't touch or see, made up of bits and bytes.

This virtuous circle becomes a focal point for the news, experiences and emotions of the world, shared at the speed of light. It is a public place; a private space; a place of greed, envy, arrogance, pity, humour and empathy. Yet it joins every human being in the world together.

> **The philanthropist Beth Canter who writes Beth's Blog suggests the 'social web' will become a platform for people to do good things and change the world; the social web will grow the web a heart. A world that is used to seeing little things happen for love and big things happen for money is moving to a place where people will self organize and come together to fight hunger or build a school, or raise money to build water wells – doing bigger things for love, smaller things for money.** [48]

The ultimate executor of the will of the people

The cloudspace becomes the melting pot of consciousness that can protect human-kind from the sanctions of power hungry governments and heartless global corporations.

Though, through thirst for power and greed they will try, leaders of governments and global corporations are unable to silence or manipulate the cloudspace ("He is powerless, however exalted his station, if he believes that he can impose his will, that he can command the tides of history").

There is no centre to the cloudspace. It has no command and control as it is a federation of opinion where each individual can pass commentary on the successes and failures of the powerful and dominate the health of corporations and nations ("he is all-powerful, no matter how lowly, if he knows himself to be responsible").

> **Emergence is a relatively new science that tries to explain complex patterns and behaviours that occur in nature like how a flock of birds or school of fish seem to move as one. Emergence is an order we might not expect to see. Usually when there's order we expect to see a leader or a general to create it; we can easily make sense of top down command and control systems where one brain controls the functions of the entire group. It's what we're used to; how we expect things to be. But what about a flock of birds or a shoal of fish? In these examples no clever fish or bird is making decisions on behalf of every other bird of fish. What we see happening is a group that has order but where decisions are shared. Scientists recognize that in the case of a shoal of fish, the fish seem to portray common decision making processes: They never move to far away from the fish they're next to, and when they see danger they change direction. A small set of engrained instructions and behaviours order the behaviours of the group.** [49]

Emergence is an important principle in social networking and the cloudspace. As scientists discover more about emergence it will no doubt help us to better understand human behaviours in the cloudspace. The implication is that as people interact, 'norms of acceptability and behaviour' emerge. This explains how humans come to create standards of acceptable behaviour in society. So, in future when the decisions made by corporations and governments clearly fall outside of what is considered acceptable to society, they are likely to be quickly brought into line by the response of people in the cloudspace.

The permanent crisis of the 21st century

The cloudspace changes every aspect of how the people of the world will *think* and *act*.

People, once distanced by race, geography, faith and belief will come together in the *cloud coffee house* where each can express his ideas and challenge the opinions and deeds of others with impunity, save the sanction of their peers.

It won't take long before this global community reaches its *new frontier* and feels the pain of a dying planet. The people of the world will realize that its over-population is the planets' *permanent crisis*.

Governments will understand that the only way to solve this problem, and others that emerge from global markets, is to seek *global solutions* through cooperation – *cooperation* on a global scale.

Though they are identified today as the co-conspirators of the planet's destruction, we will ultimately have to depend on the ability of global corporations to harness cooperation from around the world under the dominating gaze of the cloudspace. Only global corporations have global command and control systems that can make things happen on a global scale quickly. This is why it is so important that consumers insist that the corporations of the world honour their duty of care for the planet and the sustainability of communities.

The ultimate decision

Those who volunteer to bear on their shoulders the weight of responsibility for humanities' *permanent crisis* will share the load with millions of others and, through their wisdom, they will find consensus on the most difficult of decisions.

Is there a saviour in the wings?

The cloudspace amplifies.

Soon, the smallest ripple of innovation grows in strength exponentially to create a gigantic creative wave of inspiration. One person's contribution feeds another, and another.

At the moment when all hope seems lost, maybe another child somewhere will enter the *cloud coffee house* to realize their moment has come to step into the light and show what *they* can do.

That child – your child or my child perhaps – could light the spark that finds an answer to the problem that millions of people are thinking about, sharing, trying to solve.

And perhaps the Free World will go on, and be forever free.

Transcript excerpts from President John F. Kennedy's Inaugural speech

"The world is very different now.

For man holds in his mortal hands the power to abolish all forms of human poverty and all forms of human life.

And yet the same revolutionary beliefs for which our forebears fought are still at issue around the globe--the belief that the rights of man come not from the generosity of the state but from the hand of God.

We daren't forget today that we are the heirs of that first revolution. Let the word go forth from this time and place, to friend and foe alike, that the torch has been passed to a new generation --born in this century.

To those old allies whose cultural and spiritual origins we share, we pledge the loyalty of faithful friends. United there is little we cannot do in a host of cooperative ventures. Divided there is little we can do--for we daren't meet a powerful challenge at odds and split asunder."

THE FUTURESCAPE

What will it be like to live 10 years from now?

In this final chapter I describe the human experience of what it will be like to live in a world surrounded by the cloudspace through a day in the life of an *imaginary* individual, *Harry Wainwright*.

18

A day in the life of Harry Wainwright

Harry Wainwright is not unlike many of his fellow workers in 2019. He's married to Jessica and has an 8-year old son, Jason. Harry works for *Tadema* as a customer advocate. *Tadema* is a home technologies provider and support the needs of home life communities that have emerged over the past decade.

Tadema is a *tribal brand*. That means the organizations represents networks of buyers and harnesses their buying power to negotiate service agreements with suppliers. Harry spends most of his week making sure that his customers have everything they need, negotiating with suppliers on behalf of the home life groups he supports and the rest of the time seeding new products and giving feedback to suppliers. He much prefers his role today as an advocate to the *bad old days* when he was a sales person trying to push products at consumers. Harry likes to say that yesterday he represented *a single supplier to many customers* and today he represents *each of his customers to many suppliers*.

Harry likes his job because he's able to balance work and home life the way he wants to. He has a home office and can do pretty much everything he needs to perform his job role from his home workstation. His video conferencing system is installed in his conferencing room and connects to the wireless Internet service provided by his local authority. (Free-to-air wireless has been available in his area since 2010 when regional government finally succumbed to pressure from the community to support economic growth and its duty of care responsibilities. Now the local authority provides *at risk* sections of society – such as the elderly, frail, disabled and children in social care – with personal alert buttons that, when actioned, will instantly identify an individual *and their location* using wireless Internet).

Like most of his colleagues (that work for other companies), Harry prefers to work 2 or 3 days a week from the bu*siness-hub* in his village because it is the centre of village work-day activity. In the mornings when he can, Harry goes to exercise at the leisure centre annexed to the *business-hub* building. He enjoys a discount for being a *business-hub* member. Another good reason for working at the *business-hub* is the sense of belonging to a work community even though everybody has a different employer. He says the 5-minute bike ride from his house is worth it because the coffee tastes so much better from the café there.

Business-hubs have been around for a few years now. With government funding the development of village life regeneration, the Post Office took a serious interest in developing its capability as a service centre provider and the concept became popular very quickly. Having 24-hour access to post office facilities is useful. The *business-hub* means Harry and Jessica don't have to work from home all day or use their own utilities. Like a hotel, they simply book a desk at the *business-hub* for the time-slots when they want them.

On the first Monday of every month, Harry takes a car from the *allegroViaggio, a* travel services company, to go into the city to meet with his regional manager. Harry doesn't own a car himself any more, mainly because he likes to have the flexibility to choose a different style of car from *allegroVia* to suit his needs. He takes a sports car on weekends if he wants to take Jessica somewhere nice and an estate or 4x4 when he takes Jessica and James camping. *allegroViaggio* take care of the servicing issues around the car. If he doesn't use his full quota of *allegroViaggio* vouchers, Harry saves them for holidays. Last month they paid for first class rail tickets to visit their second home in Italy.

Harry loves his job because he likes helping people. His role as an 'advocate' means that he is the *mediator* for around 100 customers, all of whom he knows very well by now. His customers are community presidents of what *Tadema* describes as home life groups that develop properties and provide their tenants with a community to belong to. Everyone in the community is connected by an active social network. Paying a small amount to a home life group each month means Harry and Jessica can enjoy their home life without having the burdens of procurement, managing bill payments and having the worry of having to repair things should they go wrong. Home life groups have become major purchasers of home computer systems, air conditioning systems and integrated office products. Harry's one hundred plus customers cascade his products and services to over 180,000 households.

All of Harry's customers have access to *Tadema's* online dialogue system which means that they can 'serve-themselves' for most things using their online conversation technology, or on their mobile phone that provides touch-pad selection of services including order processing, asset maintenance and service administration. At any point in the process, customers can engage Harry via his mobile or workspace. Harry always knows who's online because their images appear on his mobile and workspace. When customers struggle to find what they're looking for or need help, Harry's dialogue system normally alerts him. It shows him the decision tree customers have walked through and the choices they've made – so he can quickly understand what it is they're trying to do.

One of the great benefits of *Tadema's* buying power is that suppliers will offer new product and service innovations for Harry to find placements for as part of their new product seeding programmes. This is good for suppliers because they get to find out more about community preferences. It also results in some early orders. For Harry, it means that his house is full of new electronics products that he normally gets to try out first. Jessica says he's a gadget man but Harry believes having a passion for his products is why his customers value his opinion so much!

Jessica leads a very different life to Harry, but they both mix their lifestyle between the home, *business-hub* and the occasional trip into the City. Jessica is a bit of a celebrity in the village because she started the Girls Are Best (GAB) club when she was ten years old. Today, there are GAB girls all over the world. Jessica started GAB by creating some cool games, story-boards and autographs on her social networks and got into visiting *PlayAreaNetworks* (these are wireless environments that support multi-player collaborative gaming and chat activities) whenever she had a free moment. What started as a bit of fun soon mushroomed as people started joining into Jessica's GAB brand. Within 2-years Jessica had more than 11,000 members.

This got the attention of suppliers that were looking for young tween networks like GAB. By the time Jessica had planned to go to University, GAB was transacting €23,000 a month in music products, tickets, books, clothes and adventure days. Jessica considered for a while passing on her presidency but, she's always enjoyed the role so much that she decided to be a full time president. Her mum naturally, thought she was crazy.

Jessica spends most of her time negotiating deals for GAB with advocates like Harry. Harry has said to Jessica many times it's lucky he specialises in home products because Jessica makes a scary customer! When James was born, Jessica again considered handing over the Presidency but the advocacy services that GAB offered were already quite good and when Jessica was expecting she knew that many of the other GAB girls were probably also facing the life changing experience of childbirth so she put more effort in providing a broader portfolio of advocacy services for young mums! One of the nappy manufacturers offered GAB free baby start packs including a high chair and car seat when they placed their first 6 months order. Another offered discounted water and energy units for 12 months.

On Mondays, Harry's day starts at 8.40am when he takes James to school. James's school has not changed too much in 10 years but Information Technology has become more embedded into coursework. No longer is IT seen as a separate subject. James has his lesson plans, personal tests and classroom activities are recorded and shared with Harry and Jessica via the cloudspace.

Harry is at his desk by 9.00am. He has a series of calls from customers and then at 11.30am he meets the home entertainment's head of a home group products supplier. They discuss a new series of wireless speakers that can also be used as vases. Much of the conversation is focused around which networks are more like to want to buy them and why. Harry agrees to take a dozen samples for user centred design studies. At 12.30pm it's time for lunch. Harry visits the business-hub retail centre and chooses Thai chicken sandwiches. As usual, he calls Jessica to find out if she's around for lunch but his social office workspace tells him that she's still on a conference call. He leaves a message to the effect that he's stopping for lunch now if she ever gets out of the home conference room!

Harry meets John Hammond and Vicky Davies, both of whom live on the same road and have children around James's age. John is a director of the Water Company NWD Plc and spends most of his time negotiating contracts with home groups and business hubs. Vicky is a customer advocate for his local authority.

Vicky co-ordinates the interactive voting systems and focus groups for the region and spends much of her time working with the presidents of local community social networks and consumer clubs to encourage them to give more time to local interest topics. One of Vicky's big successes is the village eBay market which has provided excellent opportunities for local small businesses to take advantage of the buying power of the surrounding villages. Vicky explained this morning she'd been formalizing the new voting systems that would be deployed on the cloudspace in the next few months. In the bad old days of local government in the UK, elected council members used to adopt a paternalistic view of what mattered to their customers and this led to many poor decisions on local priorities. The turnout for the central government elections of 2012 was so poor that legislation was put forward to devolve more power to regional and parish councils, and adopt new voting systems using modern technology to re-engage individuals, particularly the young. Recently, Harry has voted on every subject to do with the Environmental Services of the region. That's because Harry subscribes to the Environment Services voting group. It takes Harry less than 20-minutes a month to vote on issues that relate to his region.

After lunch, Harry joins a conference call himself. This time it is with the president of HouseWise; the largest home life group. HouseWise has experienced a number of problems with Hanso Corp's home entertainment computers and Hanso Corp have been reluctant to agree to take the products back. Harry wanted to get the full details of the complaints which have already been submitted in the dialogue management system. The main theme of complaints is associated with power interruptions and Hanso Corp is arguing that these have been caused by operator error. It's a rare occasion that issues like this one get escalated to this point given that most manufacturers are reluctant to risk losing a tribal brand. After discussing the issue with the customer advocates at HouseWise, Harry gets a clearer picture of the issues and makes the dreaded call to Hanso Corp. As it turns out Hanso are more co-operative once Harry explains the future order pipeline for their portfolio of products and Hanso agrees to upgrade the problematic home computers.

At 4pm, Harry leaves to collect James.

When he gets home Jessica is still online and they're out of food.

Harry consults *Genis*, his home computer to get a recommendation for the evening meal. *Genis* analyzes Harry's user profile and activities for the week. Then it puts forward menu recommendations based on what's in the larder! Harry doesn't find the options too interesting. He fancies an Indian dish so Harry asks *Genis* to make some suggestions. Having selected something quite delicious, Harry goes online and places a food order from *their favourite home shopping retailer* together with a collection of other groceries.

Harry sits with James to work on his homework. Shortly after Harry sits down Jessica materializes from the conference room looking jaded.

Jessica explains that she's finding a number of members migrating away from *GAB* towards *Empire* which is another *tribal brand* started (part-funded in fact) by a home shopping company in the 2000's and has become one of the largest brands in Europe. Empire has been clever at working with partners offering affinity products to provide maturing girls with the types of offers that they're interested in. Their holiday offers have been particularly popular given that they provide AirMiles for practically every purchase. Once members 'buy-in' to Empire, very few actually leave.

Jessica is debating whether it's time to keep her focus towards the mid-to-late 20's community she's grown up with, or whether she simply accepts that some of the community members are going to outgrow her GAB brand. To her utter frustration, the big issue is that she isn't 21 anymore. Her concern is that she might lose her affinity to the issues that matter most to her community. Harry comforts her saying that she's become a very good president and with so many young minds around her, it's unlikely the community will go stale. Harry reminds Jessica that as a couple they have memberships with both Empire and GAB; so it doesn't mean that just because her members join Empire, that they'll jump ship from GAB.

At 7pm the food arrives and Harry calls upstairs for James to come down from his room to eat. James has got engrossed with a community game on his Exterminator personal console. He's pressing buttons feverishly to help the England relay team (himself, Andrew next door and his cousin Philip in Kent) beat the French and Americans. He explains that if he stops now he'll let the other boys down because they'll lose. Harry switches channels on the monitor in the kitchen just to make sure James is telling the truth and then shouts up to James that he has to come off once the race has finished.

As usual they eat outside. The weather has been hot for 8-months (nothing unusual about that nowadays in England) and it's quite pleasant by this time in the evening. Normally they would have the water fountain on but Harry and Jessica have been working hard to keep down the water units they're consuming this month. The home group they buy from has negotiated a contract with the single source utility provider offering them an upgrade to their dishwasher if they manage to save a further 40 utility units this month. More reason for Harry to work from the business hub!

Harry watches the evening news on the digital television sunk into his patio table. There is a news report about growing concerns over the power of large manufacturers in the supply-chain and the risk of oligopolies forming (i.e. a market in which control over the supply of a commodity is in the hands of a small number of producers and each one can influence prices and affect competition). Jessica watches over Harry's shoulder and comments that whilst there are far fewer mid-sized manufacturing businesses than there used to be; there are many small vendors happy to provide more personalised products and services.

Another report announces the long-awaited round of trade talks between a delegation from the Economic Union and the Chinese Minister of Commerce to discuss European concerns over rocketing consumer product prices. At one time the products manufactured in China were cheaper due to lower labour costs but now, with the absence of a European manufacturing capability, European economies have seen prices rise dramatically on items such as footwear, clothing, electrical goods and toys. Some politicians and industrialists believe that China is operating an oligopoly with some of its Eastern hemisphere counterparts which is creating an uncompetitive marketing for products in Western economies that have become so dependent on China's manufacturing base. Social networks have been quick to pick up on this. There have been over 3 billion posts on the subject in just a few weeks. The consumer pressure has reached a level of intensity that the Chinese government has been forced to come to the negotiating table.

Jessica is pre-occupied with her plans for tomorrow. She's taking another half day, given that she only normally works the standard 30 hour week. Tomorrow she's promised to take James to the interactive zoo. Each of the animals has a 'Mote' (an electronic low-band radio sensor and microprocessor) connected to their collar that transmits a profile to the personal console of passing visitors telling them everything about the animal and its origins. The zoo is running a promotion with James's favourite cereal manufacturer to provide a digital scrap-book of animals. James is desperate to complete his scrap-book now that he's got all of the pages. He's never eaten so much cereal!

Harry finishes the day with a cup of cocoa gratefully received from Jessica and reads his personalized daily newspaper that brings together all of the news stories he's interested in. He reads that England have lost again at Football.

Some things perhaps will never change.

19

Final thoughts

The Green Door

The child had lived in a small dark house all of his life. It was all that he knew. His father had said, "Do whatever you like, go wherever you want to, but whatever you do, never open the green door. There's something in there. It's not safe."

The boy grew up in the house, passed the green door for many years, always keeping his distance until one day, consumed by curiosity, he steadied himself, and he opened it.

And his eyes fell upon...

...A beautiful blue panorama punctuated by puffs of white, pierced by soft rays of light. It lit the textured expanses of green that framed the snaking estuary as it led to its infinity on the horizon. Beauty everywhere he looked.

My brother told me this joke when we were growing up about a boy who never attempted to leave the house he grew up in, convinced that the *green door* would let out a gruesome creature, when in fact it was the only doorway to the outside world that he'd never seen. We all have *green doors* formed by what we believe to be true.

At the start of the 21st century we find ourselves moving towards a different society and business world brought about by the digital age, a new way of life that few can comprehend. We see the emergence of web communities, new ways of meeting people, new ways to originate and share knowledge, the breakdown of institutional control, the emerging power of the individual, new types of consumer-led markets, the migration of global manufacturing eastwards, the increased mobility and economic independence of workers leading to radical changes in working patterns and worker behaviours, scarcity of resources and the inevitable bleed through consequences of a century of 'throw-away' consumerism and 'profit before conscience' capitalism.

All these ingredients are shaping to a brave new world. Welcome to the *participative society* of the digital age powered by social networks. We're all going to be a part of it whether we like it or not.

I hope you have found this journey through the futurescape of our participative society interesting.

With the emergence of the digital cloudspace future generations will enjoy a new freedom of expression and the opportunity to build a truly global consciousness. For the first time, we can connect to people around the world who share our passions. We can relate to people who speak different languages, in different places, different cultures and religions. We're all humans and it seems we've taken until now to realize it.

I've always held a profound belief that one individual can make a difference. With social networking media we are, as individuals, more able than ever before to assert our individual creativity and inventiveness to make a positive difference on those around us.

Through this opportunity we've been given, humankind can evolve a better society. The challenge for our generation, and future generations is to *envision* what that better society should be and make it happen.

Like our ancestors, we face extinction.

Can the cloudspace help us to fight for our own survival? Through crowdsourcing and knowledge networks, can we find solutions to the life-threatening challenges of climate change, over population, impact of asteroids and killer diseases? In the words of Barack Obama 'yes we can'. But we must recognize the dangers society faces.

Let's just remind ourselves where we are:

Scientists now believe it's entirely possible that our planet is likely to increase its temperate by 5 degrees in the next 100 years which won't kill the planet necessary – it's a living organism – but it won't do humankind any good. Much of the planet we know today will be so cold or so hot it will uninhabitable.

We have a world population edging up to 7 billion and scientists estimate what's left of the planet after climate change will only offer resources to support a tiny proportion of that figure.

Those of us fortunate to live in the western world can anticipate a life expectancy of almost 100 years so long as we manage to dodge pandemics and the occasional natural catastrophe. We live in comfort while the rest of the world suffers. Every year more than 4 million people die from lower respiratory diseases, 3 million from AIDS, between 1 and 5 million from Malaria, 2.2 million from Diarrhoea and over 2 million from

Tuberculosis. These statistics don't add up. Somehow they have to.

Who will be the individuals to solve these global challenges?

Let's be positive.

The human race has survived much through the years through its ingenuity, from the ability of people to work together and its tenacious desire to survive. Hopefully we've not lost our survival spirit.

Business can itself be a positive influence on the society. We don't need to partition our lives into a 'work' box and a 'social' box. If we take the examples of ethical business models as a positive way forward, then business leaders can contribute to the solutions that will make our small world work better.

Thank you for reading Cloud Coffee House.

About the author

Ian Tomlin is a management consultant and marketing strategist.

In 2002 he founded NDMC with Nick Lawrie whose portfolio of clients includes public and private sector organizations.

His first business book 'Agilization' describes how corporations can regenerate their competitiveness by developing an ability to always fit their most profitable markets.

In 2009, NDMC released Encanvas software born of the principles presented in *Cloud Coffee House*.

Acknowledgements

I dedicate this book to my Mother-in-Law, Marg, who sadly passed away while I was writing it. Sleep well.

I'd like to say a big thanks to my publisher Nick Dale Harris and his company Management Books 2000 for publishing my business books *Agilization* and *Cloud Coffee House* and in doing so helping me to achieve a life goal.

I also want to thank the brilliant people at NDMC who have allowed me more time off to work on this book and for continuing to be a huge source of ideas to write about.

Finally, big thanks to my family, particularly my long suffering *book widow* and wife Karen for supporting me through long periods of absence from the family living room while I've hidden myself away to first research and then write this series of books in the last six years. Without Karen and my children to support me most of my dreams would never have come true.

Contributors

I thank the following people for allowing me to interview them and gain valuable insights into social networking and cloudspace technologies.

Anne Swift, CEO and founder of Young Inventors International (YII) and a serial entrepreneur who has significant know-how in the area of forming supportive communities for knowledge bohemians.

Alanna Lawrie, CEO and founder of textUhome.com and arguably one of the UK's brightest business talents having held senior marketing positions for MBNA bank and Barclays bank funded start-up YOUatwork.com.

Dr. Alpheus Bingham, founder and Chairman of INNOCENTIVE Inc. and thought leader on knowledge markets.

Dr. Martin Vasey, previously Ernst and Young Knowledge Director for the Power and Energy sector.

Henry Dotterer, CEO and founder of www.proz.com, the world's leading online community for translation professionals (one of the largest discipline specific communities of life-workers).

Jamison Roof, technology lead for User Centric Design of PA Consulting Global Systems Integration and Solutions Group.

Nick Dodds, founder and CEO of the workplace design consultancy Creative Workplace and a thought leader on how to make physical workspaces encourage workforce productivity.

Shelley Kuipers and **Sarah Blue** of Cambrian House, specialists in crowdsourcing and harnessing the ideas and innovations of unstructured groups of individuals to produce new value to organizations.

References

1   Frigyes Karinthy (1887-1938) 1929. "Everything is different". A writer who
     became an overnight sensation in Hungary. This, his forty-sixth book,
     actually flopped but then social scientists found a little short-story entitled
     "Lánceszemek," or "Chains" that led to a global debate on what eventually
     became known as 'the six degrees of separation'.

2   In 1967, American sociologist, Stanley Milgram, devised a new way to test
     the theory, which he called "the small-world problem". Milgrams'
     experiment was to ask people to pass a letter only to others they knew by
     name. The aim was to get the same letter to a named person they did not
     know living in another city. Later he coined the phrase "six degrees of
     separation" to describe his theory.

3   Mark Zuckerberg is an American computer programmer and entrepreneur
     who, as a Harvard student, created online social media website Facebook.
     http://en.wikipedia.org/wiki/Mark_Zuckerberg

4   comScore research report. July 31, 2007. "Social Networking Goes Global".
     study on the expansion of social networking across the globe.

5   Pew Internet & American Life Project. 2006. "Home Broadband Adoption
     2006". Study into levels of Internet adoption.

6   Heather Havenstein, Computer world. October 2008. "Obama still
     dominates in Web 2.0 world, Internet searches". An article that explored
     public web behaviours during the 2008 Presidential Campaign.

7   Barnes, J. A. 1954. "Class and Committees in a Norwegian Island Parish",
     Human Relations. J. A. Barnes started using the term systematically to
     denote patterns of ties that cut across the concepts traditionally used by
     the public and social scientists: bounded groups (e.g., tribes, families) and
     social categories (e.g., gender, ethnicity).

8   Granovetter, M. (1973). "The Strength of Weak Ties", American Journal of
     Sociology, Vol. 78, Issue 6, May 1973, pp. 1360-1380. Mark Granovetter is
     an American sociologist who has created some of the most influential
     theories in modern sociology since the 1970s.

9   Anatol Rapoport Professor Emeritus of Psychology, University of Toronto, University of Michigan Press. 1961. Rapoport wrote a series of papers on social networking in the 1960's and '70's.

10   Robert Putnam. 1995. "Bowling Alone: America's Declining Social Capital".

11   WikiWikiWeb was the first wiki application ever written. It was developed in 1994 by Ward Cunningham.

12   'How Top Bloggers Earn Money' Business Week. May 2008. An article describing successful blog sites and the success drivers behind them.

13   Internet News. Jan 2009. "Stephen Fry reaches 50,000 Twitter followers". http://www.techradar.com/news/internet/stephen-fry-reaches-50-000-twitter-followers-513501

14   ChildWise Monitor Report 2008/2009. http://www.childwise.co.uk/childwise-monitor-survey.asp

15   Facebook site statistics as at March 27th 2009.

16   Mike Booth's 'Somegrebloke' is an animated character that regularly features on *YouTube*. http://www.somegreybloke.com/

17   Microsoft Windows Live Spaces site statistics as at March 27th 2009.

18   Heli Hyvönen, University of Helsinki, 2008 "THE STRENGTH OF NATIVE TIES: SOCIAL NETWORKS OF FINNISH IMMIGRANTS IN ESTONIA".

19   George Orwell was an English author whose work is marked by a profound consciousness of social injustice. His novel "Nineteen Eighty-Four" was published in 1949. The novel follows the life of a civil servant named Winston Smith, a seemingly insignificant man who is assigned the task of perpetuating the regime's propaganda by falsifying records and political literature. He grows disillusioned with his meager existence and so begins a rebellion against the system that leads to his arrest and torture.

20   Robert Atkinson and Scott Andes. November 18, 2008 "The 2008 State New Economy Index: Benchmarking Economic Transformation in the States" (www.itif.org)

21   Gartner Dataquest survey. July 2005. Global forecast for mobile phones.

22   Xing site statistics March 29th 2009.

23   FORTUNE Magazine article. January 2009. "The new Valley Girls". Profiles a social network of high profile business women of Silicon Valley who use social media to sustain their professional and social network.

24   eMarketer. 2007. 'Social Network Marketing: Ad Spending and Usage' Market Research Report.

25   Joseph Boyett & Jimmie Boyett. 1998. "The Guru Guide".

26   Daniel Farey-Jones, Brand Republic 25-Sep-06, "Online shows influence over consumer buying decisions"

27   Universal McCann survey October 2008 titled "When did we start trusting strangers?" Survey on the influence of social networking behaviours on consumer buying behaviours.

28   Policy document submitted by Mr. Johan Hauknes, Norway. "OECD Business and Industry Policy Forum" 28 September 1999.

29   Cathy Benko   and   Anne Weisberg.   May/June 2008.   "MASS   CAREER CUSTOMIZATION™: A NEW MODEL FOR HOW CAREERS ARE BUILT"

30   Nasscom report on the India outsourcing market for McKinsey & Co. May 2005.

31   In 2003 the Government published a Green Paper called "Every Child Matters". This was published alongside the formal response to the report into the death of Victoria Climbié, the young girl who was horrifically abused and tortured, and eventually killed by her great aunt and the man with whom they lived. http://www.dcsf.gov.uk/everychildmatters/

32   Personnel Today article on BT survey into young professional attitudes towards corporate social responsibility. 24th March 2009. "Corporate social responsibility is more important than salary when choosing a job".

33   Businessworld article on the rise of Alter-preneurs, June 2009 titled "Meet the Alterpreneur".
      http://www.businessworld.in/index.php/Meet-the-Alterpreneur.html

34   Yellow Pages survey "Calling all business mums" 19 December 2006.

35   Business Hacks David Goldenberg. August 11th, 2008 "Obama's Productivity Advice".

36   European Commission. "Employment in Europe 2006"

37   http://www.theworkfoundation.com/difference/e4wlb/businessbenefits.aspx

38   The Economist, A Special Report (October 7-13, 2006) "The Search for Talent: Why it's Getting Harder to Find".

39   IDC Report on cloud computing 2009 -2013. A survey of IT executives, CIOs, and other business leaders.

40   Business Week article by Stephen Baker. 13th December 2007. "Google and the Wisdom of Clouds"

41   White paper written by Luba Cherbakov, IBM. 2007. "Changing the corporate IT development model: Tapping the power of grassroots computing" on ReadWriteWeb by Josh Catone, May 2008. www.readwriteweb.com/archives/forrester_enterprise_mashups.php

42   Economist Intelligence Unit survey, January 2007 and subsequent report by Forrester Research published in article "Enterprise mashups to hit $700 million by 2013"

43   J.L. Moreno. 1988. Book titled "The Essential Moreno: Writings on Psychodrama, Group Method, and Spontaneity".

44   BERR Independent Review of Flexible Working. Imelda Walsh. May 2008."Flexible Working: A review of how to extend the right to request flexible working to parents of older children".

45   Peter Drucker. 1959. "The Landmarks of Tomorrow. A Report on the New 'Post-Modern' World". Management guru Peter Drucker was the first man to describe the impact of knowledge working and workers. He also identified that knowledge workers have many activities beyond their core task which take up time and remove concentration, thereby impacting productivity and that knowledge workers require to have the capacity to manage themselves.

46   Koncept Analytics, Global Recruitment Market Report: 2009 Edition, Published: 2009/03

47   Groshan Fabiola's blog titled "Hoteling Software and Facility Scheduling" dated 6th April 2009 that publishes details od the often referenced CoreNet Global Research Center research. CoreNet Global is the world's leading professional association for corporate real estate and workplace executives serving leading multinational companies from the Fortune and Global 1000.

48   Beth Canter presentation published on authorSTREAM June 2008 titled "How the social web can help charities". Beth is the author of Beth's Blog: How Nonprofits Can Use Social Media (http://beth.typepad.com), one of the longest running and most popular blogs for nonprofits.

49   *YouTube* published this *theinquisitor* video article describing of the science of emergence "Emergence – Complexity from Simplicity, Order from Chaos" published December 2007 with comments from John Holland Santa Fe Institute.
      http://www.youtube.com/watch?v=gdQgoNitl1g&eurl=http%3A%2F%2Fwww w%2Enetworkweaver%2Eblogspot%2Ecom%2F&feature=player embedded

Other useful reference materials:

Matthew Guthridge, Asmus B. Komm and Emily Lawson. January 2008. "Making talent a strategic priority".

"Plateau Accelerates International Expansions," Business Wire, October 17th 2007).

THE CONSUMERIST. Article by Chris Walters. Feb 15th 2009. 'Facebook's New Terms of Service: "We can do anything we want with your content. Forever."'

The Economic and Social Research Council (ESRC). June 30th 2007. ESRC Fact Sheet 'Knowledge Economy in the UK'.

European Commission. Employment and Social Affairs-Knowledge Society. March 2000. 'Strategic goal for 2010 set for Europe at the Lisbon European Council'. http://ec.europa.eu/employment_social/knowledge_society/index_en.htm

Eurofound, the European Foundation for the Improvement of Living and Working Conditions. 'Fourth European Working Conditions Survey (EWCS)'. Published in 2005 (Provided data for the first ever report on Europe's 'knowledge workers').

Rosalyn Harper and Maryanne Kelly. Office for National Statistics. December 2003. 'Measuring Social Capital in the United Kingdom'. http://www.statistics.gov.uk/socialcapital/downloads/harmonisation.pdf.

"The Impact of Social Media on Purchasing behaviour". Online Testing eXchange for DEI Worldwide (2008). Survey on the influence of social networking behaviours on consumer buying behaviours.

Website links for organizations included in this book:

Amazon. http://aws.amazon.com/
Cambrian House. http://www.cambrianhouse.com/
Encanvas. http://www.encanvas.com
Facebook. http://www.facebook.com
Flickr. http://www.flickr.com
Friendfeed. http://www.Friendfeed.com
Google App Engine. The URL for Google's App Engine developer website. http://code.google.com/appengine/
IBM. The URL for IBM's Cloud Computing information website. http://www.ibm.com/cloud/ The URL for IBM's Cloud Computing developer website. http://www.ibm.com/developerworks/spaces/cloud
INNOCENTIVE. The URL for INNOCENTIVE, arguably the market leader in 'seeker-solver' knowledge-markets. http://www.innocentive.com/
Kluster. http://www.kluster.com/buy/tour
LinkedIn. http://www.linkedIn.com
Microsoft Azure. The URL for Microsoft's Azure Services Platform website. http://www.microsoft.com/azure/default.mspx
Microsoft Windows Live Spaces (MSN). http://www.msn.com
MySpace. http://www.myspace.com
Plaxo. http://www.plaxo.com
Proz. The URL for Proz.com, the online community for language professionals. http://www.proz.com/
Twiistup. http://www.Twiistup.com
Twittervision. http://www.twittervision.com
Xing. http://www.xing.com
YouTube. http://www.YouTube.com

Glossary

Agilization

My first book that contains everything business leaders need to know about how to engineer organizations to always fit their most profitable markets. (25, 26, 34)

Azure Services Portal

Microsoft's cloud computing platform. (145)

Barack Obama

President of the United States and enthusiastic adopter of social media technologies to deliver transparency of information to the US public. (15, 16, 103, 215, 217, 218)

Blogger (Blogging)

A term used to describe people who blog – i.e. create a website for the purpose of giving their opinions on a key interest topic (7, 14, 15, 31-33, 232, 234, 241)

Business Mashup

Software that knowledge workers can use by themselves to serve up the information they need to mashup existing and new sources of data with re-usable building blocks. Examples include Encanvas, Coghead, JackBe, Microsoft Popfly, Serena Business Mashups, Kapow and IBM WebSphere sMash. These applications offer organizations a way to rapidly adapt to changing business needs.

Chain Links

An article (and idea) introduced by Hungarian writer Frigyes Karinthy in 1929 describing how in future the world would become a smaller place and people would be better connected. It is thought to have sparked scientific enquiries that led to the 'six degrees of separation' theory. (13)

Click-trail	A click-trail describes the path of 'clicks' an individual takes as they browse the Web. (45)
Cloud, the	A metaphor for cloud computing suggesting consumers can access information services *from anywhere*, at any time. (4, 137)
Cloudspace, the	A metaphor for an aggregation of metainformation describing relationship ties of every person on the planet connected to 'the cloud'. (4, 73)
Cloud Coffee House	Another way of seeing the cloudspace as a virtual place where people of the world can meet 'virtually' for business and pleasure pursuits. (4,209)
Crowdsourcing	Describes the act of taking a job traditionally performed by a designated agent – usually and employee and outsourcing it to an undefined, generally large group of people in the form of an open call. Examples include *Mob4Hire*, *IdeaScale*, *CrowdSpirit*, *FellowForce* and *IdeaBlob* and *Cambrian House*. (120, 123, 178, 187, 198, 199)
Deep emotional support	The idea that people rely on a support network of (strong and weak) relationship ties to gain the confidence and ability to achieve life goals. (12, 18, 23, 64, 117)
Digital age, the	The era of digital data communications ushered in by the World Wide Web.
Economic pathway	A value chain that spans an industry. (86)
Ego-centric	A process that places 'you' the individual at its heart. (42, 43, 62, 174, 176, 178, 189)
Ego-lens	Is a concept I introduce to explain how individuals shape their perspective of the outside world and how they look upon it based on a perspective that builds over time. (41)
Egonomics	A term I created to describe the economic value of social capital in creating wealth. (62)
Ego-wall	Digital canvas used on social media sites to enable individuals to publish information about themselves. (12, 37, 41, 42, 124, 131, 136, 177, 178, 229, 232 241)
Experts Exchange	An online platform specializing in the field of IT to solve problems. An example of a knowledge market. (200)

Facebook	The world's most successful social media site. (7, 14, 15, 16, 17, 19, 22, 30, 35, 36, **37**, 38, 40, 42, 45, 49, 57, 60-67, 85, 109, 117, 119, 122, 125, 131, 133, 135, 150, 163, 188, 211, 215, 216, 225)
Flickr	Social media site designed to enable people to share their images. (36, **37**, 48, 63, 64)
Generation X	('Gen X') Refer to a generational cohort of children born after the baby boom of the late 1950's/early 1960's in Great Britain; generally taken to include children born between 1964 onwards to the early 1980's. (8, 21, 35, 225, 226)
Generation Y	('Gen Y') The generation after 'Gen X'. Its members are often referred to as 'Millennials'. There are no precise dates for when Gen Y begins and ends. Most commentators use dates from mid 1980s to early 1990s (21, 33, 34, 42, 43, 56, 82, 111-126, 179, 183, 216)
Generation Z	('Gen-Z') The generation that follows 'Gen Y', these are children of the Gen X who have grown up with the Internet (Generationi or **iGeneration**), born between the mid-1990s and through the 2000s. (8, 34, 35, 82, 179, 183, 216, 240)
Google	The world's most successful search engine company; so popular that the modern vernacular to describe searching for content on the internet is '*googling*.' (39, 43, 45, 49, 50, 66, 84, 138, 139, 146, 148, 204, 216)
Google App Engine	An applications design and deployment platform that empowers developers to easily build, maintain and scale applications using *Google*'s cloud infrastructure. (146)
Google Latitude	One of the first examples of location-aware applications platforms for mobiles. (46, 47)
Googlemaps	A popular geo-spatial mapping information service offered by Google and free to use for consumer applications (the 'catch' is Google charges advertisers and publishes their ads to people who visit *Googlemaps* online) It is a good example of the information services to come. (50,113, 141, 146)
Google Reader	A desktop *Really Simple Syndication* (RSS) reader used to read 'RSS feeds' – a form of digital communication

	often employed to distribute blogs and news-feeds across the internet. (31)
Google Wave	One of the first examples of conversation technology aimed at displacing peer-to-peer business email communications with client-server based conversation. (180, 181)
Grid computing	A means to applying large numbers of systems to a single problem. (141)
ICT	Short-hand term for Information and Communications Technology used in business. (71, 101)
Individualism	How individuals choose to assert their personality on their life-course, life-style and buying decisions on others using the Internet as the main vehicle for communications (7, 29, 34, 225, 226, 241)
Information Services	Software that manages the creation and servicing of information gathered from disparate sources within and beyond the enterprise to serve information consumers. (155)
Informediary	A person or computing process that distils the information that matters most to recipients from a mass of data. (186, 214, 228, 231)
Internet browser	Software technology used to access the Internet. Examples include *Microsoft® Internet Explorer, Google® Chrome, Firefox, Opera, Mozilla.* (50, 176)
Life workers	Individuals who find the demands of employment move beyond its rewards and as the result individuals choose to become self employed contractors serving organizations with their specialist knowledge skills. (50, 176)
Knowledge bohemians	Well educated children of Gen Y who are turning their backs on full-time employment and instead become contracted knowledge workers able to earn a living by balancing a range of different projects as part of their a free-wheeling 'alternative' lifestyle. (112, **113**)
Knowledge economy	A term – popularized by the father of management consulting Peter Drucker – used to describe an economy that produce economic benefits from the use and application of knowledge. (70-73, 75,79, 92, 150)

Knowledge management | A term commonly used to describe processes and technologies adopted by organization to harvest knowledge. (42, 150, 155, 160, 184, 188, 224-238)

Knowledge market | A place where knowledge, normally in the form of Intellectual Property, is bought and sold. (87, 133, 162, 189, 195-207, 209)

Knowledge work | A term to describe people valued for their ability to interpret and apply information within a specific subject area. Key industries where knowledge work might exist include healthcare, academia, financial services, computing, writers, publishers, science, research, design etc. (9, 56, 72, 79, 91, 93-110, 111-132, 150-155, 224-238)

Knowledge worker | Somebody who partakes in 'knowledge work'. (9, 56, 70-79, 89, 93-110, 111-132, 150, 165, 224-238)

LinkedIn | The most successful business social networking site. (7, 23, 58, **59**, 60-63, 104-105, 188, 205, 230)

Metaconcepts | Concepts that have other concepts associated with them. (40-55)

MSN | (Also called 'MSN Windows Live Spaces') One of the most successful social media sites. (29, 30, 35, 36, 39, 50, 60, 150, 179, 225,

MySpace | Social media site. (16, 22, 29, 35-38, 57, 59, 62, 64, 133, 135, 150, 215, 225)

Node | Nodes are the individual actors within social networks. (40)

OpenAd | A knowledge market serving the advertising industry. (201)

Organogram | A diagrammatical illustration of the hierarchical structure of an organization made up of names and titles in boxes connected by lines. It's a very crude way of understanding organizational design. (163-166, 172, 236, 238)

Participative age | Describes a generation of children (Generation Y) that feels disengaged by society's traditional emotional support mechanisms including family and community. As the result, they participate in social networks to seek emotional support relationships online causing the identity of the users and the creators of

	knowledge to become blurred. (14, 25, 28, 41, 42, 81, 131, 222, 226, 227, 241)
People-grid	A vocabulary used to describe social network structures. (189-192)
Peter Drucker	Peter Drucker is recognized as being the father of today's management consulting industry. In 1959 he wrote a book called 'Landmarks of Tomorrow' that introduced many of the concepts carried in this book including *knowledge workers, knowledge working* and *knowledge-based economy*. (9, 196, 224, 225, 226, 240, 241)
Photosynth	Software from Microsoft® that gathers together photographic images to create 360 degree views exampling the possibilities of where social media technologies are going.
Plaxo	Business social networking site. (23, 58, **59-60**)
Podcasting	Podcasts are a means of disseminating previously recorded sound files that people can download to their portable media player so they can listen to them later. (32)
Proz.com	A market-place that provides an international home for knowledge workers who want to exploit their knowledge skills. (202)
Relationship ties	A term used to describe emotional social ties that exist between individuals (9, 19, 36, 105, 118, 125, 131, 170-179)
RSS feeds	Really Simple Syndication (RSS) feeds are a method of distributing news stories and blog feeds across the Internet. To read RSS feeds recipients require an *RSS reader* like *Google Reader.*
Situational networks	A gated (closed) social network structure employed in business to achieve a specific outcome, normally in response to a new situation. (188, 189, 193)
Six degrees of separation	A theory that suggests 'If a person is one step away from each person they know and two steps away from each person who is known by one of the people they know, then everyone is on average six "steps" away from each person on Earth.' (13)

Skype	A Voice-overIP (VoIP) communications technology that enables people to make free calls over the internet to other people on Skype for as long as they like.
Social capital	A social science concept used to describe the influence a 'node' has on its related network (i.e. how important you are to others you have relationships with). (19, 21, 29, 35, 42, 54, 61, 62, 123, 124, 125, 235)
Social media	User generated content that is created when people share their knowledge and experiences with others. This contrasts with industrial media like newspapers where organizations produce information using methods that are much more costly and therefore out of reach to most people. (15, 22, 29-39, 42, 45,56-69, 85, 90, 109, 122, 125-129, 132,135, 181)
Social media sites	Websites that use and exploit social media. Examples include *Facebook, MySpace, MSN (Windows Live Spaces), YouTube, Flickr, Ning, BeBo, Friendster, Hi5, TagWorld, PerfSpot, Zorpia, Netlog* and *Yahoo 360*. (15, 16, 23, 24, 29-39, 45, 64, 66, 85, 90, 122, 135,150, 177, 210, 214, 217, 219
Social networking sites	Recently 'business' social networking sites have emerged that adopt similar approaches to social media sites but are purposefully designed to enable business people to share contact information. Examples include *LinkedIn, Xing* and *Plaxo*. (23, 35, 57-59, 230)
Social network	A term used to describe social structures that map out relationships between individuals. (8, 13-28, 29-39, 40-55, 57-67)
Social office workplace	What I call the new virtual office workplace technology that incorporates the new business conversation and social media technologies. (176-185)
Software-as-a-Service	(SaaS) – pronounced 'sass' – is a model of software deployment where a provider licenses an application that customers can procure on a usage basis as an on-demand information service.
Surfer (Surfing)	A term used to describe people who regularly view web pages on the Internet – so called 'surfing the web'. (7, 65, 116, 117, 119, 125, 133, 179-181, 216)

Tag clouds	Collections of words that are used to describe content. (178, 185)
Thoughtful web	A term I use to describe web-based technologies that gather information that matters to the individual filtered by the meta-information they share. (45, 46, 48, 49)
Tribal brands	An emerging consumer-driven market 'organism' born of a common expression of values held by loosely coupled communities of individuals and manifested in 'sticky values'. Tribal brands leverage their buying influence to engineer deals with suppliers prepared to meet the specific needs of their communities. Through tribal brands, individuals can collectively assert their buying power. Early examples include Fairtrade and Product RED. (24, 26, 27, 28, 82, 246)
Trust lines	Trust lines lay across social networks and point to relationship ties where trust exists. (53)
Twitter (Twittering)	Twitter is a micro- blogging website. *Twittering* is the modern day vernacular used to describe people who use the 'Twitter' micro-blogging technology to share their thoughts to other people ' followers' who have volunteered to listen in. (33-35, 60-65, 113)
Utility computing	Clusters of computers used as a virtual platform based on a metered business model. A forerunner to cloud computing. (141)
YouTube	Social media site for sharing videos. (14, 15, 30, 35, 36, **38**, 40, 57, 60, 64, 216)
Xing	(Pronounced 'x'ing) Popular European business social networking site. (23, 58, 104, 211, 228, 230)
Web 2.0	Seen to be a second generation of prolific web development where new web-based technologies are making it possible for small software companies to introduce many new and interesting ways to work with information. (159)
Wikis	A collaborative web-page that enables anyone with a rudimentary knowledge of plain text to contribute or modify content. (32)
Work-life balance	Describes the balance employers attempt to strike between the time they spend working and the time they can commit to home-life. (104)